T0361209

Building Network Capabilities in Turbulent Competitive Environments

Business Success Stories from the BRICs

Series on Resource Management

RECENT TITLES

Building Network Capabilities in Turbulent Competitive Environments

Business Success Stories from the BRICs

Paul Hong and YoungWon Park

CRC Press
Taylor & Francis Group
Boca Raton London New York

CRC Press is an imprint of the
Taylor & Francis Group, an **informa** business

CRC Press
Taylor & Francis Group
6000 Broken Sound Parkway NW, Suite 300
Boca Raton, FL 33487-2742

© 2015 by Taylor & Francis Group, LLC
CRC Press is an imprint of Taylor & Francis Group, an Informa business

No claim to original U.S. Government works

ISBN 13: 978-1-4665-1575-8 (hbk)

Library of Congress Cataloging-in-Publication Data

Hong, Paul.
    Building network capabilities in turbulent competitive environments : business success stories from the BRICs / Paul Hong, Young Won Park.
        pages cm. -- (Resource management ; 49)
    Summary: "Brazil, Russia, India, and China (BRIC) are among the largest and fastest growing economies in the world. This book presents strategies for recognizing the challenges and optimizing the opportunities for building network capabilities and competitive advantage within the context of these emerging markets. It provides a thorough review of the literature and an unparalleled abundance of fascinating case studies featuring Japanese, Korean, and indigenous business examples. The information is presented within a fully formulated theoretical framework of technological competence, customer competence, and linkage competence, as well as covering the concepts of product architecture and supply chain management"-- Provided by publisher.
    Includes bibliographical references and index.
    ISBN 978-1-4665-1575-8 (hardback)
    1. Information technology--BRIC countries. 2. Business networks--BRIC countries. 3. Social networks--BRIC countries. 4. Information technology--Developing countries. 5. Business networks--Developing countries. 6. Social networks--Developing countries. I. Park, Young Won. II. Title.

HD30.2.H662 2014
338.8'7--dc23   2014024217

Visit the Taylor & Francis Web site at
http://www.taylorandfrancis.com

and the CRC Press Web site at
http://www.crcpress.com

Contents

SECTION II　Emerging Global Firms from China, India, Brazil, and Russia

SECTION III   Japanese and Korean Global Firms in Emerging Markets

Preface

In 2012 and 2013, Psy's "Gangnam Style" and "Gentleman" received worldwide attention with their unique appeal in the global contents market. His success illustrates the integrative power of the open network via YouTube and individual core competence based on his peculiar music and dance styles. In a sense, his case is an example of building network capability in a turbulent competitive environment. With the prolonged recession in advanced economies, emerging markets—BRIC (Brazil, Russia, India, and China) in particular—are potential engines for global market growth. Recently, their performances are not as impressively sustaining as anticipated. The growth rates in India, Brazil, and Russia have slowed down somewhat. Even so, the enormous size of the customer base from these emerging markets is the strategic concern of global business firms. Their economic demographic structure is changing from a typical pyramid shape with a huge bottom tier of poor to a diamond ring structure with a tremendous consumer power base in the middle. According to the Japanese Economic Industry Bureau statistics, the total number of households in Asia with annual disposable income between \$5,000 and \$35,000 was 140 million in 1990, 220 million in 2000, and 880 million by 2008. This reflects the rapid growth of middle income groups from China, India, and the Association of South East Asian Nations (ASEAN). From a global perspective, a large share of middle income groups is distributed in these areas. With rapid economic growth and an increase in the customer base, these economies hold amazing purchasing power potential for new products and services.

In such dynamic global business environments, the source of competitive advantage is the firm's capability that offers innovative and valuable goods and services. However, the sustainable competitive strategy for these emerging markets requires substantially different market penetration approaches. Over the years Japanese and Western (i.e., US-/Europe-based) global firms entered these emerging markets much earlier—China, India, and Brazil in particular. Yet, all their stories are not necessarily so successful. Their market share is not so impressive in these emerging markets. These firms can no longer afford real success in these markets by merely offering high-quality products with sophisticated technology features at premium prices. Many Japanese firms in fact have experienced serious business failures in these nations. For example, SONY or PANASONIC of Japan have lost their market leadership in these emerging markets as they merely replicated their old business model that had been fitting US and European markets.

In contrast, Korean firms with their relatively small domestic market have implemented an adaptive product development strategy by offering products that are responsive to local market needs. Recently, the market growth rates of Samsung Electronics, LG Electronics, and Hyundai Motor in these emerging economies have become noticeable. After the 2008 global financial crisis, many global firms from Japan, the United States, and Europe reported substantial losses in their market performance. At the same time, the prevailing view was that the market success of Korean global firms would be short lived. However, after the mid-1990s, these Korean global firms are doing fairly well. Recently in Japan, serious research about Korean studies is in progress. Behind Korean global firms' impressive growth, scholars began to note the constructive roles of the Korean government and the owner-management style of Korean firms that are characterized by bold and timely investment decisions, aggressive global market expansion, and effective crisis management.

It is worth noting that Korean business strategy and management practices have their own unique features. Korean firms have made a successful transition from analog to digital to keep pace with revolutionary changes in the global markets. Korean electronic firms have achieved phenomenal growth in the context of the 1997 Asian financial crisis and the information technology (IT) bubble between 1997 and 2000. Unlike Japanese counterparts, Korean firms expanded their scale of operations for global markets and their financial performance indicators (e.g., sales, profits, and market share) vastly improved. The contribution ratio of the electronic industry for the Korean economy and the global market is substantial. In the past, steel, shipbuilding, and heavy industries were leading the annual growth of the Korean economy. At present, the contribution of the electronic industry—semiconductors, mobile phones, and thin-film-transistor liquid-crystal displays (TFT-LCDs) in particular—to the Korean economy is substantial.

The 1997 Asian financial crisis pushed Korean firms to radically restructure their business organizations and move forward to target global markets. Thus, the external shock pressures made these firms take steps toward radical change. Moving beyond their domestic operations these firms have pursued an aggressive global expansion strategy. Since 2000 the authors of this book and the research team have conducted numerous field visits to study the business practices of Japanese and Korean firms in Brazil, Russia, India, China, and South Africa (BRICS) and South East Asian Nations (ASEAN). Our observation is that the strategic core of successful global firms is in the development and deployment of their global network capabilities in emerging markets. The emerging markets display enormous contextual complexity in terms of political situations, economic policies, and the base-of-pyramid (BOP) structure of income distributions. Successful market performance in these emerging economies requires a sound understanding of dynamic environmental factors and timely investment of appropriate resources. This book puts special emphasis on three elements of network competence (i.e., technology, customer, and linkage competence) and product architecture for product development strategy as the theory base for examining successful cases of Japanese and Korean global firms and the responsive strategies of the native firms from these emerging economies.

This book of network capability covers the emerging global businesses of BRICs (Brazil, Russia, India, and China) which include Chinese and Indian electronic and automotive firms and other joint venture firms in these emerging economies. Goldman Sachs argues that the economic potential of Brazil, Russia, India, and China is such that they could become among the four most dominant economies by the year 2050. These countries encompass over 25% of the world's land coverage and 40% of the world's population. This second volume highlights these four countries that are among the biggest and fastest growing emerging markets. Many global firms have turned their attention to the emerging BRIC markets as ways to achieve alternative global competitive capabilities in view of somewhat slow business growth in North America and Europe.

This book has some distinctive features. First, it is based on the integration of relevant theories and field studies as the basis for understanding the dynamic challenges and opportunities that global firms face in emerging markets. Our research team has made numerous field visits to many firms in Brazil, Russia, China and India to meet executives, interview them and observe their manufacturing and supply chain practices. We report what we have discovered through these experiences as much as what we learned from the vast available literature. We believe that serious theory-building efforts require constant engagement with reality.

Second, this book covers beyond selected Korean and Japanese firms. Since the market focus is emerging large economies (Brazil, Russia, China and India), this book presents strategic business practices of prominent firms of these emerging economies as well as successful Japanese and Korean firms in BRICs. Since our intent is to cover the markets in BRIC, the strategic focus includes firms from global Japanese and Korean firms as well as indigenous firms from Brazil, Russia, India and China. These are based on extensive field studies in these countries and relevant literature reviews.

Third, this book presents new network capability models that include three types of competencies and the concept of product architecture. From these theoretical lenses, we analyze cases of Japanese, Korean and other global firms. In particular, these successful models display technology competence (i.e., innovative capability for offering products that fit emerging markets), customer competence (i.e., sensing capability for understanding lifestyles of customers and satisfying their needs), and linkage competence (i.e., integration capability of both technology and customer competence) (Park and Hong, 2012). Our focus is to examine the linkages between various functional design choices and their impact on competative performance (Brown, 2013). We also add the concept of product architecture in addition to these three competencies for more in-depth analyses of global firms operating in BRICs.

In brief, compared to the first book, this second book has enlarged the scope of emerging economies and the business range of global firms. The theoretical framework is also based on the integration of international business, product architecture, and supply chain management theories. Thus, this book aims to serve scholars, students, and practitioners in the areas of international business, supply chain management, and strategic management.

Paul Hong, PhD, CMA
YoungWon Park, PhD

The Authors

Dr. Paul Hong is a professor of operations management at the University of Toledo, Ohio, USA. He holds a PhD degree in manufacturing management and engineering from the University of Toledo. He also holds an MBA and an MA in economics from Bowling Green State University, Ohio, USA and a BA from Yonsei University in Seoul, Korea. He has presented and published more than 200 articles in conference proceedings and journals including the *Journal of Operations Management, International Journal of Production Research, Corporate Governance: An International Review, Journal of Supply Chain Management, Benchmarking: An International Journal, British Journal of Educational Technology, Strategic Outsourcing: An International Journal* and *European Journal of Innovation Management, Journal of Production Economics, International Journal of Operations and Production Management, Journal of Business Research, International Journal of Technology Management, International Journal of Information Management, Management Decision, Journal of Cleaner Production, Journal of Purchasing and Supply Management, Journal of Service Management* and *Business Horizons.*

He is the recipient of *Journal of Operations Management* Best Paper Finalist Award (2006) for the paper, "Role Change of Design Engineers in Integrated Product Development), Emerald Literati Network 2011 Awards for Excellence for the paper, "Integration of Supply Chain IT and Lean Practices for Mass Customization: Benchmarking of Product and Service Focused Manufacturers" and Best Paper Awards on "Flexible and Redundant Supply Chain Practices to Build Strategic Supply Chain Resilience: Contingent and Resource-Based Perspectives" and "Using Social Media for Competitive Advantage: An Empirical Study" at the Annual North American Research Symposium in Tempe, Arizona, 2012 and 2013.

He is an editorial review board member of several journals including the *Journal of Operations Management, Journal of Humanitarian Logistics and Supply Chain Management (JHLSCM),* and *Journal of Enterprise Information Management (JEIM).* Since 2006, he has been special issue editor for journals such as *Benchmarking: An International Journal* (BIJ), *International Journal of Business Excellence (IJBEX), International Journal of Services and Operations Management (IJSOM), International Journal of*

Procurement Management (IJPM), and *International Journal of Production Economics (IJPE)*. He is conference chair and international network coordinator of the annual International Symposium and Workshop on Global Supply Chain, Intermodal Transportation and Logistics—4th Symposium in Madrid, Spain, 5th Symposium in Tokyo, Japan and the 6th Global Supply Chain Conference in Dearborn, Michigan, USA. His research interests are in business ecosystem innovation strategy, global supply chain management, and international comparative studies.

Dr. Youngwon Park is an associate professor at the GCOE Project of Manufacturing Management Research Center at the University of Tokyo, Japan. He holds a PhD degree in the Department of Advanced Social and International Studies from the University of Tokyo, Japan. His articles have been published in journals including *Management Decision, International Journal of Production Economics, International Journal of Technology Management, International Journal of Information Management, Business Horizons, Journal of Business Research, Benchmarking: An International Journal, International Journal of Services and Operations Management, International Journal of Logistics Systems and Management, International Journal of Business Excellence, International Journal of Procurement Management, Akamon Management Review, Japan Academy of International Business Studies, Japanese Society for Science and Technology Studies,* and the *Japan Society of Information and Communication Research.* He has received research awards including dissertation paper awards from the Japan Association for Social Informatics (JASI), best paper awards from The Japan Society of Information and Communication Research (JSICR), research awards of the social science field from the Telecommunications Advancement Foundation (TAF), and research students awards of the social science field from the Telecommunications Advancement Foundation (TAF). His research interests are in technology management, manufacturing and IT strategy, and global supply chain management.

Section I

Research Framework

1

Research Framework:
Core Competence and Global Strategy

In Chapter 1, we provide a theoretical framework of this book. We start from Penrose theory (1959), extend to network capability theory, firms' strategy in base-of-pyramid (BOP) markets, and resource-based view (RBV) (Wenerfelt, 1984; Rumelt, 1984; Barney, 2002). We also expand competence-based theory into three types of competencies. The early form of core competence theory traces back to Smith (1776), Schumpeter (1934), and Coase (1937). This competence-based view coordinates and integrates diverse management resources toward higher levels of organizational capabilities (Hamel and Prahalad, 1990; Morone, 1993). Three core competencies are the crucial competencies that global firms need to utilize in emerging markets. And the theory of product architecture is essential in examining why certain industries use their product strategy different from others.

1.1 THE IMPORTANCE OF NETWORK CAPABILITY IN THE BRICs MARKET ENVIRONMENT

Shortly after the global financial crisis in 2009, the world economy was deteriorating on a global scale. But since 2010, it has continued to recover gradually. However, this recovery process varied sharply by countries and regions. The International Monetary Fund (IMF) forecast on the world economy as announced in April 2011 indicated that the growth rate of the world economy in 2010 registered a 5% increase over that of the previous year following a record −0.5% decrease in 2009. The gap of economic growth between the advanced and emerging economies further increased since 2011, and the imbalance in growth in various forms is emerging.

Developing economies generate half of global gross domestic product (GDP) and over 40% of world exports (Sinha, 2013). Customers in these markets are fundamentally different from those in developed markets. The customers residing in the United States are having $44,000 as a per capita income, whereas this figure in India stands out at $1,000. These markets can be termed as *mega markets with micro customers*. With the new phase of globalization where the world has shrunken from "size large" to "size medium" to "size small" to "size tiny," most of the multinational companies have targeted only the top of the pyramid (i.e., wealthiest 10%). The true potential lies in unlocking the other 90% of the pyramid as also suggested by Prahalad (2005, 2009) in his book, *Fortune at the Bottom of the Pyramid*. As mentioned by Prahalad, poor nations are incubating new business models and innovative uses of technology that in the coming decade will begin to transform the competitive landscape of entire global industries, from financial to telecom services to health care and car making.

In the words of Govindarajan (2012), a reverse innovation, very simply, is any innovation likely to be adopted first in the developing world. Instead of developing high-end products at home and adapting them for markets like China and India, companies can observe reverse innovation by developing products with the focus on the constraints of emerging markets. The price point needs to be lower, but it should deliver high value at an affordable price. Prahalad (2005) adds that reverse innovation requires a radical shift in thinking as it starts with fundamentally different ground rules.

Under these circumstances, emerging markets—BRICS (Brazil, Russia, India, China, South Africa) in particular—are perceived as a potential engine for global market growth. Recently, the rates of their growth are not as impressively sustaining as anticipated. The growth rates in India, Brazil, and Russia slowed down somewhat. Even so, the enormous size of the customer base from these emerging markets is the strategic concern of global business firms. In particular, the rapid economic growth of these nations is changing the economic demographic from a typical pyramid shape with a huge bottom tier of those who are poor to a diamond ring structure with tremendous consumer power base in the middle. According to the IMF, while advanced economies, including the United States, Euro Zone countries, the United Kingdom, and others registered a 3% increase over that of the previous year in 2010 compared to a –3.4% decrease in 2009, the emerging economies achieved 2.7% higher growth in 2009 and a 7.3% increase over the previous year in 2010. Meanwhile, most of the emerging economies such as China, India, and Brazil continued their economic growth and recovered to a level over the first quarter of 2008 before the financial crisis. The emerging economies were having a higher proportion of world nominal GDP, as mentioned above. Notably, China's nominal GDP outran that of advanced countries like the Japanese one in 2010. It is forecast that China's nominal GDP will largely outrun those of major advanced economies in 2011 and continue to do so thereafter (METI, 2011). The structural ratio in world GDP of the emerging economies is 31.2% in 2010, 34% in 2011, and 39.9% by 2014. Moreover, with the rapid growth of middle income groups, the portion of emerging economies such as China, India, and Association of South East Asian Nations (ASEAN) might grow further. A large share of middle income groups from these emerging economies would hold amazing purchasing power potential for new products and services of global firms. Furthermore, according to the Business Perspectives on Emerging Markets 2012–2017 report from Global Alliance Intelligence (GIA), by 2017 emerging markets are expected to account for 26% of global revenues on average for pharmaceuticals and healthcare companies, up from 15% today (Figure 1.1). Emerging markets are becoming large key customer markets and critical to their future of global firm operations. The 38 business managers in GIA's survey suggest that the BRIC countries (Brazil, Russia, India, and China) are still their top four most important emerging markets for 2012 to 2017, with Brazil being the clear favorite with 90% of the votes. Mexico, Turkey, Argentina, and South Africa top the list for non-BRIC emerging markets as well.

Additionally, emerging markets also show impressive results in innovation. In terms of patent data, Rupali (2013) reports that from 1987 to 2007, the number of patents has grown at least four times. The emerging economies are forging ahead and exploring new areas of market potential. Both China and India have achieved amazing patent outputs comparable to other advanced nations (e.g., United States, Japan, and other European nations). Apart from attracting offshore engineering services, the information technology sector in particular, India is attracting firms for highly functional and less expensive products with frugal engineering. India, with large domestic markets and a large population of young people, provides an ideal ground for business expansion to many firms. For instance, Tiwari and Herstatt (2012) report that IBM has entrusted its

Indian subsidiary with major responsibility in its Mobile Web Initiative to expand the web-based business, education, communication and entertainment market in India.

The landscape in emerging markets is becoming more favorable for foreign players. Rising incomes and favorable healthcare policies have spurred growth. China, for instance, allocates $41 billion for the development of new hospitals and for the refurbishment of its healthcare system in its latest Five Year Plan (2011–2015). India's government plans to improve the country's current doctor-patient ratio to 1 to 1,000 by 2015, an increase of 60%. India's federal government recently announced a $4.8 billion plan to provide more than half of its citizens with access to essential medical services. The federal governments in Mexico and Turkey have recently implemented new policies to extend healthcare coverage.

Over the next few years to 2017, global manufacturers will continue to focus on BRICS markets, with vigorous emphasis on Brazil, China, India, and Russia. South Africa, Indonesia, Turkey, and Vietnam follow the BRICS countries as "secondary" emerging markets. These four countries need to raise the level of their production capabilities. Other emerging markets include those of Mexico, Poland, and Thailand with their high production capabilities and long history of foreign direct investment by large manufacturing players.

Many global manufacturers have adapted their emerging markets approaches by developing a *BRIC + 1* strategy, a hedging strategy that involves continuing operations in the BRIC location where they have established manufacturing, while opening up just one or two factories in a secondary emerging market as a hedge. GE is one of these companies. It asserts that manufacturing prices are frequently 30% lower in secondary emerging markets than in the BRICS, but other issues frequently offset these cost increases. Another multinational giant, Unilever, has invested heavily in Indonesia. It has worked with the government and local associations and leveraged its scale of investment to develop a relationship and local support systems that will benefit the community and the company for decades to come. Collectively, emerging markets seem to offer the best hope for manufacturers for the future, with some estimates saying that they will still be growing at rates double those of the developed markets in 2025. Emerging markets, however, do not come without a variety of success factors and threats.

Increasingly, global firms emphasize these emerging markets in an effort to overcome the stagnant growth constraints in the mature market of the advanced economies. However, these markets require a radically different market approach.

Many still favor BRICS countries as their top focus between 2012 and 2017, with similar emphasis on individual markets across 10 industries according to Manufacturing & Industrial; Telecommunication, Technology & Media; Professional & Business Services; Financial Services; Consumer & Retail; Pharmaceuticals & Healthcare; Energy, Resources & Environment; Automotive; Chemicals; and Logistics & Transportation. However, 91% of firms also admit that they have not done enough for the emerging markets. Their main regrets are in relation to adaptation to local conditions, market entry decisions, and market intelligence. Over half of the respondents indicate that information on emerging markets is not readily available in their organizations. The majority (e.g., three out of four) was not sure of the accuracy and completeness of the information available to them. Japanese firms had entered these emerging economies (e.g., China, India, and Brazil) much earlier than Korean counterparts and yet not secured relatively strong market positions. With enormous confidence in their production management, the majority of Japanese firms had put quality as the forefront of their market strategy and thus offered their products with higher prices in these markets (Schonberger, 2007). Thus, Japanese firms offered the same products from the advanced markets to these emerging economies. But such Japanese firms mostly did not necessarily do well in the emerging economies. Some Japanese firms show a new success model of innovative product development according to market needs based on their unique problem solving and technological capability (Thomke and Fujimoto, 2000; Tomino et al., 2011, 2012). They do not offer outdated or inferior products to the emerging economies that are less developed. Rather, they pay very careful attention to the unique market needs of these growing markets just as they do with the advanced markets. In other words, their market winning approach to these emerging economies is not a plus-minus strategy but a multiplication strategy.

In this book, we introduce the successful examples of indigenous, Japanese, and Korean global firms in Brazil, Russia, India, and China. For this purpose, we present three types of competence and product architecture. Outstanding global firms are keenly aware of changing requirements of their organizational enviromennts (Rosenzweig, et al., 1991). The winning product strategy of global firms for these emerging economies includes technology competence (i.e., utilizing technological capability to make good products), customer competence (i.e., understanding lifestyles of customers and capturing the hearts of customers), and linkage competence (i.e., integration of technology and customer competence) (Figure 1.1) (Park and Hong, 2012). In other words, market success of global firms depends on their supply chain responsiveness in terms of effective deployment of their technology competence to fit the unique needs of the customers of these emerging economies (Roh et al., 2011, 2014). This book defines such an ability of firms to detect the needs of customers in India, China, and Brazil and translate them into the right products as sensing competence (Park, 2011a). Emerging markets also show two patterns: (1) the impact of direct income growth that impacts the rapid demand growth in business-to-customer (B to C) markets and (2) industrial or intermediate goods in business-to-business (B to B) markets based on the macroeconomic growth. In particular, industrial goods show the purchasing patterns of such products are different by regions. It is worthy to examine how firms change the product offerings according to the regional differences.

Interestingly enough, customer competence is what global firms from advanced nations find most challenging to master for their winning performance in the emerging markets. Japanese firms discussed in this book possess high levels of technology competence (i.e., product quality and safety performance capability) with their long experiences in the advanced countries. Yet, their relative weakness in customer competence in the emerging economies made them seriously unprepared for penetrating in these new markets. These emerging economies have unique market conditions that are drastically different from those of advance markets. Therefore, the crucial competitive advantage lies in their linkage competence that integrates both technological and customer competence in these emerging markets.

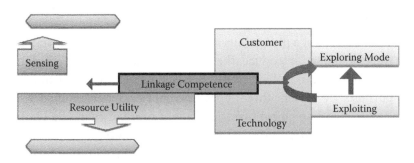

FIGURE 1.1
Three elements of core competence. (Adapted from Park and Hong, 2012.)

1.2 NETWORK CAPABILITY AND GLOBAL COMPETITIVE STRATEGY

1.2.1 Three Types of Core Competence and Global Expansion Strategy

In 2000 Malcolm Gladwell introduced *The Tipping Point: How Little Things Can Make a Big Difference*. This book became one of the bestselling books for years. This book illustrates the idea of network capability in the daily context of American life. Malcolm Gladwell (2000) focuses on three types of people that play prominent roles in making particular ideas or concepts to spread like social epidemics. The first type is the *connector*. The concept of the connector refers to those who have extraordinary levels of social contacts. For example, the size of social circles of average people among 1,000 in a random sample is about 35 people or so. In any group, at least one person has 130 to 150 (i.e., five to six times the average). These connectors play very important roles in spreading new ideas. The second type is the *maven* which is somewhat different from connectors. They are information experts. When superstores offer "special buys," most people do not remember the individual prices of the products on sale. But 0.1% of people remember the pricing details and spread the news to others. Thus, the databases stored in the minds of these mavens make a big impact on network capability. The third type is the *salesperson*. The salesperson exercises a huge influence on the customers who finally decide to purchase particular products through their timely and credible suggestions. These three type of people take quite active roles in social network distribution. The above-mentioned influential people are what in Rogers (1983) referred to as "2.5% innovators" and "13.5% early adopters."

This book examines the building process of network capability from the standpoint of global market expansion based on extensive field studies (Voss et al., 2002). Our special focus is to examine linkages between various choices of cross-functional competences and their impact on competitive performance (Brown, 2013). In other words, this book discusses how global firms successfully build their network capabilities in the markets of BRICs. The determining factor of any firm's competitive advantage is its unique resources or advantageous position (Wenerfelt, 1984; Rumelt, 1984; Barney, 2002; Rosenzweig et al., 2003; Park, 2009; Park and Hong, 2012; Penrose, 1959; Hamel and Prahalad, 1990; Morone, 1993; March, 1991;

Leonard-Barton, 1992; Henderson, 1993; Dougherty and Heller, 1994; Daugherty, 1995; Helfat and Raubitschek, 2000; Danneels, 2002). In a relatively stable business environment, it is not unusual that firms can utilize their core competence for a long period once it had been successfully built over the years. However, in a turbulent market environment the core competence of the past may turn out to be the reason for business failures.

After the 2008 global financial shock, the demise of Japanese electronics firms illustrate this point (Nonaka and Takeuchi, 1995; Fujimoto et al., 2005; Fujimoto, 2006). As firms focus on incremental innovation, architectural knowledge embedded in work routines and regular work flows rarely changes. As the internal innovation leaders depend on organizationally filtered information, their understanding of organizational architecture and absorptive knowledge become outdated. These firms are no longer able to face the challenges of the disruptive innovation of rival firms. In this context, researchers in the 1990s presented the dynamic capability theory (Teece et al., 1990; Utterback and Suarez, 1993; Teece and Pisano, 1994; Henderson and Cockburn, 1994; Teece et al., 1997; Teece, 1986; Miller and Morris, 1999; Teece, 2007; Quinn and Dalton, 2009). Firms lose their competitive advantage once their organizational governance is unable to create, store, and explore knowledge assets through their routine work processes in the form of unique innovative capability. In this sense, dynamic capabilities are defined as the systematic organic effort to capture the new innovation opportunities by connecting to the external network and to translate into organizational core capability that reconfigures and protect their knowledge assets for a sustainable competitive advantage (Teece, 1986; Snow et al., 1992; Nonaka and Takeuchi, 1995). Thus, the crucial elements of dynamic capability are organizational sensing of external environment, exploration of business opportunities, and stretch and leverage of innovative knowledge assets (Hamel & Prahalad, 1994). In this book, such dynamic capability is referred to as network capability which is further explained in three types of competence, which are market competence associated with external environment, resource securing for enhancing technology competence, and linkage competence that combines external and internal resources (Park and Hong, 2012).

First, the strengths of Japanese firms are in their technology competence that develops products with high functionality and quality. Such technology competence is based on product development capability, patent rights, multiskilled human resources, product design, and manufacturing capability embedded in organizational system and work processes. The indicators of technology competence are productivity, production lead time, time to market, number of new product projects, product integrity, and design quality (Fujimoto, 2001). Technical experts with years of experience in manufacturing floors (e.g., heavyweight project managers of Toyota Company) can recognize the level of technology competence with their intuitive understanding and careful observation of manufacturing processes (Fujimoto, 1997).

Second, in the emerging new markets relative weakness of Japanese firms lies in customer competence, which is essential to inspire customers through aggressive marketing and promotional efforts that are vastly different from the advanced US/European markets. This involves innovative methods of communicating the unique value of their products, which lead them to adopt new lifestyle patterns. Such customer competence is not for easy and quick methodical measurement. Rather, it includes comprehensive measures such as customer satisfaction ratings, repeat purchase rates, the number of new customers, market share, customer loyalty, and customer willingness to pay. Intuitively, expert managers with years of experience in the areas of customer service would be able to estimate the extent of customer competence.

Third, the ability to transform an idea into a tangible substance (i.e., linkage competence or network capability) is to integrate product concept into tangible products (i.e., linking customer competence to technology competence). However, many Japanese firms are not quite familiar with this "linkage competence" concept. Japanese firms assume that their weak customer competence is the main reason for their relatively weak position in the global markets. Thus, many firms reinforce their marketing efforts and yet they do not necessarily understand the critical role of linkage competence for their market success. Linkage competence is realized as firms attain adequate market sensing ability, develop customer-trend-sensitive managers, implement product architecture, and achieve overall product-process integrity in diverse manufacturing industries (Park et al., 2012b, 2012c; Tomita et al., 2011).

1.2.2 Core Competence and Product Architecture

A critical issue of global firms is how to effectively respond in the turbulent dynamic global business environment—particularly in the emerging markets. Product architecture is a useful concept for the analysis of rapidly changing markets. Firms focusing on finished products tend to use closed integral architecture, while component product manufacturers offering the commodity nature of products usually adopt an open modular architecture (Christensen et al., 2002; Park and Hong, 2012). As the market change is rapid, the crucial element of market success is speed. Thus, the global business environment is rapidly changing from a closed integral to an open modular environment. Thus, firms search for linkage competence (i.e., network capability) (Park and Hong, 2012).

Product architecture is the foundational element of product design. Figure 1.2 shows product architecture and system structure for product development. In general, a modular type is for a combination of separate independent parts while an integral type is for integration of complex interdependent elements (Henderson and Clark, 1990; Ulrich, 1995; Fine, 1998; Baldwin and Clark, 2000; Fujimoto, 2001). Modular types show a one-to-one relationship between functionality and structure. Therefore, each module requires independent design of each component. In contrast, integral types involve multi-to-multi relationships among interdependent parts. Any change in one part design necessarily affects other aspects and thus complex system design is a must. Common product structures of manufacturing products are hierarchical. This is why even for many modular products the basic foundational structure is integral architecture (Clark, 1985). For example, an LCD TV has integral elements in the upstream manufacturing process/front-end design process, and the

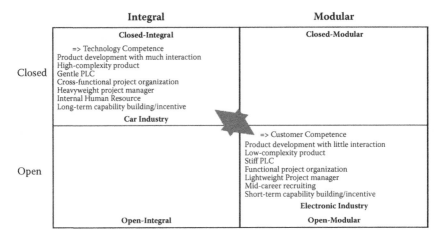

FIGURE 1.2
Product architecture and system structure for product development. (Adapted from Park and Hong, 2012.)

downstream manufacturing assembly process includes mostly modular types (Park et al., 2008; Park, 2010).

Here, two sets of parameters are as follows: (1) modular/integral (i.e., types of product architecture) and (2) open/closed (i.e., relationship extent between firms). "Open" refers to the technological specificity that defines the extent of how one firm's modules are related to those of other firms to make a particular product. In contrast, "closed" is about the incompatibility of one's modules (e.g., pure and unique components) with other firm's modules. An "open" structure allows for communalization and standardization among modules and thus a linkage mechanism among interfaces (i.e., common linkage between component parts and shared connectivity protocols for information flows). On the other hand, a "closed" structure does not allow such interface design rules among modules (i.e., unique modules of each firm are unrelated to those of other firms).

Thus, a 2×2 matrix shows four types of product architecture. An "open-modular" product indicates a modular architecture with open interface structure. Open-modular products allow combinative design of component parts. Firms are able to offer products with a high level of functionality and value potential through a smooth combination of diverse quality component parts from multiple firms (Fine, 1998; Fujimoto, 2001). Thus, maximum functionality of products is determined by the functionality potential of component parts.

In contrast, "closed-integral" products define unlimited functionality potential through complex internal integration mechanisms. In reality, the realistic functionality maximum is determined by cost and cycle time. This book notes how Japanese global firms recognize such strategic cost constraints in the emerging markets. Successful Japanese firms in the emerging markets adopt an open integral product architectural strategy (as opposed to a closed integral architectural strategy) while utilizing linkage competence. These firms determine customer needs of emerging economies and raise the level of localization (i.e., use local suppliers for majority of component parts) and yet stick to integral product architecture to ensure product quality and sustainability goals. In the subsequent chapters, based on the theoretical framework of the business competence model and product architecture strategy, this book discusses further in depth successful business strategy of Japanese and Korean global firms in BRICs.

1.3 PRODUCT ARCHITECTURE AND SUPPLY CHAIN INTEGRATION

Research is available on offshore production of multinational companies (MNCs). Classical international business approaches such as corporate advantage theory (Hymer, 1960), product cycle theory (Vernon, 1966), and OLI (ownership, location, and internalization) approach (Dunning, 1979, 1989) explain the patterns of how MNCs expand their operations in the overseas market (Hong and Roh, 2009; Shintaku et al., 2008; Park et al., 2012d).

First, we approach the MNCs' supply chain integration from the perspective of theory of comparative advantages. Transactions of information-intensive management resources (IIMRs) or intermediate goods across the national borders are possible because of three economic advantage factors (Hasegawa, 1998, 2002). First, economies of multiplants suggest that the value of IIMR does not diminish with the use in multiplants. Therefore, the common use of IIMR in multiple plants instead reduces its overall average cost. Second, joint ownership of IIMR may enhance the economies of scope and therefore realize additional profit potentials in the form of brand recognition, customers' trust, and an extended distribution channel. Third, economies of specialization may also achieve a great level of overall network system productivity when diverse sets of upstream/downstream processes within the value chain are allocated to many countries according to the differences in factor costs and economies of scale. The relationship between upstream and downstream processes is also quite interactive. For example, outputs of upstream processes are usually added into downstream processes. At the same time, information and knowledge from downstream processes are reversely put into use through the information feedback mechanisms and change the nature of upstream process characteristics. In this way, dynamic flows of intermediate goods and IIMR occur in the international value network. From the standpoint of supply chain integration it might be desirable to locate upstream and downstream processes in the same location. However, the theory of comparative advantages recognizes the values of utilizing the differences of factor costs and economies of scale through international transactional arrangements. Meanwhile, in turbulent times, configuration, collaboration, and coordination of information system to deal with supply chain complexities have been enormous challenges to global firms (Williamson et al., 2004; Abdelkafi et al., 2011; Gunasekaran, Hong and Fujimoto, 2014). In particular, supply chain integration (SCI) is one of the most important competitive strategies used by modern enterprises (Youn et al., 2008, 2012). As the main aim of supply chain management is to integrate various suppliers to satisfy market demand, supplier selection and evaluation plays an important role in establishing an effective supply chain (Vickery et al., 2003; Lee and Kimz, 2008; Lin et al., 2009; Chen, 2011; Youn et al., 2014).

Product architecture is closely related to supply chain integration. For example, increasing modularity makes it possible for module suppliers to work independently (Fine, 1998; Sako and Helper, 1998; Baldwin and Clark, 2000; Salvador et al., 2002; Sturgeon, 2002; Christensen et al., 2002; Fujimoto, 2003; Ro et al., 2007; Park et al., 2009; Abdelkafi et al., 2011; Ulku and Schmidt, 2011; Park and Hong, 2012). In particular, Ro et al. (2007) show that in response to product modularity, leading car producers reduced their supplier base. From the viewpoint of the firm like an original equipment manufacturer (OEM), the complexity of supply chain integration can be reduced through modularity strategy (Abdelkafi et al., 2011). Yet OEMs should develop trust-based buyer-supplier relationships with their module suppliers to attain high quality and reliable delivery. Examining the link between product architecture and supply chain configuration, Ulku and Schmidt (2011) also suggest that the choice of product architecture depends on firm, market, and product characteristics in addition to supply chain structure and that the optimal mapping from architecture to supply chain structure is not always one to one. They also find that a decentralized supply chain may be associated with a more integral product when the technical collaboration penalty is not excessive and suppliers have significantly superior product development capabilities. Christensen et al. (2002) also suggest appropriate decision making whether a firm's network chooses to be vertically integrated or horizontally specialized according to the changes in product architecture. A vertically integrated networked firm performs better in a market where customer requirements for product quality and functionality are not met. To develop a supply chain management alignment framework for mass customization, Abdelkafi et al. (2011) formulated 10 propositions explaining the relationships between product development and the supply chain management (SCM) framework. Their propositions concerning product architecture are as follows: (1) Modularity reduces the level of internal variety handled by the manufacturing firm. That reduces collaboration complexity from the OEM's viewpoint. (2) Modularity reduces the level of configuration and collaboration complexity.

Figure 1.3 shows how the past catch-up model has changed to a catch-up model based on product architecture and that modular products are

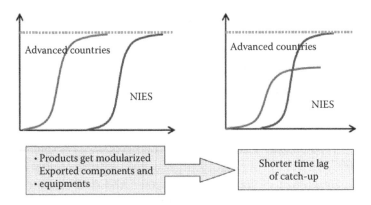

FIGURE 1.3
Foreign production transfer model by the theory of product architecture. (From Shintaku et al., 2006.)

easily transferred to the developing countries because of easy knowledge transfer on the production of equipment and component parts (Fujimoto, 2006; Shintaku et al., 2007; Shintaku, 2008; Shintaku et al., 2008). The other contribution of product architecture theory is to give a systemic view to see the integration and division of production processes of targeted products. In particular, Shintaku's product architecture theory that explains the catch-up model of Asian firms is applicable to supply chain configuration from one country to another. He points out that cellular phones adopt modular product architecture, which allows easy entry of competitors to the market (Shintaku, 2006). It is quite challenging to maintain competitive advantages in the cellular phone industry, which experiences intense price competition and rapid changes in product design. Naturally, the speed of production transfer from a leading nation to a following nation is relatively fast.

1.3.1 Network Capability Dynamics and Portfolio Strategy

This section is to examine network capability dynamics and portfolio strategy (Park and Hong, 2014). In particular, three core competence dynamics are discussed here. March (1991) emphasized dynamics of firms as learning organization and used the term *competence exploration and exploitation.* According to March (1991), exploration refers to the elements of search, variation, risk taking, experimentation, play, flexibility, discovery, and innovation. Exploitation is about refinement, choice, production, efficiency, selection, implementation, and exaction. Because so many firms tend to focus on exploiting their current competences (Levinthal and March, 1993), it is more strategically imperative to search for a balance between exploration and exploitation (Hamel and Prahalad, 1990; Leonard-Barton, 1992; Henderson, 1993; Morone, 1993; Daugherty, 1995; Helfat and Raubitschek, 2000; Dougherty and Heller, 1994; Danneels, 2002; Sidhu et al., 2007; Schulze, 2009; Park and Hong, 2012).

The idea of network capability dynamics can be further expanded in view of the concept of exploration and exploitation of competences. Figure 1.4 shows the interrelationships among customer competence, technology competence, and linkage competence in the contests of technology level and product attractiveness. Technology competence allows firms to raise the level of technology of particular products and yet product attractiveness does not necessarily follow it. On the other hand, customer competence may raise product attractiveness and yet technology level might not be enhanced simultaneously. Thus, product attractiveness and technology level have a somewhat trade-off relationship in that firms operate under resource constraints. Firms usually set their strategic priority between the resource requirements for enhancing product attractiveness and technology level and execute strategic selection/focus management for the possible maximum business impact with given resource constraints.

Such a trade-off effect becomes quite visible in the contexts of intense competition because of globalization and drastic reduction in product life-cycle through information and communications technology (ICT) innovation. If firms experience the positive outcomes of a "choose and focus" strategy, they intend to build on their successes. Firms may continue to

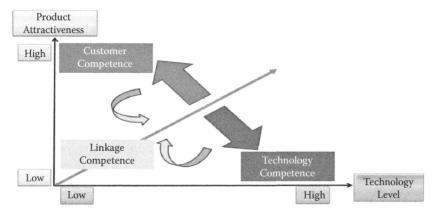

FIGURE 1.4
Dynamic mechanism of customer-technology competence.

invest their resources on enhancing "product attractiveness" based on their impressive historic records of "product attractiveness" focus. In the same way, firms with successful records of "technology focus" may not change their technology investment focus. As these investment patterns are settled over a long-term period, then these firms naturally develop either customer or technology competence.

If firms face long-term resource constraints that dictate "choose and focus" strategy, then their strategic intent might be fixed on either customer or technology competence. For example, after World War II Japanese firms have primarily focused on developing technology competence in view of their resource constraints in terms of labor and natural resources (Fujimoto, 2001). As their technology competence brought impressive results in North America and Europe in the 1970s to 1990s, they maintained their product strategy based on technology competence. Nevertheless, technology competence has a neutral effect on product attractiveness. Even products with outstanding technology competence may become unattractive and thus firms eventually lose their market share and experience business failures. In the early 1990s Japanese automotive firms pursued "extreme quality products" with no real competitive advantage and recently, a similar situation occurred with Japanese electronics firms (Fujimoto, 2003; Fujimoto and Oshika, 2006). The profit level of such firms continuously deteriorates to the extent that additional investment for new technology would not be feasible. Reckless focus on technology alone results in a downward spiral toward eventual breakdown of technology competence. Extreme technology specialization deprives firms of organizational agility. In a rapidly changing market environment, firms are incapable of adapting and thriving. For example, in the 1990s notebook PC market functionality enhancement was the key for customer satisfaction. Therefore, excellence in technology competence was a quite effective business strategy in this period. However, in the 2000s low cost as opposed to functionality improvement was the main concern of customers. Japanese firms that were too specialized in technology competence lost substantial market share to the other global firms with customer competence (i.e., ability to offer price-competitive products with a reasonable level of functionality). Several Japanese firms dropped out of the notebook PC market. Recently, Japanese firms strive to strengthen customer competence and strategically target BRICS markets. In reality, very few firms blindly pursue a "choose and focus" strategy exclusively on one particular aspect (i.e., either technology or customer competence). Most global firms seek the right balance between customer and technology competence, through linkage competence which operates through the dynamic coordinating mechanism in the 45-degree axis from the origin.

Now, let's further extend this discussion to global portfolio strategy beyond dynamic core competence. Portfolio strategy aims to strengthen core competence based on product/process/organizational architectural analysis. The purpose of architectural analysis is to implement product strategy for global competitive advantage (i.e., construction of "new business model for global market success"). For example, many global firms find it increasingly important to come up with new business models that enable firms "to catch life style of customers by the hands of engineers" by applying new product concepts in the emerging markets. This is to empower the architects of global firms (i.e., business design engineers) to coordinate the overall product development process by integrating external factors—functionality-performance-structure (components-units-modules)—based on a deep understanding of macroeconomics, changing sentiments and styles of customers through effective information sharing practices (Hong et al., 2004a, 2004b; Hong et al., 2005; Rauniar et al., 2008b; Doll et al., 2010).

However, it is not easy for design engineers to possess a deep understanding of dynamic macroeconomic phenomena, capture complex customer lifestyles and their tastes, and reflect them into the development of new products. This book aims to provide practical paths of how these design architects (i.e., super engineers) integrate vast available and relevant information (acquired through architectural analysis) and their design expertise and engineering insight (determined through trade-off of major customer requirements and internal constraints) for business successes (Hong et al., 2010a, 2010b, 2011).

Most global firms first forecast market demand and implement new product development processes. New business models need to address several key questions to be competitive in a dynamic global market environment. Will their internal technological and manufacturing capability be adequate to develop successful new products? Would extended network capability (i.e., their own plus their suppliers and strategic partners) be adequate for the growing new product challenges? These assessments require realistic simulation capability, sound business logic, and a speedy decision-making mechanism, prudent risk management, and integrative leadership mechanisms (Rauniar et al., 2008a; Hong et al., 2012b; Youn et al., 2012;. Shimizu et al., 2012, 2013; Park et al., 2013).

This book presents architectural model analytics that suggest practical examples of how to assess global market needs (based on sensing current customer mindsets and behaviors), estimate network capability, and determine specific implementation methods using real-time simulation in regard to what to make, what to buy, and where to assemble. More details on architectural simulation are discussed in Park and Hong (2014).

Figure 1.5 shows portfolio analysis that integrates architectural analytics and core competence strategy. This is useful for the examination of the relationship between architectural analytics and core competence strategy of global firms. Portfolio analysis is to use the architectural sorting process and manage core competence capability by focusing on strong integral elements. The goal is to determine who (i.e., target customers) and what (i.e., product functionality-performance structure and manufacturing processes). Such portfolio analysis provides embedded knowledge of core competence of firms and reveals complexity among architecture matrix parameters. The more the total scores of portfolio analysis move toward the upper right region, the more complex functionality is required. Firms then need to manage core competence for such high-complexity functionality products. In contrast, the lower left region is regarded as the modular dimension which allows independent design and outsourcing to external suppliers by applying various control tools (Kang et al., 2009, 2012, 2014). Thus, this portfolio analysis framework is useful to determine the customer and technology requirements matrix as well as functionality-performance-structure and manufacturing process.

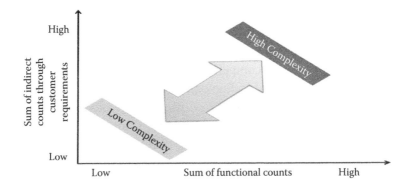

FIGURE 1.5
An example of portfolio analysis based on customer factor-functional matrix.

1.3.2 Network Capability and Intellectual Property Strategy

Starting from 2010, there has been an intellectual property war among global firms. The current bouts between Apple and Android camps accelerate into court battles. In 2012 Apple and Samsung Electronics expanded their disputes into global court bases. This suggests that today's global strategy of firms must consider how to use external resources while utilizing their internal capabilities and develop core competence. Real challenges are to what degree these global firms may claim their legitimate intellectual property rights. In 2012 the world noted the phenomenal success of Korean singer Psy and his "Gangnam Style" in global contents market. This is an example of integration of open network (i.e., YouTube) and core competence (i.e., music and dance with its unique personality and style). Behind Psy's huge success lies his intellectual property strategy as well (Oh, 2012). The success of "Gangnam Style" started with YouTube, which is free. Psy's global market strategy promoted free views and encouraged free parody video development in diverse contexts.

Intellectual property rights includes patent, trademark, industrial property right, copyright of book and music, and new intellectual rights for software. All of these are common in that the owners are given exclusive rights that protect and compensate for their creative efforts and expenses related to the development. Such legal protection and due compensation requirement is to promote new technology development, motivate creative endeavors, and contribute to larger economic development goals.

Recently, in addition to copyright, the concept of copy left is expanded to allow the widescale sharing of creative work. From the standpoint of the income stream of intellectual property rights, too restrictive protection may result in a very small number of users and therefore it is desirable to form an open network within a certain boundary. With high-demand elasticity, the price of a particular product is set somewhat low for revenue maximization. On the other hand, if a reasonably high price of a product may not decrease the overall demand level, then a premium price strategy might be more appropriate.

In the mobile operation software (OS) market, the competition pattern of Apple's iOS and Google's Android is a worthy case to note. Apple has adopted a closed strategy that limits strong hardware and software within its firm network and reaped the full benefits of its value-added products. Google's Android camp has formulated an open network strategy and increasingly dominates the OS market. Psy allowed anyone to use

"Gangnam Style" in YouTube and encouraged production of more parody videos after his song. In this way, he offered a new and exciting dance and music to billions of people and achieved worldwide name recognition. Thus, his intellectual property rights have serious implications.

Now, we may further examine the relationship between intellectual property rights and network capability strategy. From a long-term perspective, an important question is, "What type of organizational structure is more conducive to building a global open network?" In the rapidly changing external environments, various organizational concepts such as "loosely couple organization" (Orton and Weick, 1990), "organizational competence exploration and exploitation" (March, 1991), and "ambidexterity structure for contextual responsiveness" (Burgelman, 1991) are all relevant and useful.

Recent study on Japanese global firms, Itohisa (2012) analyzed how Japanese automotive firms built network capability through joint research and development (R&D) efforts with the firms within their Keiretsu. His research showed the evolution patterns of research networks of each Keiretsu in the 1980s, 1990s, and 2000s through the network and complex system analysis of joint patent data of automotive industry groups. He suggested ANS (ambidextrous network structure) as a concept that describes how firms both exploit existing knowledge within while simultaneously explore new knowledge without their Keiretsu network. ANS thus includes boundary spanner (i.e., active engagement with outside sources for new knowledge exploration), network hub (i.e., central role within the network group for existing knowledge exploitation), and keystone (i.e., network firm that combines both boundary spanner and network hub). In this sense, his ANS concept is the application of organizational role division in the organizational network level (Benner and Tushman, 2003; Tushman and O'Reilley, 1996).

After World War II, Japanese automotive firms have demonstrated noticeable evolution from "homogeneous business network groups" (i.e., network integration focus) to "complex system network groups" of traditional gasoline/diesel engine automobile group plus hybrid electric vehicle (HEV), plug-in hybrid electric vehicle (PHEV), hydrogen fuel cell (HFC) vehicle, and electric vehicle (EV) (i.e., network capability focus). This book aims to show how outstanding global firms construct network capability within their ecosystem in the context of expanding market scope to emerging economies. This naturally requires careful analysis of how firms respond to increasing environmental uncertainty and technological complexity by utilizing their domestic network or developing a global network through active strategic network capability development in the larger business eco-system (Adner, 2006; Kanter, 2012; Ramachandran et al., 2012).

1.4 STRUCTURE OF THIS BOOK

Section I is titled "Research Framework." This section focuses on how indig-enous firms from China, India, Brazil, and Russia take advantage of their market competence and domestic relational network to claim their market advantage with successful product development and commercialization efforts. The case studies of this section are based on extensive executive interviews and plant visits to China, India, and Brazil. All case analyses are based on actual case studies as well as the available business articles.

Chapter 1 is titled "Research Framework: Core Competence and Global Strategy." In Chapter 1, we provide a theoretical framework of the entire book. A careful reading of this chapter would be very helpful for readers to have an overview of this book in terms of the theoretical foundation and the overall direction of this book.

Chapter 2 is titled "Comparisons of Strategies of Established Global Firms and Indigenous Firms from BRICs." This chapter is devoted to com-paring how strategies of established global firms (United States, Europe, Japan, and Korea) are different from those of indigenous firms from Brazil, Russia, India, and China. This section examines key strategies of these global and indigenous firms with a particular focus for the competitive dynamics in the emerging markets.

Section II is entitled "Emerging Global Firms from China, India, Brazil, and Russia." This section focuses on how Japanese global firms formulate and implement their strategies in China, India, and Brazil. The introduc-tion of this first section will explain the main idea of the section (i.e., stra-tegic characteristics of Japanese global firms and their core competencies), and the overall summary of each case illustration of this section. The case studies in this section are based on extensive executive interviews and plant visits to China, India, and Brazil. All the case details are based on actual interviews/plant visits as well as from the available business articles.

Chapter 3 is titled "Strategies of Chinese Indigenous Firms." Chinese indigenous firms utilize their relatively strong competitive power with extensive regional and national market access and effective governmental relations. Chinese global firms grow out of their experiences as suppliers of Japanese and North American global firms over the years. This section highlights how Chinese firms build their core competencies and expand their market potential beyond export-driven early strategies to comprehensive products and service offerings firms targeting both the low end and mid-end of Chinese and global markets. Extensive case study details will focus on the architecture strategy of Haier for its TV market.

Chapter 4 is titled "Strategies of Indian Indigenous Firms." This chapter focuses on strategies of Indian indigenous firms (e.g., TATA). The scope of discussion includes the importance of innovative practices of offering products with low cost and standardized quality (e.g., Nano automobile development and commercialization). The utilization of India's unique IT capabilities, abundant human resources, and global management styles utilizing a global Indian business and professional network are worthy to note of these Indian indigenous firms.

Chapter 5 is titled, "Strategies of Brazilian Indigenous Firms." Brazil is a resource-rich nation that is expected to experience rapid economic growth as it will host the 2014 World Cup and the 2016 Summer Olympics. However, with its long-standing trade protection policies and real fluctuations of the currency, internal industrial foundations are relatively weak. However, with its abundant agricultural and natural resources the Brazilian indigenous firms demonstrate quite dynamic growth patterns. This section examines available literature and case studies of Brazilian firms. This chapter will highlight how Brazilian indigenous firms take their competitive positions as partners of other global firms from the United States, Japan, and Korea. Their strategies are to build up their business capabilities to the level of their global partners while rapidly building their capabilities to target their own Brazilian market and expend their target market in Latin America.

Chapter 6 is titled, "Strategies of Russian Indigenous Firms." Russia had dominated world politics and economies after World War II as the only viable rival against the United States. However, with the slow growth of the manufacturing sector, the overall economic strengths needed real changes. Even so, it is noteworthy of the emergence of the key resource-based firms. Several examples of key Russian firms are (1) AutoVaz that is the top automaker in Russia and (2) GAZPROM that occupies 20% of the global natural gas production. This chapter focuses on the relative weaknesses of the Russian manufacturing industries along with resource-based firms in the context of hybrid economic systems with both government-initiated planned industry policies as well as free-market principles.

Chapter 7 is titled "Strategies of Japanese Firms in the Chinese Market." This chapter provides in-depth case analyses of Komatzu, Yaskawa Electronics, Panasonic, and Clarion. Each of these prominent Japanese global firms experienced quite successful market positioning in China. These four firms represent heavy industries, electronics, and global auto suppliers.

Chapter 8 is titled "Strategies of Japanese Firms in the Indian Market." Increasingly, Japanese component parts suppliers sustain their global advantage by utilizing manufacturing capacities and market strategies in India. This chapter deals with the strategic practices of Japanese manufacturers, particularly Toyota, Denso, Honda, and Seiko-Epson. These firms not only use India as their production basis for the global markets but also provide successfully their own products that satisfy Indian customers.

Chapter 9 is titled "Strategies of Japanese Firms in the Brazilian Market." Brazil is another thriving emerging economy with a sizable population and a vast natural resource basis. Among emerging economies, Brazil is experiencing phenomenal growth. Japanese firms such as Komatzu (2 plants, and 10 distribution centers), Toyota (focused on Brazilian domestic demand), Bridgestone (tire manufacturers for Brazilian automobile market), and Epson (personal computer firm).

Section III is titled, "Japanese and Korean Global Firms in Emerging Markets." This section focuses on how Korean and Japanese global firms formulate and implement their strategies in China, India, and Brazil. All these case studies are also based on extensive executive interviews and plant visits to China, India, and Brazil. All the case details are based on actual interviews/plant visits as well as from the available business articles.

Chapter 10 is titled as "Strategies of Korean Firms in the Chinese Market." In China, Korean auto manufacturer Hyundai-Kia is one of the most successful firms. Korean auto suppliers (e.g., Mobis, Hankuk Tire) support Hyundai-Kia and the global competitive strengths of global auto manufacturers (e.g., Nissan, Ford). We will also introduce supply chain management capabilities of electronic firms (e.g., Samsung and LG)—the focus is their effective supplier building strategies.

Chapter 11 is titled "Strategies of Korean Firms in the Indian Market." This chapter explains the localization strategy of Korean firms (e.g., Hyundai, LG, and Samsung). It is crucial for global firms to translate their home-based technology competence into emerging-market-driven technology competence. The real key for success in emerging markets such as India is to offer products that fit the needs of customers in the local area. Korean firms utilized sensing competence first. Through leverage of market competence, they extended their technology competence.

Chapter 12 is titled "Strategies of Korean Firms in the Brazilian Market." LG and Samsung have effectively executed their global market penetration strategies through empowered local human resources. This section examines LG and Samsung's global marketing and global supply chain management with a particular focus in the Brazilian market. In view of the accelerating needs of infrastructure building (e.g., road, ports, and railroads), the global strategies of global Korean construction firms are also noteworthy in the form of consortium formation and network building.

Chapter 13 is titled "Concluding Remarks and Future Research Issues." In this book we present three essential elements of network capabilities in terms of technology competence, customer competence, and linkage competence. We then provide product architecture as an important foundation of successful product strategy in the emerging economies. All the successful global firms from Japan and Korea do not extend their product models in their respective domestic markets (i.e., Japan and Korea) and merely copy them in the emerging markets. Instead, they recognize the unique customer needs of these customers in the emerging markets (i.e., sensing competence) and offer products and services that satisfy the needs of customers. For this purpose, both global and indigenous firms develop network capabilities for their sustainable competitive advantages.

2

Comparisons of Strategies
of Established Global Firms and
Indigenous Firms from BRICs

This chapter examines how strategies of established global firms (United States, Europe, Japan, and Korea) are different from those of indigenous firms from Brazil, Russia, India, and China. Research includes collaboration and competition between global firms from the United States and Europe and local indigenous firms from emerging markets. Case examples focus on building network capability in the mobile phone industry of China and liquid crystal display (LCD) industry of Northeast Asia. Research results suggest that the key for competitiveness is to strengthen firm core competences and increase collaboration within the open network of the industry ecosystem.

2.1 INTRODUCTION

Successful firms (i.e., winners) continue to develop outstanding products that their customers value while many others (i.e., survivors at risk) are not quite capable of doing so. Clark and Fujimoto (1991) suggest that the real difference between the two lies in integration of business organization and product development processes. Firms that achieve a consistent rate of market success maintain a competitive advantage that rival firms cannot easily challenge by fascinating customers with fantastic products (Park et al., 2012a).

Customers routinely consider functionality and performance embedded in the products and other key elements (e.g., price and convenience) for initial interest. A crucial purchasing decision requires a fine balance between functional elements of products, economic rationality, and customer contexts. For consumer products, customers seek harmony between basic product functionality and their lifestyle value system. Organizational buyers of intermediate industrial products take the balance between product functionality and work system and production process quite seriously.

For example, consumer goods like Apple's iPod and iPhone experienced market success by offering basic functionality like MP3 and mobile phones and lifestyle value through an extended business network (e.g., iTunes and Web store). Apple sells Apple TV through Apple stores. Apple TV allows customers to get access to diverse entertainment options through the iCloud infrastructure and thus enjoy viewing from a large selection of content. Apple's product vision, once realized, will bring complete changes in the TV business. Customers may soon connect songs and videos purchased through Apple TV to Apple Mac, iPad, and iPhone.

Another successful example of intermediate industrial products is the factory automation (FA) sensor by KEYENCE, a Japanese manufacturing firm. The FA sensor is customized through special order to fit to each factory's unique requirements. KEYENCE, however, maintains sizable customer service operational units to readily "answer" various customer requests. The firm also effectively responds to individual customization requirements within given customer budget amounts. More than half of its 1,000 employees belong to customer service units. They visit the tens of thousands of customer sites and gather the information of embedded customer needs as well as expressed ones. In addition to their standardized customer service catalogs, KEYENCE utilizes these broad ranges of customer service information to develop and deploy new products with high customer value (Nobeoka, 2006; Park et al., 2010; Park and Hong, 2012). In brief, product integrity is a much larger concept than product essential functionality and technical performance. This requires an organizational sensing structure and product development process that recognize unexpressed customer values.

The recent prolonged recession in North America and Europe turned the attention of global firms to emerging markets like BRICs as possible global engines for growth. Emerging markets show relatively fast economic growth and the change speed among income groups is rapid. The accelerating growth rates of middle-income groups transform the economic structure from a pyramid shape (i.e., vast size of low income groups with relatively small high-income groups) of poor nations of the past to the diamond structure of advanced nations (i.e., relatively large middle-income groups and an even level of high- and low-income groups).

According to Japanese Economic Industry Bureau Statistics, the total number of households in Asia that have annual disposable income between $5,000 and $35,000 was 140 million in 1990, 220 million in 2000, and 880 million by 2008. This reflects the rapid growth of middle-income groups from China, India, and the Association of South East Asian Nations (ASEAN). From a global perspective, the large share of middle-income groups is distributed in these areas. With rapid economic growth and increase in customer base, these economies hold amazing purchasing power potential for new products and services.

Product strategy for these emerging economies requires linkage competence that combines technology competence for high functionality-quality-performance-driven products and customer competence for high customer needs, lifestyle, and values-based products (Park and Hong, 2012). The obvious obstacle for global firms from advanced nations to penetrating emerging markets like BRICS is customer competence. In particular, many Japanese global firms have relatively high technology competence through their long product development experiences for customers from North America and Europe that expect high quality, functionality, and safety requirements of their products.

In contrast, these global firms experience patterns of business that are new. Sensing different customer needs and translating them into successful products is key for strategic positioning in these emerging markets. To enhance customer competence in the emerging markets, these global firms need to develop customer experts with sensing capability and utilize an information technology (IT) infrastructure. For business-to-consumer (B-to-C) product markets, it is important to assess what particular types of products customers prefer to purchase through direct customer visits and marketing research in retail stores. The size of demand in B-to-C consumer markets is directly related to the increase of personal incomes. The growth rate of business-to-business (B-to-B) markets (i.e., intermediate industrial goods) is in keeping up with the economic growth of emerging economies, but its purchasing pattern is different by regions.

2.2 GLOBAL SUPPLY CHAIN MANAGEMENT (SCM) STRATEGY AND SPECIALIZATION

2.2.1 Supply Chain Management in Emerging Markets

This section discusses supply chain management (SCM) topics in emerging markets. It includes (1) integration between demand chain and supply chain, (2) product/service development fitting emerging markets, (3) differentiation of supply management style and inventory management, (4) consideration of marketing channels, (5) logistics strategy different from advanced markets, and (6) strategy considering local government policy and institutional rules such as Free Trade Agreement (FTA) and Trans-Pacific Partnership (TPP).

Supply chain management considers all of the information exchange and the movement of goods from manufacturer, wholesaler, and retailer to all the suppliers on the extended supply chain. To successfully meet all the requirements of customers, SCM applies a total system in managing information, materials, and services (Chase, 1998; Li and Wang, 2007; Park and Hong, 2012).

It is possible for focal firms to reduce their innovation expenditures and minimize risk factors through collaboration with the partners in a business ecosystem (e.g., suppliers with unique technological and manufacturing capability even in other countries). What is critical for competitive advantage is how such focal firms seek, find, and involve these resourceful and competent suppliers in their network. They must combine knowledge assets of many suppliers in its network. Thus, the integrating ability of a focal firm is important in any network (Brusoni and Prencipe, 2001).

However, it is not sufficient to simply bring in such suppliers into a network and integrate them as network members. Instead, sustainable competitive advantage requires perpetual network coordinating capability. In this sense, coordinating mechanisms of Japanese automobile manufacturers (e.g., encouraging competition among suppliers while promoting long-term trust relationships) have contributed to the formation of successful networks (Asanuma, 1997). Li and Wang (2007) focus on coordination mechanisms that influence the goals of a supply chain member. An effective value chain management requires managing incentives within the supply chain (Narayanan and Raman, 2004). Sahin and Robinson (2002) also discuss the value of information and physical flow coordination.

In the emerging markets, in contrast to past practices in the advanced markets, the patterns of SCM are noticeably dissimilar. Products made are not necessarily sold. SCM requires product planning, development, production, sales, and service based entirely on customers. Firms need to construct their supply chains for their competitiveness in global markets. Global firms move factories and their sales hubs to overseas as well. The immediate challenges to these firms are how to integrate their domestic and global operations. SCM is not to focus on individual firms but to direct attention to the management of entire value chains of firms. Firms need to approach the flows of products not from an individual firm perspective but from a global perspective considering all the network structural relationships associated with the products. The crucial aspect of the global supply chain is how to integrate all the external network firms with a focal company. Global supply chain management, therefore, allows firms to respond to changing customer demands beyond a particular geographical market. Moreover, global firms in emerging markets must manage risks. What level of risk does each of the following post to your company when planning or implementing expansion in emerging markets? For companies expanding their operations into the emerging markets, the success of their global supply chain initiatives is determined by the rigor of their approach to managing operational, tax, and regulatory risks in these jurisdictions. As a reflection of continued concern over challenges facing companies in emerging markets, more than 70% of respondents rated the risks of operating in his region as "very high" or "high." The risks that ranked highest included logistics and distribution capabilities (83%), reliability of suppliers (81%), finding and retaining qualified talent (77%), and import/export restrictions (77%).

2.2.2 Supply Chain Management and Product Architecture

In turbulent times, configuration, collaboration, and coordination complexities of the supply chain have been the variables that matter (Abdelkafi et al., 2011). In particular, supply chain integration (SCI) is one of the most important competitive strategies used by modern enterprises. As the main aim of supply chain management is to integrate various suppliers to satisfy market demand, supplier selection, and evaluation play an important role in establishing an effective supply chain (Lee and Kimz, 2008; Lin et al., 2009; Chen, 2011).

Product architecture is deeply related to supply chain integration (Fixson, 2005; Nepal et al., 2012). Ro et al. (2007) show that in response to product modularity, leading car producers reduced their supplier base. From the viewpoint of the firm like an original equipment manufacturer (OEM), the complexity of supply chain integration can be reduced through a modularity strategy (Abdelkafi et al., 2011). Yet OEMs should develop trust-based buyer–supplier relationships with their module suppliers to attain high quality and reliable delivery. Examining the link between product architecture and supply chain configuration, Ulku and Schmidt (2011) also suggest that the choice of product architecture depends on firm, market, and product characteristics in addition to supply chain structure and that the optimal mapping from architecture to supply chain structure is not always one to one. They also find that a decentralized supply chain may be associated with a more integral product when the technical collaboration penalty is not excessive and suppliers have significantly superior product development capabilities. To develop a supply chain management alignment framework for mass customization, Abdelkafi et al. (2011) formulated 10 propositions explaining the relationships between product development and the SCM framework. Their propositions concerning product architecture are as follows: (1) Modularity reduces the level of internal variety handled by the manufacturing firm. That reduces collaboration complexity from the OEM's viewpoint. (2) Modularity reduces the level of configuration and collaboration complexity. In particular, Shintaku's (2006) product architecture theory that explains the catch-up model of Asian firms is applicable to supply chain configuration from one country to another.

2.3 CASES OF COLLABORATION BETWEEN GLOBAL FIRMS AND INDIGENOUS FIRMS

2.3.1 Global Supply Chain Collaboration between Apple and Foxconn

Effective supply chain management requires adequate information sharing beyond the organizational boundary. Firms take caution in selecting the right supply chain partners. Constructive collaboration with suppliers assumes timely responses to customer needs for mutual competitive advantage. Otherwise, the wrong kind of supply chain partnership might damage all parties involved. This section examines how Apple, a global electronic firm, integrates its global supply chain through a Chinese supplier.

Apple keeps its core competence within and integrates the supply chain with its suppliers. In particular, Apple maintains a collaborative relationship with Foxconn, a global electronics manufacturing service (EMS) firm. In general, a global firm develops a partnership with an EMS firm for three reasons: (1) to meet mass production requirements and timely adjustments for demand fluctuations through adequate production capability; (2) to achieve total cost reduction goals in terms of factory operation costs, maintenance expenses, labor costs, and inventory costs; and (3) to achieve global production responsiveness with adjusting production hub locations according to product life cycle changes and fluctuating major market demands. In this sense, EMS plays effective roles for supply chain management in emerging economies.

According to AMR's supply-chain evaluation report, Apple, holding the number one global leader position for three years straight from 2008, maintains a supply chain partnership with Foxconn, an EMS firm. Apple, the largest customer of Foxconn, has 16% of market share of the electronics market (e.g., smartphone) in China. Apple manages the long-term global supply chain costs by using the interior production facilities of Foxconn for the Chinese domestic market while utilizing Foxconn's coastal facilities to target global markets. Over the years, Apple has released a set of impressive products such as the iPhone and iPad. These products received enthusiastic responses from global customers with fresh design ideas and superb customer values. Apple successfully implemented supply chain management for inventory control, product components' quality, and a short cash cycle (Nikkei, 2012). Apple, a US firm, does not manufacture the iPhone from the United States. Apple instead adopts *fabless* methods and outsources production without having its own manufacturing facilities. The merits of fabless methods are to avoid massive capital investment and huge operational costs related to complex production processes. Instead, Apple focuses its core efforts in design/development/marketing functions. Its speed management strategy allows flexible production volume control. Apple's fabless methods require careful selection of its suppliers and manufacturing partners for its global SCM.

Apple outsources all production processes to Foxconn, a Taiwanese EMS firm, for several reasons: (1) labor costs are cheaper in China than in the United States; and (2) suppliers of iPhone component parts are concentrated in Asia. Apple's sourcing list suggests that 70% of all the component parts are from firms located in Asia including Japan and South Korea. Since most of the component parts are from Asian countries, it is prudent to use Foxconn in China as the primary manufacturer and achieve effective cost advantage through managing supply chain processes from procurement to production. In this way, the strategic alliance between Apple (i.e., strength in product design and marketing competence) and Foxconn (i.e., manufacturing capability) is an example of a successful SCM model. Recently, Apple and its China manufacturing partner, Foxconn, agreed to improve wages and working conditions at factories accused of being sweatshops, a move that could set a new higher-cost benchmark for other Western users of Chinese labor. Foxconn will hire tens of thousands of new workers, eliminate illegal overtime, improve safety protocols, and upgrade worker housing and other amenities. Today's graphic looks at different aspects of the Apple-Foxconn workforce.

Certainly, fabless methods also have disadvantages. Because there is no direct management authority over production processes, total cost increases are probable with inadequate inventory control, component parts increase, and long cycle time. Apple, however, effectively manages these potential problems of fabless methods. Apple implements very strict product life cycle (PLC) management to avoid any unnecessary level of finished goods inventory of each life cycle. Thus, a rumor among customers was circulating saying that once all the inventory is gone, then Apple releases new products. Apple also uses Apple stores—direct sales and distribution stores. Apple sells its products to the final customers and offers after-sale services and completes customer-focused supply chain management. Although Apple restricts the sales of its products to direct sales offices or distribution networks, its customers appreciate Apple's unique marketing strategy. Apple stores offer high-quality after-care services through direct customer contact. Apple monitors the precise levels of inventory through its direct sales offices in real time. Apple also listens to its customers—their needs, interests, changing tastes, and lifestyle requirements.

As of September 2011, Apple's 357 stores report annual sales of $14.1 billion, which is 13% of total sales of $108.2 billion. Each sales office has average sales of $43.30 million which is 4.9 times that of Japanese key retail store, Uniqlo (Nikkei Newspaper, 2012). For this reason, Apple plans to increase six stores in China (including Hong Kong) to 25 stores in 2010 (China Press, 2010). In summary, Apple's production is outsourcing to Foxconn, an EMS firm, and does not have any of its own manufacturing plants. Its sales methods are to stay close to its customers and maintain very strict real-time inventory control along with superb product design and planning.

2.3.2 Growth Process of the Chinese Mobile Phone Industry

In response to the 1999 government industry policy, Chinese local mobile phone makers started their mobile phone manufacturing efforts (Kimura, 2007, 2010). With lack of technological know-how, they built a domestic marketing network with products supplied by global firms. For example, Chinese firm T started as sales distribution agents of Samsung Electronics and other global phone makers and continued to expand their distribution network. From 2005 and forward, it offered its own brand of mobile phones in its distribution channel (Marukawa et al., 2006; Shiu et al., 2008). These Chinese firms used design houses for cost-cutting purposes and concentrated marketing efforts. By 2007 it became the market leader in China offering its own domestic brand and thus exceeded Lenovo's market share.

However, as the low-cost mobile phone market in China required tremendous volume demand, competition among global firms from the United States and Europe and large numbers of small and medium firms intensified (Kimura, 2010). With an increase in the number of mobile phone makers, the business environment of the upstream industry also improved through the wide availability of design house services (i.e., by firms specialized in upstream chip set supply and development/design) and easy access of product platforms for makers with limited technological capacity. As a result, many Chinese firms entered mobile phone markets. With continuous improvement in upstream and downstream sectors, the Chinese mobile phone industry experienced drastic improvement and growth (Jin and von Zedtwitz, 2008). In such upstream and downstream integration, many other US/European integrated circuit (IC) makers also became deeply involved in searching for business opportunities for growing Chinese customers.

Take, for example, Texas Instruments (TI). From 1995 to 1996 Nokia requested TI for process development that includes ARM core and by 1998 it started using TI chip sets (Marykawa, 2006; Shiu et al., 2008, MMRC-DP-226). From the mid-1990s, mobile phone manufacturers (e.g., Nokia) stopped internal IC system development for direct access system and instead outsourced the processes. Nokia secured its own customized chip sets from TI. Thus, Nokia utilized TI's cutting-edge semiconductor process technology and introduced mobile phones with new communication standards for 2.5. Generation GPRS, 2.75 Generation EDGE, and 3 Generation WCDMA ahead of its rivals in the global markets.

TI, however, did not intend to supply customized base band IC for particular firm use only. Rather, its goal was to become a supplier of base band IC for setting industry standards just as Intel did for CPU standards. For this reason, in 1995 TI sought a strategic collaboration with Japanese Panasonic (at that time Matsushita Communication Manufacturer). In 1992 Panasonic started marketing the first GSM mobile phone and by 1996 it developed its own operation system (OS) and chip sets as well. Yet, at that time, the failure rates of its own chip sets were relatively high and chip sets from TI were fitting to mini mobile phones with high performance quality. Panasonic accepted TI's request and from 1996 it embarked joint development projects. After 1997 Panasonic adopted TI's chip sets for its products. For their joint development efforts, Panasonic provided protocol and stack while TI offered digital signal processing (DSP) and semiconductor process technology. Different from Nokia, Panasonic permitted TI to sell base band IC (developed jointly) to mobile phone makers other than Panasonic. Strategic partnership with Panasonic provided TI to expand the user scope of its chip sets as the technological platform for many other firms. Later, Chinese mobile phone makers also adopted TI's chip sets after seeing broad acceptance by many mobile phone manufactures in the world.

It is noteworthy that MediaTek provided platforms that makers with limited technological capability could also handle. Base band IC and protocol stack made by MediaTek in the late 2004 accelerated the vertical specialization process in the Chinese mobile phone industry (Shiu and Imai, 2010). The reason is that MediaTek products have a higher level of platform integration than those by American and European makers. Chips by American/European makers require customers to develop multimedia functions on their own and embed inside of IC. In contrast, base band IC chip sets by MediaTek are sold in packages with adequate technical support from the moment of purchase. Therefore, firms using base band IC chip sets made by MediaTek can develop mobile phone development much faster than using base band IC chips by TI.

Meanwhile, mobile phone makers that occupy downstream positions in the Chinese phone industry produce their products in response to market needs at the right time. Such makers use the design house for their independent product development strategy and still need to possess the technological capacity for building their own platform. Besides, building their own marketing competence and internal technological know-how is essential to maintain domestic advantage and global competitiveness.

2.3.3 LCD Industry: An Illustration of Supply Chain Structure in East Asia

Two major IT industries—semiconductor and LCD industry IT—in East Asia, the market share of Japanese global firms have been steadily reduced since 1990s. Meanwhile, Japanese firms still maintain their relative advantage in component parts and intermediate industrial goods (Shintaku and Park, 2012). In the LCD industry case, the IT supply chain structure is quite noticeable. The transfer of production centers from advanced nations to emerging economies is explained by the flying geese model (Akamatsu, 1962) and product life cycle model (Vernon, 1966). These two models suggest that new products are introduced and tested in the advanced markets first and then as product cycles become mature, the production sites are gradually moved to developing countries.

However, such a transfer time period that takes from advanced countries to emerging economies has been reduced substantially with the drastic reduction in product life cycles in general. It is not uncommon that the products introduced in the advanced countries are quickly and even simultaneously available in emerging economies. In particular, such patterns are prevalent in the electronics industry including LCD TVs, mobile phones, digital cameras, and light disk drives (Shintaku, 2006).

Figure 2.1 shows the LCD industry structure of Northeast Asia. Japan, Korea, and China assume somewhat different structural positions in the LCD TV industry. In 2000, the LCD TV market was formed in Japan, North America, and Europe. By 2005, the sizable market in China invited many Chinese firms to increase their own production. Meanwhile, within

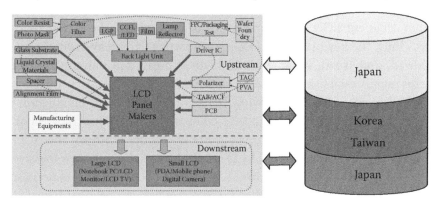

FIGURE 2.1
LCD industry structure of Northeast Asia.

the LCD industry, LCD panel production is centered in South Korea and Taiwan beyond Japan. By the late 2000s, the small size of panel production occurs in China as well. The Chinese government vigorously invites Japanese, Korean, and Taiwanese firms to build huge, large-size panel production facilities in China. Yet, Japanese firms still maintain their lead in LCD raw materials and facility construction know-how (Park, 2010, WIAS).

As shown above, such a complex vertical structure demonstrates diverse international division of roles in keeping up with the rapid product demand pattern transfers from advanced nations to emerging markets. Similar patterns are noted in basic components of light disk (e.g., light pickup and chip sets), chip sets, and final component portions of mobile phones (Shintaku et al., 2007; Shintaku & Park, 2012). The key factor that impacts the production transfer speed is product and process architecture. In general, modular type of products and their component parts have fast transfer speed, while integral products and their component parts show relatively slow transfer speed (Shintaku et al., 2008).

A careful analysis of international division of roles in the LCD industry suggests that every structural level (i.e., finished component parts/materials, intermediate component parts/materials, and basic component parts/materials) has distinct product architectures. In Japan, suppliers of raw materials and facility makers usually worked together for new product development. With gradual deterioration of Japanese competitiveness on finished goods and device makers, Samsung and LG of South Korea (once they had been no more than Japanese upstream customers) acquired manufacturing systems from Japanese manufacturers through aggressive investment. In a relatively short time period, they established visible global market leader positions.

Afterward, Taiwanese panel makers received technology transfers from Japanese LCD panel makers who also entered the global market. Thus, the key players in LCD panel markets are firms from Korea, Taiwan, and Japan. From the mid-1990s, Korean and Taiwanese LCD firms rapidly established their own solid LCD industry infrastructures for which Japanese firms had provided a full range of relevant manufacturing systems and supplied necessary component parts (Shintaku, 2006). Meanwhile, Sharp of Japan, Samsung and LG Philips of Korea, and AUO and CMO of Taiwan are global LCD market leaders through their massive investment. Upstream competitive advantage (i.e., components/materials/facility system) cannot be easily transferrable because original patented technology is secured through independent processes in a black box. Such integral product architecture is not for the target of rapid catch-up.

However, Korean/Taiwanese firms attained such a short-term catch-up in the LCD panel business because their massive investment was heavily focused on products/processes with modular architecture. Downstream LCD TV shows somewhat more complex structures. Recent TV market share indicates that Samsung and LG are global leaders with their successful vertical integration of LCD TV and panel manufacturing. Most core component parts of LCD TV are modularized. Therefore, Chinese and Indian firms are capable of becoming market leaders in the years to come once serious quality issues are properly handled. In brief, the LCD industry has three levels of structures of which LCD panel makers are in the middle. Even in these three level structures, upstream components/materials are all dominated by firms from Japan and other advanced nations.

2.4 CONCLUSION

Chapter 2 examines case examples of the Chinese mobile industry and the LCD industry of East Asia. This is to study how global firms build their network capability through strategic collaboration plus vigorous competition involving local suppliers in global market contexts. First, any global firm must define and strengthen its core competence boundary within its industry ecosystem and seek for strategic partnership through an open network. In the case of the mobile phone industry, the obvious trend is toward open/modular/vertical specialization. The vertical integration business model is now of the past and increasingly global firms switch to a vertical specialized business model. Since specialized semiconductor firms offer the upstream base band IC chip set platforms, design house and EMS firms appear to allow global mobile firms to move away from their past vertical integration model to more diverse business models instead. The first case is about the strategic partnership between Apple and Foxconn. Increasing market segmentation, vertical specialization, and open networks enable even relatively small mobile phone manufacturers to "sow and reap" with their own products in the global markets. Besides Apple, other firms such as Google (i.e., recent acquirer of Motorola and user of Android OS), RIM (Research in Motion), and HTC (i.e., relatively small smartphone makers) display an impressive level of business success in certain customer segments by offering an enormous range of applications and service options.

In contrast, indigenous firms from emerging economies (e.g., China and India) build collaborative supply chain relationships with well-established global firms and steadily strengthen their core competences for their long term growth objectives. Foxconn, for example, collaborates with Apple and strengthens its core competence as an EMS firm. This is true with Chinese local mobile phone manufacturers. Recent phenomenal growth of PC makers and IT firms from China are noteworthy. The IT industry shows relatively rapid technological knowledge transfer, and thus no firm is able to sustain its competitive advantage for an indefinite time (Henderson, 2003; Yasumoto, 2010). Product system completion and performance outcomes do not depend on the superiority of individual structural elements but in the integration of the final product system (Clark and Fujimoto, 1991). Such a tendency is more obvious in industries with extreme modularization and an open system network (Prencipe et al., 2003; Jacobides et al., 2006; Gawer, 2010; Yasumoto, 2010).

Going with the waves of global open ecosystem development, even the relatively small size of firms (if possessing adequate strengths in any of the areas such as strategic planning, technological ability, product development potential, brand, new applications and service system know-how) find opportunities for success in global markets through building network capability that might complement their relative disadvantages. As seen in Apple, the gap between firms excelling in vertical specialization/open network ecosystem and those that are not would become quite visible. Increasingly, a technology-intensive industry ecosystem requires rapid growth and thus coordination ability among network firms is crucial for long-term business successes and failures (Teece, 1986; Christensen et al., 2002; Evans et al., 2006; Gawer, 2010; Yasumoto, 2010). In emerging economies, global firms stand firm on their competences and take advantage of their coordination mechanism with their strategic partners. Both in advanced and emerging markets, an enormous range of market segmentations requires firms to pursue successful global market strategy by combining a complex set of options such as promoting horizontal product distribution, expanding their economies of scale, deploying external development/productive resources, and seeking network collaboration. Increasingly, competitive advantages of global firms lie in the complex sets of network capability that include market needs sensing competence, network coordination ability, and technology/knowledge exploration capability within their ever-expanding network ecosystem.

Section II

Emerging Global Firms from China, India, Brazil, and Russia

3

Strategies of Chinese Indigenous Firms

Chinese indigenous firms utilize their relatively strong competitive power with extensive regional and national market access and effective governmental relations. Chinese global firms grow out of their experiences as suppliers of Japanese and North American global firms over the years. This section highlights how Chinese firms build their core competencies and expand their market potential beyond export-driven early strategies to comprehensive products and service offerings firms targeting both low-end and mid-end Chinese and global markets. Extensive case study details will focus on the architecture strategy of Haier for its TV market.

3.1 INTRODUCTION

Chinese indigenous firms utilize their relatively strong competitive power with extensive regional and national market access and effective governmental relations. Chinese global firms grow out of their experiences as suppliers of Japanese and North American global firms over the years. This section highlights how Chinese firms build their core competencies and expand their market potential beyond export-driven early strategies to comprehensive products and service offerings firms targeting both low-end and mid-end Chinese and global markets. Extensive case study details will focus on the architecture strategy of Haier for its TV market.

3.2 CHINESE ECONOMIC CONTEXT

China is a rapidly developing country with more than 56 different national groups including the majority of Han (93%). It has rich natural resources such as coal, oil, and steel as well as abundant human resources. Since 1978 China has pursued reform-minded, economic development policies and has sustained high annual growth for years. Under Deng Xiaoping's reformist agenda, Chinese economic priorities were to develop Eastern Coastline Regions first and after a while substantial regional disparity became a serious national issue. Chinese central government moved toward balanced economic development. Therefore, massive investment in the development of the western and central regions allows rapid economic growth. After 2002, Hu Jintao's government stressed the need for social harmony and made serious efforts to remove the huge differences in standard of living between urban and rural areas. Xi Jinping's government continues the development policy of interior rural regions and accelerates the vast differences between the eastern coastline areas and interior western areas.

Since 2000, China has experienced high growth rates in export and foreign direct investment (FDI). Massive investments in fixed assets and social infrastructures have supported industrialization, urbanization, and revitalization of rural areas. With an increase of the items of cutting-edge technology products and enhancement of competitiveness of Chinese export items in global markets, China has maintained more than 10% of annual GDP growth even after the global financial crisis since 2008 (Lee, 2008). Additional financial meltdowns in Greece and European shocks slowed the annual growth rates, but China remains one of the most steadily growing economies in the world. This is primarily because of a huge domestic market that consistently grows over the years. The Chinese government is committed to expanding the size of domestic demand through its variety of policy initiatives. In spite of sizable growth in social welfare expenditures, after the mid-2000s the Chinese government has improved the budget definition through expanding the tax basis of its growing economy. High rates of economic growth also involve the rapid hike in the real estate market, increasing food prices, and money supply growth, which are all crucial macropolicy issues in the coming years.

3.3 CASE STUDIES OF CHINESE FIRMS

Since 2000, the brands of Chinese global firms have become much more visible in global markets. The scale of the Chinese domestic market is the largest in the world. In keeping up with the large domestic market impact, the growth speed of Chinese firms is also rapid. With expansive fiscal expenditures, enormous inflows of durable goods are noted including TVs and automobiles in the leading cities in China. With the simultaneous brand market growth is obvious in relation to the drastic changes occurring in the retail-based logistics and leisure industries. Chinese state-owned enterprises are increasingly privatized. These firms accept the branding standards, and their advertising and promotional expenditures increase accordingly. As a result, the size of the Chinese advertising market has already surpassed that of the United Kingdom, Germany, and Japan. In this way, Chinese firms had exceeded many of the Western product brands through their price competitiveness and logistical advantages in the Chinese market. With their relatively obscure reputation among Chinese consumers, they pursue innovation in the quality of products and services.

Chinese firms may dominate their domestic market with their brand products. The key is effective implementation. Chinese brands are more familiar to Chinese people than are Western brands. For example, TCL decorated its mobile phones with imitation diamonds for the Chinese customers who like to communicate their sense of dignity. At first, foreign global firms laughed at the idea but soon they also adopted this concept (Meyer et al., 2004). More Chinese firms are growing as global brands. Haier is an outstanding example. In this section, a short case study of Haier is introduced.

3.4 CASE STUDY OF HAIER

3.4.1 History of Haier

December 26, 1984, is regarded as the birthday of Haier. In 1984 Haier was at the brink of bankruptcy with huge losses. As Zhang Ruimin assumed the position of CEO, Haier started showing rapid growth. From 1985 on, Haier changed its product focus from washer producer to refrigerator manufacturer. Haier's business growth strategy suggests three distinct patterns: the initial period (1984–1990) was mostly for the introduction of several styles of refrigerators. After 1991, Haier expanded its product lines that included refrigerators, air conditioners, and white household electronics brands (i.e., refrigerators and washers), and other black household product lines (e.g., TVs and personal computers).

Starting from 1998, Haier moved forward beyond China for global market orientation. Initially, it established distribution centers in the United States and Europe. From 2005 it accelerated the global market orientation. It empowers the native managers for decision making so as to develop products that fit the target market needs and thus implements its global brand strategy. Specifically, from 2005, in the course of implementing high-end product development strategy, Haier has developed diverse premium products that satisfy global customer requirements. Haier developed refrigerators that fit the specific country market needs. For example, Haier introduced high-end premium quality products including temperature-flexible refrigerators (with temperature monitoring devices) in the United States, refrigerators with no middle barriers in France, and energy-saving refrigerators in Italy. At the same time, for rural customers in China, Haier developed cost-competitive refrigerators with special design features that address issues of frequent electricity leakages and voltage fluctuations and damages by rats that sneak into the refrigerators (Figure 3.1).

Summary of Haier's Defining Events for the First 10 Years

December 1985	76 refrigerators that failed inspection tests were destroyed by hammers. Quality-mindset revolution in Haier. Established Mr. Zhang's leadership. One hammer that was used to destroy the refrigerators was named "Haier Jujubu" and stored in March 2009 as a national treasure in the national museum. Afterward, Haier received a technological transfer contract with Rifhel of Germany and started producing high-end, premium refrigerators.
December 1991	Qingdao Refrigerator acquired Qingdao Freezers and Qingdao Air-conditioners and established Qingdao Haier.
September 1992	Haier was ISO9001 certified.
December 1992	Qingdao Haier Cooperatives changed into Haier Cooperatives.
November 1993	Refrigerator business unit was listed on Shanghai Stock Exchange.
May 1995	Haier Industrial Complex complete. Second Haier established
July 1995	Acquired Hongsung Electrical Co. and established Qingdao Haier Washer. By 1998, Haier acquired and merged 18 companies and laid the foundation for global diversification.

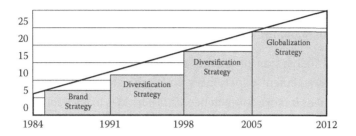

FIGURE 3.1
Haier's business growth strategy.

In 2011 Haier acquired Sanyo Electrical Co.'s washer and refrigerator division for Japanese and household electronic division for four Southeast Asian country markets (i.e., Indonesia, Malaysia, Philippines, and Vietnam). With this strategic move, Haier's strategy made a drastic turn toward global markets from 2012. Haier presented a three-step strategy for global markets. Its vigorous expansion to global markets started from 2001 when China became a member of the WTO (World Trade Organization). Haier's business motto was, "Strive to be a global brand maker that customers from China and the entire world admire." Haier's business slogan is "Inspired Living."

Haier's founder and CEO Zhang Ruimin said, "The aim of most of Chinese firms is to export their goods and earn foreign currencies, but Haier's exporting goal is to create and sustain Haier's brand reputation" (Meyer et al., 2004). He is the ardent believer of the brand power. The hammer that is on display in the lobby of the headquarters (i.e., "use hammer to destroy any goods in defect") suggests the commitment for world-class service programs that assure the loyalty of its global customers. The motto of Haier's market entry strategy is, "Do first what is difficult." After developing sufficient production capabilities, Haier entered US and EU markets. Thus, all Haier's products sold in the United States are labeled as "Made in America." In this way, by 2005 Haier has attained 10% market share in the large refrigerator market in the United States and its high market growth is maintained thereafter.

3.4.2 Strategic Management System: Four Phases of Development Strategy

Haier's strategic management system is explained into four distinct phases of development.

3.4.2.1 Quality Strategy (Comprehensive Quality Management) (1984 to 1991)

This period focuses on producing refrigerators only. It is to accumulate business management experiences and cultivate comprehensive quality management as its core competence. This period is to lay a solid foundation for future growth. One symbolic incident—"Hammer Events"—occurred in December 1985. Haier's CEO gathered its employees and demolished 76 refrigerators that had quality defects. The sales prices of these 76 refrigerators were as large as two months salaries of the entire workforce. At that time, one unit of premium brand refrigerators was worth 800 Yuan, whereas one month of worker's wage was no more than 50 Yuan. Thus, these refrigerators with even slight quality issues were rated as a second or third brand and sold to "reasonable customers" who wanted them at lower prices. Yet, by using "Haier Hammer," the firm did away with those practices. The hammer was accepted as a national memorial treasure in March 2009 and is now being preserved in a national museum. This period became an era of Haier's quality revolution and huge transformation in the business mindset among the management and employees of the firm.

3.4.2.2 Brand Strategy Phase (OEC Management) (1992 to 1998)

This period was to diversify its businesses from a single refrigerator manufacturer to a competitive manufacturer of complex product lines. As its expansion strategy, Haier adopted the strategy of "Eat fish that has experienced shock." This means that fish seems to be dying not out of internal corruption but having received a major shock. The firm had a good hardware system but software aspects were not yet well developed. Haier was implementing management system breakthroughs. Based on this strategy, Haier acquired and merged 18 other firms including Hongsung Electricals and Educk Washers and thus Haier expanded its business capabilities for global market positioning.

Haier also adopted an OEC management system. OEC is derived from keywords such as "Altogether, Everyone, Everything, Everyday, Control, and Clear." OCE management principles are expressed in phrases like "Complete each day's work by the end of the day." Work units examine each day's performance results. Any improvement needs are set aside as the next day's target goals. To all employees, 3E cards (Everyone,

Everything, Everyday) are also distributed. These OEC management rules include "Work Flows and Improvement Management" as follows:

1. Worker Tasks and Improvement: Upon completion of daily work, each worker checks the status of seven areas (i.e., production volume, quality, wastes, prototype, safety, production, and labor rules), records them on a 3E card, and submits it to his/her team leader.
2. Supervisor Tasks and Improvement: Each production floor supervisor examines a single product line and manufacturing floor every 2 hours daily. Any problems detected are recorded in a daily log.
3. Managers check "Work Tasks and Improvement" and "Supervisor Tasks and Improvement."

Haier has also implemented a 6S Movement by adding "Safety" to Japanese 5S (Sorting, Set in order, Systematic Cleaning, Standardizing, and Sustaining) Movement. The 6S Movement (Sorting, Set in order, Systematic Cleaning, Standardizing, Sustaining, and Safety) recognizes outstanding employees with a 6S mark. Other workers naturally learn from their examples. Three worker motion transformation is also adopted for labor management.

The 3E Haier Management Control System classifies workers into three groups (i.e., outstanding, acceptable, and testing). Testing employees are either being laid off or are on a waiting list, whereas outstanding workers receive additional premium benefits and become candidates for advanced training opportunities.

3.4.2.3 Diversification Strategy Period (1998 to 2005)

In this period, Haier has expanded its distribution channel, establishing service centers and marketing its products in major international markets. Haier's brand is steadily positioning in key market segments in terms of brand recognition, credibility, and reputation. Thus, Haier's efforts are moving toward further expansion and enhancement. In this stage, Haier's market chain management as its source of core competitiveness is becoming important.

In Haier groups, a new "market chain" concept was initiated for the purpose of encouraging a competitive spirit within. It is to introduce "the market chain" within Haier. This market chain refers to implementation of the concept of "external market competition and market transactions" into the firm's internal processes. For example, the workers in early manufacturing processes are called vendors, those in the subsequent manufacturing processes are customers, and work contents are known as products. Thus, even the relationships among internal work processes are defined by strict supply contracts. Furthermore, another management method, "SST management," was also applied in this period. This SST stands for the first letters of "suo chou: seeking maintenance to the next processes" (S), "suo pei: discover defective parts and request compensation to the workers of previous processes" (S), and "tiao zha: stop the delivery to the customers at the location where defective parts are discovered" (T). The characteristics of Haier's human resource management are fairness and integrity. Thus, people are promoted not by human relationship factors (e.g., those from same country and same language groups), but are based on competence and performance results.

3.4.2.4 *Global Brand Strategy Period (2006 to Present)*

For the international diversification period, China remained the center of the operations. For global brand strategy, Haier is now targeting the entire world. In keeping up with the globalization of the world economies, Haier examines the primary brands of each nation and instead focuses on creating its own brand products as competitive alternatives for global customers. Continuous upgrading of their products and enhancement of its competitive capabilities are all the more imperative and "individual-goal combination" and "T Style" of new management control systems are being introduced.

The "individual-goal combination" can be explained in this way. "Individual" refers to a strategic business unit (SBU), which is able to independently implement innovation strategies. "Goal" is about attaining the number one competitive market position in every target market. "People" become SBUs that work in the designated markets. Thus, "individual-goal combination" intends to achieve direct market advantage with all Haier's customers.

"T Style" is a management method that accomplishes the objectives of "individual-goal combination" and budget system that realizes competitive market performance targets. The entire processes of Haier Groups from order receipt to order fulfillment involve 13 different aspects. "T Style" focuses on "4 T": T (time), keep delivery time requirements; T (target), number one market position; T (today), daily improvement of OEC management; and T (team), teamwork for achieving goals.

In this period, the main emphasis is on Haier's SBU. Instilling SBU management mechanisms with all the employees has been its top strategic priority. The concept of SBU was initially used by GE from 1970. SBU is one business unit in terms of total firm strategic goals. Within the boundary of Haier's overall business strategy framework, each SBU can take a realistic investment decision for its number one business priority. Each SBU also examines business patterns, customer characteristics, growth potential, competitive rivals, technological capabilities, production modes, future prospects, and commonalities with other SBUs, its uniqueness and resources control.

From September 8, 1998, Haier started reconstructing business process redesign (BPR). Its ultimate goal is to transform its employees from the status of being managed to actively realizing innovation players. The focus of SBU is to connect the individual goals into the firm's performance targets. Haier has many functional-specific SBUs such as market SBU, research and development (R&D) SBU, and manufacturing SBU. Market SBUs are further divided into regional SBUs and customer segment SBUs. With increasing value of market demand, market SBUs take the position of central core among all SBUs. Haier expands the value of customers and employees while each SBU is divided into smaller units. Recently, total value management (TVM) is another of Haier's strategic business slogans. The key of TVM is V (values). Through innovation of employees, Haier intends to enhance value-added products, and the global brand enhancement goals are divided into the specific responsibility aspect of each individual employee.

3.4.3 Haier's Product Strategy

3.4.3.1 Haier's Product Development Speed

A unique aspect of Haier's new product development is the rapid increase in the number of new products. In 1985 when Haier started its business operation, its main product was one type of refrigerator. By 2000, its product lines included refrigerators, washers, air conditioners, dishwashers, air cleaners, color TVs, mobile phones, and a wide range of personal computers (PCs). The number of new products introduced to markets increased from 60 models in 1995 to 252 models in 1998 and 382 models in 2002. Haier deploys one model per day to markets (Fujimoto et al., 2005).

3.4.3.2 *Champion Quality of R&D Organization*

In 1984 Qingdao Refrigerator (i.e., Haier's earliest name) established a technology department in a mountain as the starting point of its product development efforts. Key personnel of Haier first received training in Liebherr (a German firm) and acquired crucial product development competences. In 1991 Qingdao Refrigerator acquired and merged both Qingdao Refrigerator and Qingdao Air Conditioners. Their R&D organization was called "Refrigerator Research Institute" from which Refrigerators/Freezers/Air Conditioner Projects were separately organized for more independent innovation outcomes.

In 1995 Haier adopted the patterns of other diversified global firms from the United States and Europe and built three floors of comprehensive R&D systems. The first floor is the Central Research Institute that started in 1998. It established collaborative development alliances with the 28 firms from Japan, Europe, and the United States. Its focus is on basic research and commercialization of cutting-edge technologies into wider applications. The second floor has 14 different product development institutes and maintains independent profit centers by product lines. The third floor houses the production prototype centers that resemble production processes of various factories. In the production floor Haier implements the improvement of production technology and process innovation. Haier also achieves cost reductions for new products through effective use of raw materials.

3.4.3.3 *Haier's Global Competitiveness and Its Product Strategy*

Haier's international market strategy is illustrated by its slogan: "Go overseas. Find the 'gap' products and seize the market." Its product strategy is to find "gap" products that refer to the products with unrealized market potential because of lack of value awareness of its competitors such as small refrigerators, apartment computers, and desk refrigerators. Its channel strategy is to focus on small appliance shops and toy shops. Haier once made the record sales of 7,000 air conditioners within 7 hours in the United States. These "gap" product markets accounted for Haier's 50% and 20% market share in the United States.

Haier's domestic market strategy is about "going local" by meeting domestic demand by offering popular products with low cost and high quality. Its product strategy is in line with the local needs. Its channel strategy is the large-chain supermarket.

Attempts are also made to pursue a high premium market strategy. Some of the examples are as follows:

1. Haier Home. This is to offer kitchen appliances as a set to customers. Chinese consumers do interior design for their mansion apartments on their own. Haier offers a comprehensive set of electronic range, stove, rice cooker, and dishwasher along with interior design options. For example, Haier makes its brand of kitchen cabinets along with design services.
2. Built-in Appliance. An example is a built-in refrigerator along with kitchen cabinets. Other samples of built-in appliances include built-in kitchen furniture and kitchen set interior design. The target customers for Haier Home and Built-in Appliances include not only individual customers but also corporate and industry users as well.

3.5 LENOVO CASE

Lenovo was established in 1984 as a producer of PCs and other supplementary computer equipment. It started as agent distributor of foreign manufacturers. In 1990 it first introduced its own PC brand to the market. From 1994 its PC sales doubled each year for the next 4 years. By 1997 it became the top PC maker in China. From 2000, it diversified its product lines and expanded its global operations. In 2004, Lenovo acquired IBM of the United States and became one of the top three PC makers along with Dell and HP. Afterward, it consolidated IBM's management resources and enlarged its market scope to the United States, Europe, and Japan. Based on a successful Chinese business model, it expanded to emerging markets, including India, Russia, Brazil, and Middle East.

3.5.1 Early Market Experiences and Global Market Entry

According to Lenovo's official statement, it was founded on November 1, 1984. The Chinese government approved Lenovo's incorporation on the same day. The first meeting in preparation for starting the company was held on October 17, 1984. Eleven staff members of the Institute of Computing Technology, Chinese Academy of Sciences, attended. The 200,000 Yuan used as start-up capital and the initial approved name was the Chinese Academy of Sciences Computer Technology Research Institute New Technology Development Company (Wikipedia).

At this time, Lenovo did not have its own products. Thus, it sold products made by other firms such as sport shirts, roller skates, shoes, quartz-type watches, and color TVs. Through various trial and error, it reconfirmed independent management resources to develop macrocomputer and technology management from Computer Technology Research Institute (CTRI) and concentrated on offering computer-related services.

CTRI earned 600,000 Yuan in profit by transferring memory functions of macrocomputer development projects and application software to new Technology Development Cooperatives. It also earned another 700,000 Yuan by transferring the business activities including testing, repairs, education, and training related to the 500 IBM PCs that the Chinese Academy of Science purchased. Afterward, its sales grew up to 73,000,000 Yuan in 1987.

In 1988, with additional 300,000 Hong Kong dollars, it established Hong Kong Lenovo. It kept selling products of foreign brands and produced Intel 286 motherboards and achieved production system integration. It also became the sole agent for US AST and started distribution of AST products in China. Through these activities, Lenovo established an information-gathering infrastructure for the overseas market and mastered computer technology of advanced nations and kept focusing on developing domestic sales distribution channels.

3.5.2 Establishing Lenovo's Brand and Pursuit of Its Unique Customer Base

In March 1990, Lenovo became successful in developing its own brand of PC products and received the Chinese government's permission to produce 5,000 units in the first year. Its main component parts, except the motherboards made by Hong Kong Lenovo, were the same as those of AST products. At that time, the revenues received from sales of finished PC products were protected by 50% import duties. Thus, Lenovo's brand products were comparatively cheaper than those imported (i.e., AST products) in the same distribution channels and their sales steadily increased over the years. However, from 1991, Taiwan-made inexpensive products swept through Chinese markets along with other foreign brands of IBM and HP. Besides, government support through exemption of import duties dropped from 50% to 20%. Thus, Lenovo's market share was negatively affected. In this changing market context, Lenovo focused on supplying PCs for Chinese users in its competitive strategy against other foreign PC makers. It kept developing low-priced and highly specialized new products for small- and medium-sized enterprises, educational institutions, and family users.

In the course of implementing such a competitive market strategy, in 1992 Lenovo established a technology information-gathering research center in the US Silicon Valley. In this way, its research center in Beijing designed motherboards through the support of its Hong Kong–based operations and high-level analysis of changing customer global needs. As Lenovo kept up the innovation pace with the global market leaders in terms of utilizing the cutting-edge technologies and continued to develop a variety of PCs—regular desktop, notebook, servers—it soon became a comprehensive computer manufacturer and services provider.

3.5.3 Diversification of Its Businesses and Enhancement of Global Competitiveness

From the mid-1990s, Lenovo utilized its distribution channels and started marketing PCs and other related products made by global firms from the United States, Europe, and Japan. By selling global brand products, Lenovo was able to recognize the domestic market trends and developed its brand of printers and diversified other product lines. In this way, Lenovo strengthened its customer competence while enhancing its technology competence, and thus it was becoming a world-class company that realizes excellent product concept into outstanding products. However, its technological capabilities were still behind the global leaders, and its products were no more than imitations of other global brands.

From 2000, Lenovo poured a huge investment into its R&D areas. Yet, its market share was relatively small compared to the global leaders such as Apple and IBM. Thus, Lenovo sought its business diversification through M&A (mergers and acquisitions) and strategic alliance. With vigorous technology exchange programs, it began manufacturing mobile phones and OA (office automation) products. Furthermore, it enlarged the scope of strategic alliance with other global firms. For example, it collaborated with CISCO in the areas of communication and Unix product development. It also had technology exchange programs with IBM and CA for software development. With Intel, Lenovo established Lenovo/Intel Future Technology Research Center and engaged in joint research on Internet technology. From 2001, Dell sold its products directly in China and penetrated with BTO, Lenovo's market share dropped from 30% in 2011 to 27% in 2004. In response, Lenovo engaged in direct sales and introduced BTO (build to order) as well.

3.5.4 Lenovo Acquired IBM PC and Expanded Its Global Target Market

In December 2004, Lenovo with its annual sales no more than $3 billion, acquired IBM PC (annual sales of $13 billion in exchange for $650 million (cash) and $600 million (Lenovo's stock) and $500 million (debts). Through this, Lenovo gained all the R&D research centers of IBM PC, manufacturing facilities, distribution channels, patents, and two R&D centers in the United States and Japan and 9,600 employees in 160 countries. Thus, Lenovo became quickly an industry leader with 7.6% of global market share. To maximize its M&A effects, Lenovo moved its headquarters to New York and its business language to English. It responded with prudence to serve its customers, employees, and distribution channels. In this way, its sales and profits increased steadily. Lenovo also hired Dell's executives and applied Dell's management practices and accomplished drastic cost reduction and expanded the new market segments. Lenovo also hired competent professionals from diverse countries and implemented its global strategy. Lenovo constructed successful business models in China first, then strengthened its market scope to emerging economies including India, Brazil, Russia, and the Middle East.

3.6 CONCLUSION

In this chapter, two cases (Haier and Lenovo) highlighted the growth of global firms from China. These firms have a relatively short history of developing technology competence. They strengthened their customer competence first to achieve their domestic advantage and adopted network capability strategy through strategic alliance with other global leaders to achieve rapid technology catch-up. Lenovo achieved its global leader status through the acquisition of IBM PC for the rapid growth as a global leader.

4

Strategies of Indian Indigenous Firms

This chapter focuses on strategies of Indian indigenous firms (e.g., Tata). The scope of discussions includes the importance of innovative practices of offering products with low cost and standardized quality (e.g., Nano automobile development and commercialization). The utilization of India's unique information technology (IT) capabilities, abundant human resources, and global management styles utilizing global Indian business and professional networks are worthy to note of these Indian indigenous firms.

4.1 INTRODUCTION

This chapter focuses on strategies of Indian indigenous firms (e.g., Tata). The scope of discussions includes the importance of innovative practices of offering products with low cost and standardized quality (e.g., Nano automobile development and commercialization). The utilization of India's unique information technology (IT) capabilities, abundant human resources, and global management styles utilizing global Indian business and professional networks are worthy to note of these Indian indigenous firms.

4.2 INDIA'S ECONOMIC GROWTH PATTERNS

Over the years India has recorded different annual growth rates—from 4% in 2000 to 2002, 7% in 2003 to 2004, 8.2% in 2005, and 8.9% in 2006 to 2008 and somewhat slowed after the 2009 Global Financial Crisis. Since then, the Indian economy has shown steady growth rates (Lee, 2008). The reason for its fast growth after 2000 is the acceleration in social infrastructure development, the vitalization in economic zones, the return of outstanding human resources to domestic industries, and the increase in consumption spending through expanding middle-class segments.

First, the Indian government and Indian firms plan to pour massive spending into infrastructure development since 2000. The Indian government concentrates its efforts in expanding roads/highways, electricity, and communication networks. The Golden Quadrilateral Project is a prime example. This project is to connect four major cities of India from north to south and east to west including Mumbai, New Delhi, Calcutta, and Chennai with superhighways that are 6,000 km long. In the course of completing this huge project, the multiplier effects on employment creation, demand growth in related industries, and reduction in logistics costs would be enormous. Another example for communication infrastructure network, Reliance Communications Inc., India's largest telecommunication firm, announced its plan to spend $1.5 billion for 3 years starting from January 28, 2007, to construct deep sea cables (connecting 60 countries in the world, for a total length of 115,000 km, simultaneously processing 2.5 billion telephone voice recordings). Furthermore, the Indian government plans to build an additional 18 nuclear plants starting from April 2007 as part of the 11th 5-year planning cycle.

Second, they plan vitalization of the Special Economic Zones. From 2000, India established special economic zones (SEZs) in various areas. The firms that locate in these SEZs receive special privileges in the form of exempting 100% corporate taxes for the first 5 years and in the following 5 years, 50% exemption of corporate taxes as well as other tariffs, state sales taxes, services taxes, and federal sales taxes, regardless of the sources of investment capital. By 2004, 42 SEZs were created, and in March 2006 an additional 148 new SEZs were established. These new SEZs would focus on petrochemical, biotechnology, IT integrative industries, seaports, and heavy chemical manufacturing industries. As building these comprehensive infrastructures continues, India started attracting a massive inflow of new direct foreign investment, which had been somewhat slowed over the years. In this regard, the Indian government also relaxes various regulatory requirements to encourage these foreign investors.

Third, returning superior human talent back to India is a goal. Recently, many overseas Indian talents that have been prominent in the areas of semiconductors, automotive, pharmaceutical, and jewelry design chose to work in India instead. Thus, a massive influx of high-quality human resources contributes to raising India's industrial competitiveness. Such changes are the direct response to the priority hiring and high compensation policies of Indian firms. Semiinias (having been established by Indians living in the Silicon Valley of the United States) invested $100 million for a SEZ located in Southern India and established semiconductor assembly and quality inspection facilities. Since 2007 the firm has produced semiconductors—the first in India. Furthermore, after the mid-2000s these Indian firms moved beyond the supplier status of original equipment manufacturers (OEMs) and instead using their own capital pursued M&A of other foreign firms and enhanced the competitiveness of Indian industries as a whole. For example, Wipro, one of the largest IT software firms in India, acquired the integrated circuit (IC) design engineering firm Newrojic of Australia in 2005 and in 2006; it also became the owner of Quantic of the United States, which specializes in automotive and airplane design and continued to expand its global business market potential.

Fourth, a drastic increase in consumption with the expanding middle classes was desired. The rapid growth of Indian firms has impacted the improvement of employment and overall labor wages. As the size of the middle classes multiplied, the base of consumption for disposable consumer goods is rapidly enlarging. An accelerating level of production of cement, capital goods, and iron occurs in response to the consistently expanding investment and construction boom. Corresponding increases in the wages of the middle classes have contributed to the sales growth of disposable consumer goods such as automobiles and cellular phones. For example, as of June 2006, the number of mobile phone users exceeded 100 million. Since then, the subsequent phenomenal growth reports 180 million in 2007 and 500 million by 2010. Automobile ownership is rapidly growing as well. According to the Indian government's report of automotive industry growth plans published in January 2007, the annual automobile production volume in India is expected to grow from 1.5 million ($34 billion) to 3.9 million ($145 billion). About 25 million in new employment is expected in this period.

From the mid-2000s, the profit rate in the manufacturing sector increased more than 30% with the corresponding increase in per capita productivity. Thus, the wage level for skilled workers and managerial personnel shows an annual increase of 10% to 15%. However, rising general prices with such wage hikes would result in inflationary pressures in the

Indian economy. Accelerating consumer loans and enormous investment increases for urban infrastructure development further contribute to the rising general prices. Naturally, the building and housing market reported an extraordinary level of asset appreciation. On top of this, India's sustained trade deficit with oil and capital goods imports are another factor for India's long-term fiscal risk.

4.3 CASE STUDIES OF INDIAN FIRMS

The role of the Indian brand in Asia is entering the maturity state. The world pays attention to China, which has become the number two economic power in the world. Many researchers regard India as a real potential rival to China. In particular, India, in contrast to China, is known for the development of unique industries and brand products. Fujimoto (2006) noted that Indian firms pursue product strategy with their unique integral architecture approach in contrast to the product development patterns of Chinese firms that tend to imitate Japanese or other Western firms and thus choose more or less open modular architecture.

India's particular strength shows in soft skill areas based on huge knowledge assets and creativity capabilities (Meyer et al., 2004). India's knowledge advantage shows in well-known brands like Nicholas Piramal/Bioon in the areas of Wipro technologies, healthcare, and bioengineering. These firms are successful in developing the global number one technology service firms with the slogan of "Applying Thought." Furthermore, India's brand growth in fast-moving consumer goods is phenomenal. The Indian leading firms provide an outstanding brand mix of customer-friendly goods and penetrate the upper-middle-income segments in which non-Indian global firms assume the market leader positions.

Tata Motors is one of the flagship companies of the Tata conglomerate (Rupali, 2013). Tata Motors attracted international attention with the announcement of the Tata Nano, the world's lowest-priced car, in January 2008. Bajaj Auto is the second largest player in the Indian motorcycle market and the leader in the executive segment with nearly 60% market share in 2007. Bajaj Auto was the second-largest two-wheeler company in India in financial year 2009–2010 and had sales of Rs. 119 billion during 2011.

Titan attributes its success in the jewelry business to its ability to manage the entire value chain from design to manufacture, to sale and delivery with high quality and reliability. Titan believes that the first mover advantage it has achieved through the creation of this integrated model will remain unchallenged for some years to come.

Pantaloon has been successful in building several private-label brands across the company. Pantaloon has also lent its experience to nontraditional retail formats (e.g., it has taken a controlling stake in Mother Earth, a craft and artisan-based retail chain being set up in large cities). The company has forged a deep professional relationship with Idiom, a Bangalore-based design firm. Idiom has about 180 designers and has become a think tank and incubator for the company.

In 2002, Biocon decided to enter the new drug development arena. The strategy was to use the profits generated by the generics business (statins, immune suppressant) to fund innovation-led drug development programs. The company intended to manage the risk of its R&D strategy by targeting proven targets (e.g., epidermal growth factor receptor, EGFR), proven molecules (e.g., insulin), a focus on biologicals (which had lower risks of facing toxicity problems), and using its integrated biopharmaceutical manufacturing facilities to be able to develop proof-of-concept quickly and then scale up manufacturing (the annual reports of Biocon from 2004 to 2011). Tata Group and Mahindra are two major Indian global firms. In this section, we briefly introduce these two firms.

4.3.1 Tata Group

In June 2012 Tata Motor Company, after its surprising introduction of the $2,500 nano-automobile as a symbol of nano-innovation, presented a $20,000 electric car development plan. This is half the price of any electric cars that have ever been considered. This is to speed up the widespread demand for electric cars through the mini-electric cars at reasonable prices of $20,000. Tata Technology, Tata's IT affiliated subsidiary, reported its completion of "the initial feasibility study on electric mobility (eMO) with Daso System, France's 3D software specialist firm. Four-passenger-mini-electric mobility (eMO) is possible under $20,000" (Kim, 2012). Tata Group does not disclose the details of financial commitment for eMO or its market introduction date but featured eMo's test drive video in its company home page.

In 2009, Tata kept the global auto industry's attention for its development of a super inexpensive $2,500 nano-automobile. Although the demand for the nano-car was not as revolutionary as expected, recently its 2012 demand in India has increased up to 30% compared to that in 2011 in response to the recent recession in the Indian economy. In 2010, Tata also announced its plan to market "India Car Vista" (an electric motor that is substantially larger than the 2009 nano-electric auto) in Europe, but it has not yet been realized.

In the US market, Nissan's Leaf (a pure electric car) is priced at $35,000 and GM's Chevrolet Volt (plug hybrid) is sold for $39,000 (Kim, 2012). As most of the global electric car developers focus on how to extend the short driving range per electricity charge, Tata's competitive strategy has been directed to price reduction, down to half of that of the competitors by applying new automotive design and manufacturing process methods.

Tata's strategy is somewhat similar to that of US-based Apple. Apple is primarily a marketing firm just like Nike, P&G rather than a high-tech consumer manufacturer (Chosun Biz, 2012). Apple's marketing secrets include pricing strategy as well. Apple first determines the price level that fits to the target customer expectations and implemented process innovation to cut down the manufacturing costs. Its strategy is pricing first and then development details.

In his 1960 *HBR* article "Marketing Myopia," Theodore Levitt, a Harvard Business professor who was commonly referred to as "a father of marketing," discussed the basic aspects of Apple's marketing strategy with his focused case study of Ford Motor Company's mass production system. Henry Ford was successful in creating enormous wealth by developing a mass production system for Ford Motor Company. People tend to think that Ford merely reduced the production cost through economies of scale production methods. Thus, he was able to introduce a car at $500 and customers were more than willing to purchase such cars. In Ford's time, $500 would have been worth $7,800 today. However, Levitt's point is different. Ford first conceived the idea of selling millions of cars to the consumers. His conclusion was to reduce the price up to $500 per car. To fulfill this pricing objective he came up with the mass production method. This is the core idea of Levitt's paper. In 2010 *HBR* again selected his paper as one of the "10 Must Reads Essential." Henry Ford also often emphasized pricing strategy as of first importance. Yet, people still misunderstand that Ford's mass production methods reduced the production costs and thus he could sell his cars at a very low price. Pricing first is to make customers and market first. Successful firms must study their customers in depth and determine the right prices for their customers and follow through with appropriate product development, design, and manufacturing methods. It was the pricing strategy that Steve Jobs, Apple's founder, emphasized as he introduced MacBook Air and iPad. As he unveiled the pricing strategy detail with $999 for MacBook Air and $499 for iPad, some critics of the same industry commented that they were killer prices. However, Apple regarded it appropriate to create its own business ecosystem.

India's Tata Group went one step further and disclosed the price goals first and then involved in technological development for the products (Chung, 2012). In 2003 Ratan, Tata's chairman of the board, announced the people's car production plans and determined the price as 100,000 rupees ($2,500). After 5 years of bone-crushing R&D efforts, Tata finally introduced the Nano car in 2008. In fact, the Nano development project started with the unintentional promise by words of Tata Group's chairman. In the Motor Show in Geneva, one reporter of the *Financial Times* persistently asked about the future cars to the Tata chairman. He happened to say that future Indian people's cars should be no more than 100,000 rupees. Then, in his article the reporter spread the news that Tata's chairman promised to introduce a future car at 100,000 rupees ($2,500). According to Tata's business philosophy, "A promise made must be kept," Ratan's words put into practice through implementing the Nano road map afterward.

After the Nano road map announcement, Tata's motto, "Price first and production second for our people," became the core value of Tata's management. In 2009, Tata Group also introduced "Tata Swach" with which a five-member family could drink purified water for 200 days at no more than $25. In 1950, as Ford Motor successfully implemented a mass production system, then all other US auto manufacturers made massive capital investment for mass production. In a matter of time, the US automobile industry faced serious trouble with their "blind" focus on mass production, apart from the market reality and customer needs. The timeless lesson from Ford, Apple, and Tata is that firms must first define their marketing goals and then innovate all the means to achieve the predetermined goals. Then, the door for greater market opportunities will naturally open.

4.3.2 Mahindra & Mahindra Limited (M&M)

In the past, competitive Indian firms from emerging economies pursued rapid growth through strategic alliance with global firms from advanced nations. The strategic initiatives of these firms include new product development for the large number of low-income customers at the base of the pyramid. They exert tremendous efforts to catch up with the well-established organizational practices of advanced global firms and make their own core competent system elements. In this sense, Mahindra & Mahindra Limited (M&M) is quite noteworthy (Sirkin et al., 2008).

In 1954 the chairman of M&M presented a bold idea. It was to collaborate with Renault and manufacture and market French cars in India. In 1945 M&M was already selling automobiles (e.g., industry vehicles) for diverse customer segments and yet did not produce passenger cars for customers in general. Instead of developing cars alone, he preferred to utilize the accumulated know-how of Renault. This Harvard MBA regarded this strategy as most appropriate. In the auto industry it was quite common for firms to form strategic alliances, participate in joint ventures, and receive education and training support in administrative services and manufacturing functions. In the 1950s, the business context in India was not conducive to implementing bold strategies because it was only several years after independence from British rule. India's domestic regulatory and legal barriers kept other global firms from making innovative investment decisions.

It was 40 years afterward that India's business environment showed substantial changes. In 1996, M&M established a joint venture with Ford Motor Company and invited US auto manufacturers into the Indian market. The business project itself did not bring a huge success in sales and profit. Through this joint venture M&M enhanced its internal capabilities—particularly in the areas of product design and project management. Thus, by 2002, M&M could develop Scorpio (a SUV—diverse purpose sports car) on its own. As this car became very popular in India, M&M started selling in other foreign markets as well.

Based on the successful experience with its strategic alliance with Ford, M&M dared to move into additional collaboration projects with other global firms. Through a joint venture with UK's British Telecom Co., M&M established Tech Mahindra, which specializes in major outsourcing projects. In 2007 M&M made a public offering and recorded another huge success. M&M also started from ground zero for the automobile mold business, invested $250 million for acquiring other Indian, British, and German firms. Within 3 years after starting the firm, it is now positioned as the number five firm in the world in this line of business. M&M began another joint venture firm with North American International Truck & Engine to produce mid- to large-sized trucks in India and export to other markets as well. In 2005, M&M established a 51–49 joint venture with Renault and started manufacturing and distributing the Logan model in India. The Logan model fit Indian customers' needs so well that as soon as the model was introduced to the Indian market in April of the same year, it became the top seller. In August 2010, M&M also acquired Korea's Ssangyong Motor Company (SMC). Although China's Shanghai Locomotive owned 49% of Ssangyong's ownership, M&M managed to acquire 50% of SMC's ownership. By November 23, 2010, M&M completed the contract for acquiring SMC's stocks up to 70% with $522 million and entered the global Jeep market.

M&M also proceeded in its goal to become the global top player in the tractor market. In fact, India's tractor market is the largest in the world in terms of sales volume—bigger than that of China and the United States. M&M's tractor is known for below 80 HP and its position in the Indian market for 23 years straight with about 40% of market share. The price range starts from $10,000. The scope of product offerings is also very rich, and its distribution network is closely connected with the vast customer and social network base. For example, M&M collaborates with banks in many regions and provides financing options and loan terms that fit the regional and specific customer requirements. M&M's distribution and logistical network for agricultural machinery product lines is very well developed with 510 dealers and 1,175 service centers.

M&M carefully designed its tractors for small, self-employed Indian farmers. The size of average US farms is several hundred acres. In contrast, Indian farmers have no more than 3 to 4 acres of land. In India, tractors are used for the clearance and reclamation of both existing and additional farmland. Tractors are crucial for moving huge rocks, smoothing the rough surface roads, irrigating in rice fields, threshing wheat and barley (Sorghum), and preparing for golf courses. In vast India, different regions adopt a variety of agricultural methods. The quality dimensions of soil and harvest patterns are so different that the customer usage expectations for tractors are quite varied as well. M&M considers all these factors and develops tractors to fit the complex market needs accordingly. In this sense, M&M's customer-oriented product development is comparable to that of Komatsu—the global construction equipment manufacturer that offers products for changing customer needs and attractive financing options. M&M is also aggressively acquiring firms from China and Iran and search-ing for more joint venture opportunities to expand its global market advan-tages. M&M provides a very successful business model in that it continues to enhance its market expanding capability, strengthen customer compe-tence, and strengthen its needed technological competence through joint venture, merger, and acquisitions, and thus achieves linkage competence for domestic advantage and global competitiveness.

4.3.3 Big Bazaar

It is vital for the strategist while planning a sustainability strategy to understand the emerging market and its culture and scenario in the environment surrounding these emerging markets (Yoo et al., 2006; Roh et al., 2008). Let us take the case of Big Bazaar, the company that was the pioneer of the hypermarket concept in India with the launch of Big Bazaar in Kolkata in September 2001. The Big Bazaar model was a hypermarket concept created for India rather than a blind imitation of hypermarkets in the West. It was designed to combine the look and feel of an Indian bazaar with the convenience of organized retail shopping.

Some of the distinctive features of the initial Big Bazaar models were as follows:

1. Location in crowded areas well connected by public transportation rather than suburbs
2. An effort to retain the chaos and feel of a bazaar
3. Sourcing through consolidators identified for different product categories
4. Concerted efforts to bring in customers who were apprehensive of shopping at modern retail outlets
5. Sale of products in a way that is aligned to the buying habits of the Indian housewife, such as the opportunity to get grain freshly ground or inspect staples and grains before purchase
6. Customization to local market needs: In August 2002, the company launched Food Bazaar within Big Bazaar stores to sell vegetables and fruits. By 2006–2007, Big Bazaar had opened 50 stores across India (Source: http://en.wikipedia.org/wiki/bigbazaar).

4.4 CONCLUSION

In this chapter we discussed two Indian global giants—Tata Group and M&M—that illustrate the successful cases of Indian indigenous firms. The innovations by Indian companies like Tata Group and M&M show that a nationally developed product can have international as well as rural effect, Innovation is not only restricted to product, but it has crossed its boundaries by innovation in marketing, packaging, and also managing logistics (Rupali, 2013). Innovation distinguishes between a leader and a follower as rightly said by Steve Jobs. Those who want to sustain will think and do things differently rather than doing different things. Korean firms in India offer another aspect of emerging market innovation by concentrating efforts not on product development but on product delivery. In short, this innovation relied exclusively on moving beyond the current markets to challenge the existing market share of current providers.

These two firms, as discussed in this book, have a relatively short time period to develop their needed technological capabilities. Thus, they first focus on knowing the market needs and developing customer competence. They make persistent and prudent efforts to achieve rapid catch-up of technological capabilities through external network strategies in the form of joint ventures, mergers and acquisitions, and creative financing arrangements.

5

Strategies of Brazilian Indigenous Firms

Brazil is a resource-rich nation that is expected to experience rapid economic growth as it has recently hosted the 2014 World Cup and will host the 2016 Summer Olympics. However, with its long-standing trade protection policies and real fluctuations of the currency, internal industrial foundations are relatively weak. However, with its abundant agricultural and natural resources, the Brazilian indigenous firms demonstrate quite dynamic growth patterns. This section examines both available literature and case studies of Brazilian firms. This chapter will highlight how Brazilian indigenous firms take their competitive positions as partners of other global firms from the United States, Japan, and Korea. Their strategies are to build up their business capabilities to the levels of their global partners while rapidly building their capabilities to target their own Brazilian market and expanding their target market in Latin America.

5.1 INTRODUCTION

Brazil is a resource-rich nation that is expected to experience rapid economic growth as it has recently hosted the 2014 World Cup and will host the 2016 Summer Olympics. However, with its long-standing trade protection policies and real fluctuations of the currency, internal industrial foundations are relatively weak. However, with its abundant agricultural and natural resources, the Brazilian indigenous firms demonstrate quite dynamic growth patterns. This section examines both available literature and case studies of Brazilian firms. This chapter will highlight how

Brazilian indigenous firms take their competitive positions as partners of other global firms from the United States, Japan, and Korea. Their strategies are to build up their business capabilities to the levels of their global partners while rapidly building their capabilities to target their own Brazilian market and expanding their target market in Latin America.

5.2 BRAZIL'S ECONOMIC CONTEXT

Brazil, like China and India, has received the world's attention as a leading nation among emerging economies not only because of its strategic geographical location and enormous labor resources, but also because of their unique advantage lies in their abundant natural resources (Sirkin et al., 2008). Brazilian firms reap the benefits of having rich natural resources such as iron ores, water, and endless miles of vast fertile land. The food-processing industry naturally flourishes and other manufacturing industries are rapidly growing. For example, Embraer has become the number three aerospace manufacturer through inexpensive labor resources and tremendous innovation competence.

5.3 BRAZILIAN FIRMS

5.3.1 Embraer

In 1945 Brazil made the transition from dictatorship to republic governance. The first step was to formulate macroeconomic plans. Establishing Embraer was one of numerous strategic initiatives (Sirkin et al., 2008). These ambitious efforts included constructing the large comprehensive steel mill plants and the government decision to build airplanes and other aerospace component parts with Brazil's domestic capabilities. To fulfill these goals, in 1946 the Brazilian government opened the Aerospace Technology Institute (ATI) in San Josedos Campus and in 1950 started the Aero-Engineering College (AEC) to educate and train needed engineering talent.

For the next 25 years, these two organizations—ATI and AEC—have accumulated ample knowledge and supplied numerous high-quality engineers. As a result, in 1969 the Brazilian government established Embraer—the state-owned firm. For another 20 years, Embraer applied existing technology know-how from private firms and developed innovative design skills and developed a bimotored turbo full-rope passenger airplane. The representative models were the nonsecret, structural, 19-passenger, short-distance airplane (EMB110) and the secret structural 30-passenger airplane (EMB120 Brasilia). EMB120 Brasilia is known for building with Embraer's unique design capabilities. In the late 1980s, Embraer started developing a new model, CBA123. It was intended for use of connecting flights between small cities and large metropolitan areas. After testing in various ways, the project was discontinued because the manufacturing costs were too high and not competitive enough. Afterward, using available technologies Embraer strived to develop brand new design features. Through such efforts engineers in Embraer noticed new jet engine design possibilities that might result in a faster and cheaper jet aircraft than the turbo full-rope aircraft. This new one could show improvement both in noise and vibration level and thus perform well in the bumpy current.

Without any prior experience in jet engine development, in 1989 Embraer launched a 45-passenger, short-distance jet engine craft (ERJ145). However, before the completion of this project, the aerospace industry experienced a big recession. Brasilia, the primary model of Embraer, was deemed outdated and its sale was drastically dropped. In response to the deteriorating cash flow, most of the subsidy of the Brazilian government supported the manufacturing and marketing of current models, and thus additional new R&D efforts were negatively affected. With increasing government deficit, many of the state owned enterprises were privatized, and on December 1994, Embraer changed the ownership structure as privately owned.

In 1995, Mauriochi Boterho assumed the CEO position for Embraer that was on the verge of bankruptcy. He made innovations as the crucial lifeline saver for the organization and poured in resources to complete the discontinued ERJ145 project. Bombardier, its rival, already invested heavily on short-distance CRJ (Canadian Regional Jet). With an unexpected surge in demand for short-distance jet aircrafts, Embraer also had chances to revive. Thus, Embraer dared compete with its product in the market and focused on matching cost performance with that of its rivals.

By 1992, the niche market for 35- to 50-passenger jet aircraft was virtually in the unexplored state. However, Embraer entered the market as the second follower. Its 1996 model of ERJ145 generated enormous market response. In 1997, it introduced mini 37-passenger EIR 135 and 44-passenger ERJ140. Embraer also offered a military jet and business charter jet (Regacy). Based on the huge success of ERJ145, Embraer decided to develop the next-generation, short-distance jet aircraft—70- to 110-passenger aircraft (ERJ145). However, these new models were in the competitive turf of the well-established industry leaders—Boeing and Air Bus. However, Embraer was steady in challenging these new models based on their small passenger capacity. At that time, it was customary to lengthen the aircraft as the number of passenger requirements increased from small to large models. The problem with ERJ145 was that because the original design was such that increasing the passenger capacity to 20 to 50 would result in making the aircraft too long and thus too costly to produce. Besides profitability, comfortability was also an issue. The engineering project manager who worked on the ERJ145 project from 1990 to 2005 commented: "It was important to communicate to design engineers the perspective of end users. Otherwise, the project team decision based on available technology options without any due regard to the convenience factors of the users" (Sirkin et al., 2008).

Thus, the source of the real issue was lack of customer competence of design engineers. Most engineers proceeded with their product development work based on technology competence alone. The quality and performance issues from customer perspectives are too often not adequately addressed. At that time, the rival Bombardier's 50-passenger CRJ was in the process of implementing the extended circle-shape design in which passenger seats are positioned in four rows. However, design configurations of passenger seats in four rows would make each seat space too narrow and there would remain little compartment storage above for 22-inch suitcases. The Embraer's engineers decided to try a new design named "double bubble." The most efficient structure for any aircraft is through circular design. In this way, an airplane minimizes the overall impact of air pressures. Yet, circular design makes too much unusable space in the middle section. This is the reason why the routine airplane design feature is elliptical instead. Even so, an elliptical design fits large aircraft, but the small to medium one in the same design would end up having too small of a freight space below the aircraft. In the past, as a compromise solution the design of a short-distance jet plane adopted an oval yet approximately circular shape to secure adequate compartment storage above the passengers and freight space below the aircraft. However, passengers at the end section of each row find it somewhat uncomfortable to sit. So Embraer combined two frames into one as a new design feature. The design for the upper half of the aircraft dedicated for the passenger seating section is by big frame, and the lower half of the freight section is by small frame. In this configuration, compartment areas above both passenger seats near windows have enough space for suitcases, and the small frame handles the passenger bags and freight volumes. As this new design combines two different sizes of circle, the aircraft ensures the comfort of passengers, reduces the airflow resistance, and secures adequate storage spaces. This is the way Embraer 170 was brought into the market. The airline companies could afford to offer competitive prices and the passengers enjoy the pleasant experiences. Thus, the Embraer 170 series became a huge success.

Since then, Embraer has been successful in developing six to eight executive jetliners whose target customers are busy business executives. Because of the high profit margin, the executive jets are extremely competitive. In collaboration with BMW, Embraer chose luxurious and stylish interior designs for the six to eight executive jets. This allowed Embraer to diversify its product lines by offering both the low-cost and cutting-edge jetliners for general passengers in the highly reliable and safe world-class commercial executive jets. Embraer is now positioning as the global number one passenger aircraft manufacturer for seat capacity under 120.

Success factors of Embraer include unique innovation, low wages, and advantageous foreign exchange rates. One crucial factor is the management and engineers with linkage competence through which it develops products with high customer impact. Had they not considered the comfort for the customers, "double bubble" technology would not have been born and Embraer 170 would never have made Embraer become a world-class firm.

The light jet market has seen new market entrants come and go, but Embraer has bucked the trend by not only registering a sizable backlog but also by delivering a viable product on time and on budget (*Aircraft Value News*, 2010). The NBAA show was the venue for an order for 50 Embraer Phenom 300 light jets from NetJets with options for another 75. The Phenom 100 and 300 have accumulated backlogs of approximately 400 and 200, respectively, and now represent formidable competition. With considerable experience in aircraft manufacturing and the financial and engineering expertise to deliver a variety of corporate jets, there exists an expectation that residual values of this type will perform well. The Aircraft Value Analysis (AVAC), having recently launched a new corporate jet future value module for its aircraft value reference, indicates that the Phenom 300 will have a residual value of approximately 70% after 10 years, a much higher percentage than that attributed to any commercial jet. Used values of the light jets have not been performing well during the current cycle as potential owners have found difficulty in finding financing. Whereas previously, buyers were able to secure 100% or more financing for used aircraft, a deposit of 20% is more the norm along with greater emphasis on the ability to pay.

However, the product support and ability of Embraer to deliver on time have provided much reassurance for owners and financial institutions. The move to the fractional ownership as a result of the NetJets order for 50 Phenom 300s creates some valuation difficulties due to sometimes higher utilization levels.

Recently, African airlines adopted the same strategy as their larger competitors on other continents: using large aircraft on all but very short flights. More recently, however, Brazilian firm Embraer has had great success in marketing its small- and mid-sized aircraft (African Business, 2013). They can prove more commercially viable on the mid-range routes that are the basis of the African aviation industry. Airbus and Boeing continue to dominate the global aviation industry, but Embraer has managed to cement its position as the world's third-biggest manufacturer by specializing in smaller aircraft.

Embraer signaled its commitment to the region when it appointed its first vice president for commercial aviation in the Middle East and Africa in 2011, Mathieu Duquesnoy. He predicts that the firm will double its sales revenue in Africa over the next 20 years, but this is dependent on the Yamoussoukro Decision actually being implemented. Under Yamoussoukro, African governments agreed to open up their airline sectors to cross-border competition. As discussed elsewhere, the decision was reached in 1999 and was due to be implemented within 3 years but has still not come fully into force.

There are currently about 670 large- and medium-sized aircraft based in Africa. Estimates vary but most sources predict that this figure will double by 2030. Embraer is obviously keen to promote the advantages of mid-sized aircraft. Duquesnoy says, "If deregulation does not happen, the African skies will continue to be dominated by old, oversized aircraft and airlines will not be able to address the demand for better linking of the continent's large airports." The chief executive of aviation IT firm Locatory, Zilvinas Sadauskas, commented, "There remains wide growth avenues for short to medium-haul airline service within Africa—a market aptly tailored for Embraer jets." About 124 Embraer commercial aircraft operate in Africa, based in 24 different countries, comprising 49 Embraer 120s, 38 ERJs, 30 E-Jets, and seven 110s, while E190S are now also being introduced.

The other side of the Brazilian firm's business is military aircraft, which it has supplied to eight air forces, most recently Mauritania, which received an unspecified number of A-29 Super Tucano light-attack aircraft at the end of last year. The company's head of defense and security Luiz Carlos Aguiar said: "With this delivery, we are broadening our ties with the African continent, where this aircraft has generated great interest" (African Business, 2013).

Other Embraer customers in Africa include Kenya Airways, EgyptAir Express, and Linhas Aéreas de Moçambique (LAM). LAM has taken delivery of the first of three Embraer 145s that it will lease to provide services around Mozambique and within the Southern African Development Community (SADC). The 145 has seating for just 50 passengers and so can be deployed on routes that would not justify larger aircraft. The South African firm Airlink, which operates 11 Embraer aircraft, is to set up an Embraer service center in Johannesburg, while there is already another support center for the Brazilian company's aircraft in Morocco, which is operated by Air Atlantique.

Yet another center is planned for Kenya, where Kenya Airways has ordered 20 E-Jets. Kenya Airways Chief Operating Officer Mbuvi Ngunze said, "Soon we might be able to announce something substantive from a training point of view. That will bring advantages in terms of timing, costs and flexibility. This is something we are working on, so watch this space. On spares, we are working with Embraer to deliver a service centre, but these things depend on critical mass" (African Business, 2013).

5.4 CONCLUSION

This chapter examined the case of Embraer as an example of a Brazilian indigenous global firm. It had a relatively short period of accumulating technology competence. Thus, it strengthened customer competence as of first importance and strengthened it through strategic network capability alliance with other global firms. As it paid attention to customer convenience, brand new innovation was possible. It did not remain for the past technology applications but grew as the exploring technological new frontier for its global eminence in its chosen global market segments.

6

Strategies of Russian Indigenous Firms

Russia has been a dominating factor in world politics and economies since World War II and, politically, the greatest rival to the United States. Since the breakup of the Soviet Union in 1991, the Russian Federation, as it is now known, has struggled with slow economic growth in several industrial areas; with the manufacturing sector being one of the most challenging. Contrasting these years of slow growth in manufacturing, Russia sits atop vast natural resources where deep reserves of natural gas and oil have become not only the primary export commodity of the nation, it is literally the fuel driving the Russian economy. This chapter studies two companies who have and continue to demonstrate a resource-based approach for sustainable growth. Aided by Foreign Direct Investment (FDI) each plays a significant economic role in the Russian economy: AvtoVAZ, the largest automotive manufacturer in Russia, and Gazprom, representing 20% of Russia's natural gas production.

6.1 INTRODUCTION

Russia had dominated the world politics and economies after World War II as the only viable rival against the United States. However, with the slow growth of the manufacturing sector, the overall economic strengths needed real changes. Even so, it is noteworthy of the emergence of the key resource-based firms. Several examples of key Russian firms are (1) AutoVaz (number one automaker in Russia) and (2) Gazprom (yields 20% of global natural gas production). This chapter focuses on the relative weaknesses of Russian manufacturing industries along with resource-based firms in the context of hybrid economic systems with both government-initiated planned industry policies as well as free market principles.

6.2 RUSSIAN ECONOMIC CONTEXT

In contrast to Brazil, the Russian economy with its considerable human resources, geographical advantage, and substantial natural resources has taken a much different path toward economic growth. Peter the Great in 1703, recognizing the Russian Empire's geographical disadvantage as compared to other European countries and capitals, began significant infrastructure investments to create a city that would rival any world capital, St. Petersburg. After World War II, and utilizing its rich natural resources, Russia became a superpower among nations and, along with the United States, affected global politics and economies.

However, in the 1990s Russia, in the course of confusing political transitions, experienced a moratorium. With the dissolution of the Soviet Union in 1991, political transitions among governing bodies brought unique changes, resulting in a moratorium of defining an economic direction for the new Russian Federation. Since 2000, Russia experienced positive annual gross domestic product (GDP) growth; for example, during the time period 2003 to 2006, the annual rate averaged 6.9%. In 2006, the rate of the oil price increase was somewhat slowed, but with vigorous investment and consumer spending increases, Russia still maintained 6.7% of annual growth. Even after 2007, the upward trend of international oil prices continued. In light of increasing oil prices and even with the threat of global warming, the construction boom in Russia continued unabated; in other words, oil exports were driving Russia's economic growth. The increasing real disposable income of the Russian middle class spurred consumer spending, and the first quarter of Russia's GDP showed hefty 7.9% annual GDP growth. This section is devoted to describing the characteristics of the Russian economy (Lee, 2008).

6.2.1 Energy-Dependent Economic Structure

Energy (e.g., oil and natural gas) represents in excess of 30% of Russian GDP and 66.2% of total exports. With such a reliance on one industry for economic survival, any unfavorable market shocks to energy prices can have a devastating effect on the overall economy. According to the International Monetary Fund (IMF), the elasticity between oil prices and GDP growth rate is 0.15% to 0.2%. For example, 10% price hikes in oil prices are expected to impact Russia's GDP growth up to 1.5% to 2%. Furthermore in 2003, as a result of the political issues related to Yukos, its assets and subsidiaries were nationalized to strengthen state control of all energy industries. After the Yukos incident, foreign direct investment in Russia slowed and the total oil production noticeably dropped. Import expansion occurred as a result of the ruble appreciating in value, and it is estimated that the growth elasticity between oil prices and GDP growth rate was somewhat weakened, hovering at around the 0.1% level.

From 2004 the Russian government established an Oil Price Stabilization Fund to expand economic revitalization in other areas such as balanced regional development, social infrastructure investment, and information technology (IT)/aerospace/space industry growth. In particular, the government secured 300 billion ruble in the form of investment/venture fund and development bank and promoted social infrastructure development. From the mid-2000s Russia's domestic market expansion encouraged the greater inflow of foreign direct investment (FDI) for food, construction, logistics, and automotive industries. Annual import volume of heavy machinery and equipment also rapidly increased in keeping with large inflows of FDI and expansive capital investment of manufacturing firms.

6.2.2 Aggressive Public Expenditures

The Russian government has adopted an aggressive public expansion policy to achieve sustained economic policy. From 2008 on, the Russian government changed its public expenditure planning to intermediate term (3-year period), increased the public expenditures 16.2% in 2006, and exceeded 18% in the period 2008 to 2010. President Putin announced in his April 2007 annual State of the Union Address key national investment priorities such as public welfare improvement (e.g., housing/retirees pension) for $250 billion ruble (0.8% of GDP), social infrastructure (e.g., domestic highways) for $100 ruble (0.3% of GDP), establishment of a development institute for 300 billion ruble (1.0% of GDP), and aerospace/shipbuilding/nanotechnology for 180 billion ruble (0.6% of GDP).

Furthermore, out of the Oil Stabilization Fund, the Russian government sets aside any excess monies beyond 10% of GDP as a Fund for Future Generation by investing in potential high-yield global investment portfolios. Based on their huge foreign reserves the oil producer nations in the Middle East and Asian nations such as China and Singapore have maintained national funds to secure higher annual yields through investment in natural resources asset and global instruments accounts. As of 2008, such a Russian national fund amounted to $32 billion. However, the Russian economy has many practical challenges to overcome for its long-term economic growth. The most critical one is that its economy is very vulnerable to political changes. From the 1990s, the political circumstances too often affected the Russian economy in a drastic fashion. In 2012, the Russian people reelected Putin as president in the hope of restoring Russia's influence in international politics. His nationalistic policies are expected to generate a greater level of conflicts in the European Union, Eastern Europe, and Commonwealth of Independent States (CIS) nations and thus uncertainty in international politics may naturally intensify.

6.3 RUSSIA'S AUTOMOTIVE INDUSTRY

During the Soviet Union era, more than 5,000 automotive-related firms were in operation. With the dissolution of the Soviet Union, many of these firms disappeared either through bankruptcy proceedings or restructuring efforts. With such drastic reorganization processes, the Russian automotive industry has become stronger than before. At present, three million people are employed either directly or indirectly in the automotive industries. The automotive industry is emerging as one of the most important manufacturing industries in Russia.

6.3.1 Current Status of the Russian Automotive Industry

6.3.1.1 Passenger Car Production and Sales Statistics

In 1997, overall sales volume of passenger cars was approximately 1.5 million units, following the 1998 to 1999 economic crisis, total unit production (both Russian domestic and Russian domestic with foreign investment in 1999 fell to 1.1 million. Afterward, with high global oil prices, the Russian economy experienced a favorable turn and in 2001 the sales volume was restored to the level of 1.5 million cars and has been in the process of consistent growth thereafter.

The Russian passenger car market can be classified into three types (domestic, foreign new cars, and imported used cars). In 2001 to 2002, the sales of imported used cars showed a drastic increase. In 2002, it was 29.2% of the total car sales. With double increases of custom duties for imported used cars in 2002 to 2003, Russian customers changed their preference to foreign new cars instead. Cars produced by Russian domestic auto manufacturers have decreased considerably compared to the sales of imported used or new foreign cars.

6.3.1.2 Domestic Production and Sales Record

In 1997 passenger car unit production volume returned to the prior years' higher volume reaching 985,000. In 1998, with an economic recession, it went down to 936,000. Since then, it slightly grew and by 2000 the total production exceeded 1,000,000. Furthermore, in the mid-2000s, during economic recovery through rising oil prices, there was a surge in demand for passenger cars in Russia but customers mostly chose imported used cars or new foreign cars. Thus, domestic production volume did not show any real improvement.

As of 2012, there are 13 passenger car manufacturers in Russia. Eight out of these thirteen firms (one discontinued its production) target purely the domestic market. The other five firms are foreign global firms. The top leading firm among these Russian domestic passenger car manufacturers is AutoVAX whose market share is about 70% with absolute superiority. Domestic competitor companies to zhmash-Avto, GAZ (Gorky Automobile Plant), KAMAZ, and UAZ (Ulianovsk Automobile Plant) divide the remaining market share.

Since 2003, global auto manufacturers such as Ford Russia, GM-Avto-VAZ, and Hyundai Russia also built assembly plants in Russia and market their brand cars for Russian customers. These companies' passenger cars target fairly stable market profiles; approximately 50% of total sales are comprised of low-priced, small cars selling in the range of $6,000 to $8,000 (USD). As incomes rise, the desire for more premium cars also increases which helps to create new market opportunities for both domestic and foreign manufacturers.

6.3.2 Growth of Russian Indigenous Firms: AvtoVAZ

AvtoVAZ has become the major domestic car maker in Russia. By creating foreign joint ventures, utilizing idled manufacturing facilities, and leveraging the available production capacity for OEM parts, AvtoVAZ has become the primary driver to revitalize Russia's automotive industry. There are the contract manufacturing operations of three Russian OEMs: GAZ, Avtotor, and Sollers (Automotive Manufacturing Solutions, 2013).

Foreign carmakers are investing heavily in expanding their manufacturing footprint in Russia, not just through contract deals and utilizing existing facilities, but also in building and developing their own manufacturing hubs, complete with supply chains. VW, Nissan, Hyundai, PSA, and Mitsubishi have all expanded their manufacturing operations in Russia and they are building cars.

As of 2012, the joint venture of AvtoVAZ and the Renault–Nissan group has created a 30.6% market share, far exceeding that of the Volkswagen group at 10.9% and General Motors at 9.1%. Even without Renault and Nissan sales in its total, AvtoVAZ's Lada brand still manages to be easily the country's number one nameplate with just under 18% of the market. The carmaker sold 608,205 Lada vehicles in 2012 in the CIS, of which 537,600 were in Russia (Automotive Manufacturing Solutions, 2013).

Renault operates its own plant, Avtoframos, which builds the Duster, Logan, Sandero, Fluence, and Mégane models. The company holds 94% of the suburban Moscow facility, with the remainder owned by the city council.

The Renault group's investment in Avtroframos is second only to the investment made with its alliance partner Nissan to form the AvtoVAZ–Renault–Nissan joint venture. The maker of Lada vehicles says it is aiming for annual production of one million cars by 2017, though to attain that goal it must continue to add several new model series to its profit for the previous year (Automotive Manufacturing Solutions, 2013).

The first step in the rebuilding and ongoing expansion of the Lada brand was the launch of the Cranta, a small sedan that uses the Renault BO platform from the first-generation Dacia Logan, itself derived from the second-generation Renault Clio. A major investment was made at the Togliatti plant to build this replacement for the long-running 2105 to 2107 series. The car, which went into production in November 2011, is powered by a Renault-derived 1.6-liter four-cylinder engine.

Cranta production takes place not only at Togliatti but also at the IzhAvto plant in Russia's Udmurtia region, which AvtoVAZ bought during 2011. The company said in December 2011 that it would invest €4 billion into the facility, lifting production capacity to 300,000 vehicles per annum. Cranta assembly began there in June 2012.

Following the launch of the Cranta, AvtoVAZ discontinued its best-selling model "Kalina" due to its dated body design and lack of technologically advanced options as compared with competitive products. These small, five-door hatchback and wagon models, each of which premiered at the Moscow motor show in August 2012, are based on the Granta sedan. Series production of both began at Togliatti in May with the first customer cars delivered in June.

Until recently, most suppliers largely shipped to Russia from other countries but production of the first Nissan model (the Almera) within the AvtoVAZ Togliatti complex has encouraged some vendors to establish local operations. Sanoh is one such example, having brought a factory in Togliatti on-stream in February. The tubing maker says it plans to open two further sites this year. Kinugawa Rubber also plans to build a plant in Togliatti, its first in Russia. The firm intends to begin making automotive sealing parts for Nissan by the end of fiscal year 2014 (Automotive Manufacturing Solutions, 2013).

The example of how AvtoVAZ has reinvented its supply chain illustrates the ways in which foreign manufacturers and tier suppliers continue to influence seemingly all aspects of an ongoing rebuilding of the local manufacturing base. The Togliatti Special Economic Zone (SEZ) of automotive parts manufacturers integrated with RNPO (Renault–Nissan Purchasing Organisation) to produce parts for the Renault–Nissan's B platform—a design for compact and sub-compact passenger cars. With several Togliatti SEZ manufacturers focusing on foreign parts production, those suppliers that have been dependent on former Soviet era designed domestic cars are finding it difficult to continue operations.

In 2012, Nissan entered into a memorandum of understanding with Renault to form an alliance with AvtoVAZ's primary shareholder Russian Technologies to increase its stake in the Lada badge. Initially it was not clear what Nissan's intentions might be, as it already had its own production plant in St Petersburg. However, it soon became obvious that the company planned to use the vast, idled production capacity in the Togliatti SEZ to aid in building low-cost cars.

The first product for Nissan to come down the line at the Lada works was the Almera. This heavily modified version of the second-generation Nissan Bluebird Sylphy sedan was revealed to the world's press at the Moscow motor show in August 2012. Production began a slow ramp up in December 2012, with the first cars delivered to buyers 3 months later.

Nissan engineers, working with others from both Renault and AvtoVAZ, modified the Bluebird for local conditions, with particular attention paid to the suspension, which was strengthened for Russian roads.

Renault–Nissan set a very ambitious production target for AvtoVAZ, for the Almera was based on the many outdated Lada models traveling the Russian roads and were soon to be retired from service as consumers sought new replacements with more advanced features and contemporary designs. The car also has steel plates on its underside for added protection. No sooner had the Almera began to reach Russian dealers than Nissan announced it would launch its revival of the low-cost Datsun brand in Russia with two models to be built from 2014 on, again using Togliatti as a manufacturing base. The Nissan/Datsun production line at Togliatti has a "potential capacity" of 350,000 units, according to Nissan.

The ownership and technological influence on AvtoVAZ from the Renault and Nissan alliance has been significant; however, this does not preclude the importance of the existing and first joint-venture AvtoVAZ developed with a foreign automotive manufacturer, i.e., General Motors. The firms are again collaborating for the successor to the Chevrolet Niva, a compact 4 × 4. Volume production of a new GM-developed model is expected to commence in the second half of 2015.

Last year, 62,981 Chevrolet Nivas were manufactured at Togliatti, a 9% year-on-year rise, and the company says it plans to produce 62,500 vehicles in 2013. In 2012, the directors of the JV approved a $200 million expansion of the Togliatti plant that builds the model. This will see annual capacity rise from 98,000 to 120,000 units. The AvtoVAZ-GM production facility is separate from the others, which build Lada and Renault-Nissan Alliance models. Although the Association of European Businesses has cut its growth forecast for the Russian market following a recent fall in sales there is optimism. "Market participants are concerned about this situation, and expect continued slow demand before a potential improvement in the second half of the year," AEB chairman Joerg Schreiber stated in mid-June (Automotive Manufacturing Solutions, 2013).

If Russia is unlikely to witness its previous exponential growth rate of 20% in the short term, most analysts seem to agree with the AEB that the economy and vehicle market will nonetheless post substantially improved performance compared to Europe.

Overall, the consensus is that the market has much potential to return to growth—it has come a long way over the last two to three years thanks mainly to government decrees 166 and 566, which have lowered vehicle prices by encouraging foreign OEMs to localize production.

6.4 RUSSIAN ENERGY INDUSTRIES

6.4.1 Growth of Russian Indigenous Firms: Gazprom

Based on the abundant natural resources and Soviet-era technology capabilities, Russia exports natural gas and other lightly manufactured goods (e.g., made of aluminum). It is not unusual for several natural resource-based firms to reinvest in new businesses out of their available capital funds that have accumulated over the years. For example, Gazprom, a representative Russian energy firm headquartered in Moscow, conducts diverse lines of business not only in Russia but also in the entire European Union.

Gazprom is the largest gas company in the world, employing over 410,000 people and paying taxes that account for 25% of the Russian budget (Kupchinsky, 2006; Alon and Dwyer, 2012). The operating scale of Gazprom also positions it as the dominant natural gas supplier in Russia. It owns the infrastructure of the entire Russian pipeline network and thus controls the only means of transmission for both domestic and export consumption; in essence, giving Gazprom a distribution monopoly among its peers. Gazprom was established in 1989 from the Soviet Gas Ministry as part of the privatization program. The initial managers were individuals who previously had overseen state-run businesses and had no prior experiences with market-driven business practices (Freeland, 2000). The company is now trading on the London Stock Exchange and through American Depository Receipts (ADRs) (Table 6.1).

As a global energy company, Gazprom segments its core businesses into the following: 1) geological exploration, 2) production, 3) transportation (or transmission), 4) processing, 5) sales, 6) gas condensate, 7) power and heat generation. Gazprom views its mission in the reliable, efficient, and balanced supply of natural gas, other energy resources, and their derivatives to consumers. Gazprom holds the world's largest natural gas reserves. The company's share in the global and Russian gas reserves makes up 18% and 72%, respectively. Gazprom accounts for 14% and 74% of the global and Russian gas output accordingly. At present, the company actively implements large-scale projects aimed at exploiting gas resources of the

TABLE 6.1

Gazprom among FT Global 500 in the World in 2013

Global Rank 2013	Global Rank 2012	Company	Country	Sector	Market Value ($ m)	Turnover ($ m)	Net Income ($ m)	Total Assets ($ m)	Employees
1	1	Apple	US	Technology hardware and equipment	415,683	156,508	41,733	176,064	76,100
2	2	ExxonMobil	US	Oil and gas producers	403,733	420,714	44,880	333,795	76,900
3	13	Berkshire Hathaway	US	Nonlife insurance	256,802	14,824	427,452	288,500	156,280
4	3	PetroChina	China	Oil and gas producers	254,619	352,367	18,511	347,898	548,355
5	11	Wal-Mart	US	General retailers	246,373	469,162	16,999	203,105	2,200,000
6	9	General Electric	US	General industrials	239,776	144,796	13,622	685,300	305,000
7	4	Microsoft	US	Software and computer services	239,602	73,723	16,978	121,271	94,000
8	5	IBM	US	Software and computer services	237,725	104,507	16,604	115,240	434,246
9	12	Nestle	Switzerland	Food producers	233,792	100,640	11,584	134,635	339,000
10	10	Chevron	US	Oil and gas producers	230,831	222,629	26,179	230,320	62,000
57	31	Gazprom	Russia	Oil and gas producers	101,421	155,892	38,696	394,870	417,000

Source: Financial Times, FT Global 500; Czarny et al. (2009).

Yamal Peninsula, Arctic Shelf, Eastern Siberia, and the Far East, as well as hydrocarbon exploration and production projects abroad.

Gazprom is a reliable supplier of gas to Russian and foreign consumers. The company owns the world's largest gas transmission network—the Unified Gas Supply System of Russia with the total length of over 168,000 kilometers. Gazprom sells more than half of overall produced gas to Russian consumers and exports gas to more than 30 countries within and beyond the former Soviet Union. Gazprom is the only producer and exporter of liquefied natural gas in Russia.

The company is among Russia's five largest oil producers, and it is the largest owner of power-generating assets in the country. These assets account for 17% of the total installed capacity of the national energy system. Gazprom pursues the strategic objective of establishing itself as a leader among global energy companies by entering new markets, diversifying its activities, and ensuring reliable supplies.

This firm, under the direct control of the Russian government, is organized in the form of vertical integration. It is the largest natural gas firm in the world. Its production volume amounts to 24% of total global natural gas production and maintains 23% of ownership of the total available natural gas. In Russia, Gazprom produces up to 85% of Russian domestic natural gas and controls all domestic natural gas pipelines. Its business growth records are also impressive. In 2005, it increased the other source of natural gas reserve by 54%, 44% of crude oil, and 38% of small- and large-sized pipelines.

With its enormous energy resources ownership, Gazprom is very decisive in implementing its pricing policies. It controls the natural gas market with prudence and brings steady inflows of cash revenues to Russia and its affiliated firms. Gazprom supplies 25% of natural gas to EU countries. Thus, Gazprom exerts tremendous energy influence on the economies of countries in the European Union and other neighbors such as Ukraine. For instance, Gazprom constructed new pipelines in Germany and made contracts with EU countries to supply natural gas by 2036. Dependency on Russian exported natural gas by EU countries continues to grow. In the first decade of the 21st century, imported natural gas from Russia accounted for 40% of demand and it is forecasted to reach 70% by 2020.

Here, we will look into Gazprom's key projects, operational system, cooperation structure, and customizing business strategy (Scannel et al., 2000; Tan, 2001; Tomino et al., 2009; Yang et al., 2011). First, Gazprom's key projects included Shtokman, Blue Stream, Nord Stream, Altai, and

Sakhalin II, in which it was found that the destinations included the strengthening of natural gas exports to the eastern US coast, Canada, and Mexico LNG, and that the cooperative partners included corporations in France, the United States, and Norway. The Blue Stream project, specifically, had the purpose of reinforcing the oil conveyance equipment in Turkey and improving pipeline calibers to achieve the export volume of 16 bcm each year. Last, the building of the world's largest pressurization station had the purpose of developing markets in Southern Europe, for instance, cooperating with ENI, the Italian energy giant, to provide access to the market in Southern Europe.

Additionally, in order to reduce the risk of natural gas conveyance in Europe, Gazprom collaborated with German BASFAG and E.ONAG6 on constructing undersea oil pipes so that it could stabilize and create a reliable natural gas export to Western Europe as well as increase exports to Europe. Of these projects, particularly deserving notice is the ALTAI7 project, which revealed that Russia intended to develop a new market—China. The reason was that China's demand for natural gas would increase, as estimated, from 47.5 bcm in 2004 to 91 bcm in 2008. Russia will utilize long-term contracts and 2800-km-long pipes to achieve transference of 6.8 bcm of natural gas each year. This signaled to us that Russia has wanted to develop markets outside Europe since 2006. Moreover, once the market in China is operational, Russia can also have access to the Japanese market for diversification of the market risk and enhance its position in the world as a supplier of natural gas.

The above-stated projects of Gazprom required the work of vertical and horizontal strategic integrations; hence, Gazprom had over 43 partners in joint ventures in 2007, more than double in 2006, and these had not yet included what Gazprom would venture overseas with its own capital. It is especially noteworthy that Gazprom has already set foot in the United Kingdom, Romania, Vietnam, the United States, and even Venezuela, by 2007, virtually owning footholds all over the world; of the 20 covered countries, 13 were European. This attested that apart from reinforcing its market share in Europe, Gazprom was clearly seen, in 2007, with the policy of development toward other markets like Asia, America, and Australia. While the natural gas industry grasped a stable position, Gazprom engaged in a diversified business strategy, for example, entering the banking industry (Gazprombank), information technology (Informgaz), transportation (Gazpromtrans), and the insurance industry (Sogaz), to name a few. Thus, it can be clearly seen that Gazprom intended to benefit from vertical and horizontal integrations by the strategy of joint venture or sole ownership, as well as diversify the corporate risks by multiple businesses. Therefore, if the policy of Gazprom privatization successfully improved the domestic economy, then, in addition to the natural gas industry, we should consider the potential of Russia's aluminum and petroleum industries. As we know, aluminum will be among the most important resources in the next industrial revolution. Utilizing the Gazprom business model for aluminum and petroleum raw materials, will allow Russia to achieve similar economic results.

6.4.2 Comparison of Gazprom with Other Firms

The non-Gazprom gas producers (NGPs) doubled their share of the Russian domestic gas market between 2000 and 2010 and have continued growing since then. For several years especially, Novatek expanded. More recently, Rosneft has emerged as a key player, not least through its purchase of TNK-BP. With rising costs of Gazprom's queue of greenfield developments, any delays in Gazprom's investment program may be compensated through increased NGPs production.

The NGPs are ready to fill the gap, may be allowed to do so, and are already increasing their market share in an increasingly competitive market (Lunden et al., 2013), but the overall contribution these countries and industries make to the Russian economy are much greater than those efforts of the past.

6.5 CONCLUSION

This chapter examined the cases of AutoVaz and Gazprom as examples of Russian indigenous global firms. Even though Russian firms show the slow growth of the manufacturing sector, it is quite noteworthy of the emergence of the key resource-based firms. AvtoVAZ may be progressing toward ever greater integration within the Renault–Nissan sphere of influence and ownership, but that does not spell the end for a long-standing joint venture with General Motors. Gazprom engaged in a diversified business strategy and intended to benefit from vertical and horizontal integrations by the strategy of joint venture or sole ownership, as well as diversify the corporate risks by multiple businesses. Thus the strategic actions taken by both firms were designed to strengthen their related network capabilities and through the alliance with other global firms, customers, and countries, each firm improved its technology competence, customer competence and linkage competence.

Section III

Japanese and Korean Global Firms in Emerging Markets

7

Strategies of Japanese Firms in the Chinese Market

This chapter provides in-depth case analyses of Komatsu, Yaskawa Electronics, Panasonic, Clarion, and Toyota. Each of these prominent Japanese global firms experienced quite successful market positioning in China. The case studies of Japanese firms in China suggest that their successful business strategy is not a replication of their domestic product strategy in Japan but supply chain management that is characterized by sensing Chinese customer needs, deploying their unique technological capabilities and collaborating with Chinese suppliers.

7.1 INTRODUCTION

In the previous chapter, the three elements of network capability are presented as technology competence, customer competence, and linkage competence. A firm's network capability is essential to the successful development of product strategy and product architecture as discussed in the case studies of Japanese firms found in Chapters 3 to 5. This chapter focuses on the practices of Japanese firms in the Chinese market. In particular, the stories of Komatsu, Yaskawa Electronics, Panasonic, Clarion, and Toyota are discussed.

7.2 STRATEGY OF KOMATSU CHINA

7.2.1 An Overview of Komatsu China

In 2010 NHK (the National Public Broadcasting Organization) reported that Komatsu was the most outstanding firms among those Japanese firms operating globally. Its phenomenal success is based on strong performance in the emerging economies such as China, Brazil, and India. In this chapter, we focus on Komatsu China during different time periods. Komatsu's earliest Chinese market entry was in 1956 to 1978 in which the finished products made in Japan were mostly exported to China (Park and Shintaku, 2014). In the next period (1979–1994), Komatsu's strategic priority was set to develop Chinese partners with whom it was willing to support technology innovation for Chinese state-owned firms. During this period, Komatsu offered the in-depth technology know-how of nine affiliated construction firms and three industrial equipment companies. Afterward, during the period of 1995 to 2000, Komatsu developed joint sales/marketing programs through foreign direct investment (FDI) in China. Komatsu deployed used construction equipment in the southern regions to keep up with the growing Chinese construction market.

From 1995, Komatsu involved Chinese partners for joint sales efforts in Chinese markets while attempting the integration of Japanese quality/production control methods with Chinese management practices. At that time, Komatsu built several plants and then expanded foundry operations in the Shantung province and Shanghai regions. From 2001, Komatsu started penetrating the Chinese market in a large scale. After China became a member of the World Trade Organization (WTO), Komatsu established regional-center firms. As a part of its global market strategy, Komatsu built its own sales/services network in the name of Komatsu China in 2011. As of 2011, there were nine manufacturing centers, three sales/marketing centers, and one other corporation unit. It also has 32 distribution centers. With the absence of Chinese distribution channels, 32 distribution centers have been established with one center serving each province. All these centers are established through Chinese local capital, and the total number of employees in 32 centers is 6,000 with an average of 200 people per center. In this way, Komatsu China grew rapidly since 2000. Although in 2004 the Chinese government's macroeconomic policy stopped land development projects, Komatsu's growth remained unhindered because of its early recognition and preparation for possible external business environment change prospects. For example, a sensor system called KOMTRAX (a wireless monitoring device attached to construction equipment) reports operation stoppages and geographic locations on all construction machine equipment. Due to production issues, the introduction of KOMTRAX experienced a delay of three months; however, once these issues were solved the number of units being installed on equipment quickly grew. This growth was aided in part by the Chinese government's massive economic stimulus into infrastructure projects which required the extensive use and purchase of construction equipment. As an affinitive beneficiary of this stimulus, Komatsu China revenues in March of 2011 represented 21% of all Komatsu global revenues (Figures 7.1 and 7.2).

7.2.2 Structure of KOMTRAX of Komatsu China

The KOMTRAX system was initially developed for preventing theft through the use of GPS (Global Positioning System) to monitor the location of construction and mining equipment. As the technology advanced, KOMTRAX

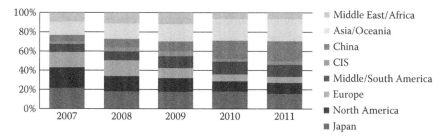

FIGURE 7.1
Sales rate of global Komatsu.

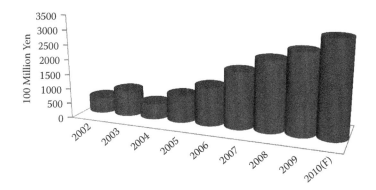

FIGURE 7.2
Komatsu China growth.

became useful to monitor machine productivity, human resource deployment in operating the construction equipment, and overall equipment operation data analysis. Introducing the KOMTRAX product to the Chinese market through establishing a domiciled presence that integrates Japanese and Chinese operating practices is one example of a business model successfully used in an emerging market such as China. KOMTRAX is a standard feature on all construction and mining equipment; KOMTRAX revenues are produced through communication usage fees that are essentially billed in advance to the purchaser. When a piece of equipment is purchased, three years of up-front communication usage fees are assessed and added to the equipment cost; for example, the assessment in China is 600 (yen) per annum or 1,800 for the 3-year communication agreement. Communication frequency occurs once per hour, notifying the equipment owner of the equipment's vital statistics and with the information being transmitted in one of three ways: (1) daily and dispatched every morning to a designated e-mail account or URL; (2) text message delivered to a mobile phone; or (3) using the Wireless Application Protocol (WAP) system, remote access to the data via the website through a mobile phone or pad application to view the information in a graphical format.

7.2.3 KOMTRAX's Usage Patterns in Emerging Markets

Usage data is delivered by the KOMTRAX system daily and every hour (24 hours, 7 days a week, 365 days a year), which is of great value to the distribution center offices that manage equipment servicing and for the equipment owners seeking to protect their assets at all times. Komatsu collects comprehensive data (e.g., diverse usage patterns) through this system installed in all the construction equipment sold. This system is used primarily in Japan, North America, and China and additional such system usage is considered in other regions as well. Komatsu China in particular uses KOMTRAX for (1) theft prevention, (2) rental management, (3) production planning based on demand forecast, (4) credit management, (5) operation cost, and fuel efficiency. Since KOMTRAX is connected to customers, distribution centers, manufacturing plants, and sales offices, it allows regular monitoring of maintenance needs and overall machine efficiency controls.

In general, operating expenses of construction equipment are more than three times initial purchase cost. Automatic internal data collecting mechanisms, however, may reduce unnecessary movements and breakdowns, assist distribution centers to arrange component parts exchanges at the right times, and help take appropriate measures for inventory cost control. The KOMTRAX system, with simple data entry of an ID number, can pinpoint the location of particular equipment in the video screen. This is possible because all equipment with the KOMTRAX system also contain the receiver of GPS. A real-time check of engine usage patterns (i.e., either in use or not) allows Komatsu headquarters to examine the total operation times and hours taken for specific tasks. Other maintenance check details (e.g., the level of engine pressures and temperature performance) are all available. In case of theft, it is reasonable to identify how and where the equipment is being transported.

Komatsu is able to visually evaluate the operation hours and operation costs of its construction equipment on computer video screens. For example, using comparative labor costs to operate a 20-ton hydraulic shovel, the variances between China and Japan are quite significant, with China being much lower; whereas lost production time and cost in China are much greater than Japan due to the number of hours a piece of equipment may remain idle due to breakdowns occurring and speed of repair taking longer than in Japan. Such detailed information sent through KOMTRAX is quite useful for the owners of the equipment and allows Komatsu to better forecast overall demand as well as maintenance management.

Then, how is a demand forecast obtained? Komatsu headquarters readily has access to performance details of particular bulldozers in a certain area (e.g., the actual tons of earth removed to a certain distance in terms of kilometers). This is possible through the data system attached in all construction equipment, which automatically store required information according to preprogrammed instructions. In this way, KOMTRAX provides all the required information of high value for Komatsu Japan that includes an overall demand forecast that determines actual production schedule planning. Such an information network mechanism is extremely helpful for responding to the changing market reality of emerging economies like China.

As mentioned before, in April 2004 the Chinese government implemented tight fiscal control that temporarily halted operation of much Komatsu equipment that naturally influenced the stoppage of actual production lines in China. Sakane, the Komatsu chairman, pointed out that their firm inventory control was substantially better than that of the Chinese and Korean rivals that had not attached GPS systems to their products. For almost half a year or so, Komatsu could save a large sum of unnecessary inventory-related costs. This is what the KOMTRAX system did for Komatsu's operational excellence.

The KOMTRAX system is being applied in after sales services. Sakane said, "Out of ten daily engine run hours only six hours might be devoted to actual operation. If so, why not advise the customers to stop the engine when it is not under operation hours?" Such detailed advice is possible through the KOMTRAX system. In addition, timely delivery of required parts occurs within 24 hours through the KOMTRAX system, which reports regular maintenance need details. Such on-time delivery is possible through KOMTRAX's advance diagnosis of maintenance needs of particular parts of every Komatsu product. Such maintenance service arrangements are expanded for customers in emerging economies as well. As of 2011, more than 95% of "the next morning delivery" regions include Japan, the United States, Germany, and France. With an increasing number of the component parts distribution centers, Komatsu plans to extend such reliable maintenance services to China, Brazil, Indonesia, and India within the next 2 years. This action is to protect any customer who purchased equipment prior to the global financial crisis that began in 2008. In fact, Komatsu sold a large number of dump trucks (i.e., "living mining machine") used for the exploration of natural resources such as copper and coal and hydraulic shovels between 2007 and 2008. Thus, their maintenance needs (i.e., replacement of component parts) became extensive as their total running hours came close to 15,000 to 20,000. As of March 2010, Komatsu has 35 parts distribution centers in the world from which all the required maintenance items for large trucks and hydraulic shovels (e.g., tires and engine parts) are supplied. In China the average timely delivery within 24 hours from the actual need is about 90%, with a target rate of 95%. In China, two parts distribution centers are in Beijing and Shanghai. With an additional 1 to 2 billion (yen), two or three more such distribution centers will be built in anticipation of continuous market growth.

Banks also find KOMTRAX useful in the risk management of loans. For a Chinese bank loan evaluation process, Chinese bankers give high marks for Komatsu's construction equipment because equipment installed with KOMTRAX reports operational details of the machines and thus the risk of management is relatively low. Should loan defaults occur, being able to track the location of the equipment used to collateralize the loans is very valuable. In case of temporary loan payment delay up to 3 months, the banks and the retailers have an option to stop machine operations. Ninety percent of the time the customers immediately resolve any loan payment issues.

A radio-controlled (i.e., unattended) dump truck is the next innovative step of the KOMTRAX system. This product is being marketed in Chile

and Australia for 300-ton trucks that operate without attending drivers. These unattended dump trucks are useful for mines located 3000 to
4000 m above sea level. By hiring drivers, additional accommodation for
their family members requires extra facilities for lodging, hospitals, and
schools. In mining operations, their work is repetitious and predictable;
the risk for human accidents is fairly high.

Komatsu China products are very appealing due to the technological
superiority being offered to customers with the concept of darapaton
(i.e., 1 ton unit based running cost). In terms of running costs, Komatsu's
darapaton is very low, much below the purchasing cost of the particular
equipment. Compared to the product performance of rival firms, Komatsu
products indicate consistently better efficiency in terms of work volumes,
operation hours, maintenance costs, operational capability, speed level,
and operational productivity.

Komatsu China maintains distribution centers like other Japanese firms
and collects relevant information from the individual users of the products. Komatsu's KOMTRAX enables Komatsu to configure customized
service offerings to the individual buyer of the products. Other rival firms
are unaware of the needs of their individual customers unless they receive
specific service requests. In contrast, by utilizing the KOMTRAX system,
Komatsu China designed proactive service systems for its entire customer
base. In this way, Komatsu instituted win-win relationships among distri-
bution/service centers, customers, and manufacturing facilities.

7.2.4 Competition with Local Chinese Firms

This section considers competition with indigenous firms and localization
strategy. Currently, civil engineering (i.e., earth moving) systemization and
efficiency allow role changes of the hydraulic shovel. The usage of "wheel
loader" equipment has diminished over recent years in favor of "hydraulic shovels." As of 2010, Komatsu's market share of the hydraulic shovel is
20% which places it in the number one position in the industry. However,
Chinese local firms entered the hydraulic shovel market as well. The market
growth trend of the hydraulic shovel shows steady increases each year—16%
in 2006 and 27% in 2010. Thus, Chinese firms' market progress is visible.
It is expected that their market share will exceed 30% after 2010. Chinese
firms are not able to make key engines or hydraulic parts, but they import
from Japanese firms such as Kawasaki and Isuzu, and the overall quality is
reasonable. Caterpillar also competes in the hydraulic shovel market against

Komatsu. Other global competitors are Korean firms such as Hyundai and Doosan. It is important to note the growth of Chinese local firms and Korean global firms. In the Chinese market, for example, the price comparison of 20 ton classic 20 can be stated as below, assuming Komatsu's price is 100, Chinese local makers 85, and the Korean maker is 75. Korean firms offer their products 25% lower than Komatsu and their overall quality is comparable to those of Komatsu.

In the low-end market (e.g., wheel loader), Chinese and Korean construction equipment manufacturers overwhelmingly dominate the market (Figure 7.3). Chinese firms take 50% of market share. Wheel loaders by Chinese makers are sold at one third the price level of Japanese products. About 10 Chinese firms produce somewhat identical products from design concept to manufacturing processes. Komatsu continues to differentiate through high-end, premium quality.

The overall Chinese construction equipment market is segmented into three areas: (1) basic (i.e., bulldozers), (2) intermediate (i.e., wheel loaders) and (3) premium (i.e., hydraulic shovels) product categories. A substantial difference exists between premium products (e.g., hydraulic shovel) and intermediate-range products (e.g., wheel loader). Japanese manufacturers dominate the premium products market, and local Chinese makers supply intermediate products. Chinese local manufacturers have begun to gradually enter the hydraulic shovel market. With this changing market environment, Komatsu China is all the more specializing in its premium products division. By utilizing an IT system such as KOMTRAX, Komatsu is differentiated in its service offerings and has expanded its market share. Komatsu China assesses the operational status of its construction equipment through KOMTRAX and achieves high value-added sales performance. Komatsu China offers products that report substantially lower operating expenses compared to those by

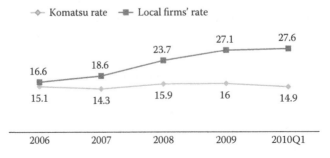

FIGURE 7.3
Market share comparison of Komatsu China and other local firms for wheel loader.

other rival firms. Komatsu products show comparative strengths in the areas of annual operating costs, work volumes, operational hours, maintenance costs, speed, and operating efficiency.

Korean and Chinese firms also produce bulldozers. Compared to those by Komatsu, the performance levels of their products are somewhat lower in terms of operational efficiency and durability. However, with the low cost advantage of these products, these firms still pose a threat to Komatsu's market share. It is to be seen how Korean and Chinese firms compete against Komatsu in the emerging markets for the coming years.

7.3 STRATEGY OF DAIKIN CHINA

Established in 1924, Daikin Industries (Daikin) has celebrated its 90th anniversary in 2014. As of 2013, its annual sales are 1,783.1 (Yen in billion) and net profit of 91.9 (Yen in billion). Its main business segments are 86.8% of air conditioning/refrigeration, fluorochemical industries 9.6%, Oil hydraulics/special equipments 3.6%. The major source of revenues is air conditioning and refrigeration business units. (Note: As of July 1, 2014, 1 USD = 102.08 Japanese Yen).

Daikin Industries, an air-conditioner manufacturer, is the largest Japanese maker of its kind. In 2003 Daikin was already the market leader for family-use air conditioners in Japan. In the 1970s Daikin also marketed floor and ceiling types of air conditioners. In the 1980s, it built the broad set of technological capabilities through which it introduced diverse production lines including multi-air-conditioning systems for buildings, large-scale temperature control system devices, and high-reliability compressor design, direct digital control (DDC), and communication control (Jin, 2007).

Daikin also strengthened its marketing business unit, strategic support of the recruitment and training of air-conditioner professionals in its distribution centers, public relations, and promotion activities for premium customers. In China, major global air-conditioner manufacturers fiercely compete for their fair market share, and 60% of this industry is for room air conditioners. More than 50 firms from Japan, the United States, Germany, France, the United Kingdom, and Korea join with other local Chinese makers in this competitive battleground. The central air conditioners are about 20% of the total air-conditioner market. The market leaders are mostly US firms. The other 20% is for business offices among which Daikin holds 30% of the market share.

7.3.1 Daikin's China Market Strategy

Daikin's China market entry started somewhat later compared to other Western and Japanese firms (e.g., Carrier, Yoko, and Train). Among the Japanese rivals, Daikin was the last that started Chinese operations. In June 1994, Inoue, Daikin's president, anticipated that China would be the largest potential market in the world as well as the global factory of the world (Jin, 2007). Accordingly, Daikin formulated a China market strategy and implemented specific steps for market positioning. In the same period, China became a member of the World Trade Organization (WTO). The Chinese government implemented a lower tariff, provided incentives for foreign direct investment, and maintained open market policies.

For their China production hub, Daikin chose Shanghai based on the principle of "Produce near Customers." Since Daikin's strength is in heat pumps (i.e., air conditioning and heating), the Zhejiang region with four distinctive seasonal variations and a large market of numerous coastal cities was most appropriate as the location for its manufacturing center. Its motto was, "For entire China market, start with Shanghai." The Shanghai region also has strong industrial foundation infrastructures with abundant skilled resources and component parts manufacturers. At that time, the Chinese government was switching its economic policy focus from Guangzhou (South West Region) to Shanghai (South East).

In the 1990s, the Chinese air-conditioner industry experienced explosive consumer market growth. Numerous global/domestic makers entered and competed for their fair share of the China market. By 1995, there were more than 300 air-conditioner manufacturers in China which overflew their products in air-conditioner markets. The Shanghai City Government implemented policies intended to curb the additional entries for the already crowded air-conditioner industry. Daikin, therefore, concentrated its business on a business-building air-conditioner package. For its air-conditioner product line, Daikin started two parallel productions. The demand forecast of the Chinese business line was largely uncertain, but Daikin was decisive in building a huge manufacturing basis for business-purpose air conditioners.

In November 1995, Daikin established an air-conditioner joint venture firm with a Chinese machine maker (state owned) that was experiencing a prolonged sales slump with no dependable supplier partners on its own (Jin, 2007). The overall power influence of this Chinese partner was minimal because it was busy with its restructuring efforts and its knowledge on air-conditioner design and manufacturing was quite limited. Thus,

Daikin China managed to keep the number of Chinese managers (no more than 18) and could overcome undesirable Chinese state-owned practices (e.g., lack of quality management mindset and organizational disciplines), improved the working relationship with Shanghai City government, and implemented the Daikin style of decisive, speed management.

7.3.2 Product Development Strategy of Daikin China

Daikin maintains 63 major global airconditioning production centers. The Production and Technology Unit (PTU) under the airconditioning production headquarters oversees these 63 production centers globally. PTU is responsible for three main functions: (1) overseeing the cutting edge technology development, developing innovative production methods/technologies for new products/components functionality/quality/cost, and deliverfing a steady stream of new products with differentiation; (2) applying mass (i.e., economies of scale) production technologies (line engineering) and efficient production methods into product features and process designs and achieving performance requirements in terms of high quality/short lead time/low costs; (3) expanding global scale applications of new production technologies/production methods and support to build new production facilities and transferring front-end *monozukuri* know-how. For this, Daikin has been adopting production methods known as PDS (Production of Daikin System) and introducing it to the plants globally.

From April 1996 Daikin China started production training in its temporary facility and searched for its customers (Jin, 2007). By March 1997, it moved to the new manufacturing facility for large-scale production. Yet, there was no real sales increase. From 1998, the Shanghai market showed a drastic change in demand patterns which spread out to the neighboring coastline cities. More customers no longer were content with in-house, small air-conditioner units; instead, diverse customer needs required larger air conditioners for high-rise business buildings, apartments, and individual homes with more than 100 square meters. Increasingly, hospitals, universities, and banks installed high-performance air-conditioner units for their large offices.

In terms of business air conditioners, Daikin has world-class technological capabilities (Jin, 2007). In Japan, Daikin leads in market share of business units (as of 2004, 43%). Daikin Shanghai, instead of being concerned about the market moves of its rivals, consistently built on its strengths and introduced newer models in the Chinese market based on its core competences. Its Chinese strategy clearly reflected its global product development strategy. All the new product designs were prepared in Japan, and their efforts focused on reducing overall new product development costs for its global products.

Daikin also organized a Chinese market team that specialized in the changing needs of Chinese customers (Jin, 2007). The products sold in China were made to fit Chinese customer contexts. Relentless efforts were directed to improving product performance and doing an innovative redesign of Chinese models. For example, in view of unstable voltage power in China, Daikin installed an automatic voltage restoration feature for each air conditioner for Chinese customers. In response to the dignity-conscious psyche of upper-middle-class customers in the areas of Beijing, Shanghai, and Guangzhou, floor-type air conditioners (i.e., 170-cm high and 50-cm wide) were developed, and they were an instant hit in the market (Jin, 2007).

In recent years sales in China has substantially increased. Figure 7.4 shows that the relative importance Daikin China is similar to that of Dainkin Europe—around 18% in terms of global sales percentage as of the end of 2012.

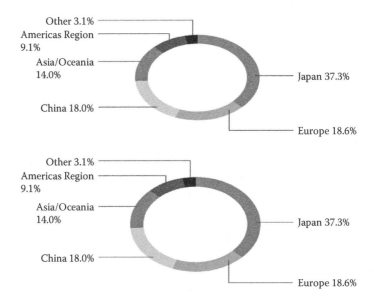

FIGURE 7.4
Sales by geographical segments (air-conditioning and refrigeration equipment). (From Daikin Annual Report, 2012, p. 31.)

7.3.3 Brand Marketing Strategy of Daikin China

In the mid-1990s, the popular air conditioners for Chinese stores were mostly a floor type. For differentiation from rivals, Daikin developed an integrative car-set-type model that contains both an interior unit (attached to the ceiling) and an exterior unit (connected to the outside) (Jin, 2007). At the same time, Daikin promoted the advanced nature and premium quality of its products to appeal to potential customers and increased the actual market size. Daikin's aggressive marketing force was its sales engineers (SEs) who were overwhelmingly in larger number. As of 2003, Daikin has 30 distribution centers. Each distribution center had about 230 SEs (Jin, 2007).

Daikin did not use the traditional Chinese distribution channels. Instead, it built its own sales network. Each distribution center handled the initial installation, sales, and after-sale services as well. All the staff members in the distribution centers received "two-night and three-day" intensive training by expert engineers for assuming any service requests from customers. To avoid the issues of bad accounts receivables, Daikin Shanghai insisted on a cash-only policy for all of its transactions. Under such a sales policy, no distribution centers carried excessive inventory beyond the actual demand. Daikin did not have to worry about the credit problems of its customers.

Daikin's SEs concentrated their activities in shopping centers or libraries in the newly developed areas and listened to questions and suggestions from interested users (Jin, 2007). SEs responded to their questions, both technical and sales aspects, and presented the practical details of the available products while answering all their questions. SEs also regularly conducted seminars for the customers and explained the performance and key features of the products. SEs also contacted the construction field offices and helped their managers to understand Daikin's product advantages and thus supported them to adopt Daikin's products from the design processes of the residential and business-purpose facilities. Through these comprehensive and well-coordinated promotion activities, SEs expanded the customer basis in the Chinese market.

The point of Daikin's brand strategy is how to keep outstanding customers. Daikin strengthened service aspects of its business and offered year-round (i.e., 24 hour/365 day) services (Jin, 2007). Thus, its customers could receive immediate service attention from Daikin. In China, customers regarded Daikin's products as the "Benz of Air Conditioners." In this way, Daikin deployed the highly differentiated and cutting-edge products for Chinese customers. Naturally, the profit margins relative to sales volumes of its products are consistently higher than those of its rivals.

7.3.4 Strategic Talent Development That Supports Global Monozukuri (i.e., Japanese Manufacturing)

Dakin focuses on developing three types of strategic talents that support its global *monozukuri*: (1) technological engineers with specialized expert skill-set; (2) top leadership candidates for global business units; (3) competent local talents. The qualification for technological engineers and top leadership for global business units are engineers with ten years of experiences within the firm.

In particular, there has been a critical shortage of veteran engineers that are able to train young engineers for radidly expanding business opportunities such as China. Thus, Daikin emphasizes that young aspiring engineers develop common strategic skill set requirements from the early years of their career.

For the top leadership positions in global business units, engineers with at least ten years of work expericiene first master the essential knowledge of production, finance and accounting and start working as bridge persons in between Japanese headquarters and overseas business units. In the past, Daikin had prepared these top leadership candidates with essential monozukuri practices, but not necessarily other skill requirements such as management/HR/finance/insurance/strategy/banking and financial institutions. Thus, many leaders had faced enourmous difficulties in their overseas assignments. At present, Daikin is implementing strategic integration between Japanese headquarters and global business units through this new education and training initiatives.

Finally, since 2003 Daikin has been promoting production independence in each overseas plant through local talent development program, which includes basic education and intermediate training. For basic education and training, Daikin invites local talent to Japan for two weeks and offers extensive training in principles of manufacturing assembly/repairing/painting processes. At the end of 2013, more than 150 have successfully completed such a training program, intermediate trainng targets local managers in global business units and invites them to Japan to get involved in the actual production lines with Japanese engineers in the areas of production planning and facility development. By 2013, 22 people have completed such training as well.

7.4 STRATEGY OF HONDA GUANGZHOU

In 1980s Honda expanded its global production. From the 2000s Honda started production in China. As of 2012, Honda established three automobile

TABLE 7.1

Honda China's Automotible Production Volumes

Names	Guangqi Honda Automobile Co., Ltd.		Honda China Automobile Co., Ltd.	Dongfeng Honda Automobile Co., Ltd.	
Investment Ratio	Honda 50% Guangzhou Train Group 50%		Honda 65% Guangzhou Train Group 25% Dongfeng Motor Corporation 10%	Honda 50% Dongfeng Motor Corporation 50%	
Production Plants (#)	Guangzhou (1)	Guangzhou (2)	Guangzhou (1)	Wuhan (1)	Wuhan (2)
Production Capacity	240,000	120,000	50,000	240,000	60,000

plants in China. (1) Guangqi Honda automobile Co., Ltd. by 50:50 joint venture of Guangzhou Train Group and Honda, (2) Honda China Automobile Co., Ltd. by 65:25:10 joint venture by Honda (65), Guangzhou Train Group (25), and Dongfeng Train Group (10), (3) Dongfeng Honda Automobile Co. LTd. by 50: 50 Joint Venture by Honda and Dongfeng Motor Corporation (See Table 7.1 for other details). In this section, we focus on the business strategy of Guangqi Honda automobile Co., Ltd. and the design engineering support by Honda Engineering China Co.,Ltd. (EGCH).

In 1998 Honda formed a 50–50 joint venture with Guangzhou Train Group (GTG). The market share is still small, but its production/sales are steadily increasing. With the 2012 China-Japan territorial dispute, just like other Japanese firms experienced drastic sales reduction, Honda Guangzhou also struggles with a sales slowdown.

7.4.1 Honda's Entry Strategy for the Chinese Market

Honda's production in China was somewhat behind that of its global rivals. As of 1998 when Honda started its production in China, firms such as Volkswagen (VW) and General Motors (GM) formed joint ventures and their operations were in full swing. From the late 1990s, with the WTO membership, the Chinese government relaxed previous strict control policies on the automotive industries and encouraged market development.

From 1994 Honda started component parts production with Dongfeng Motor (i.e., joint venture) around Guangzhou areas. After the pullout of Peugeot Motors from Guangzhou, Honda gained the right to produce passenger cars in China, winning out over GM and Hyundai.

The reason why Honda chose Guangzhou as its primary production hub was that in cities like Shanghai, Beijing, Tianjin, and Changchun, other global firms such as GM, VW, Toyota, and Chrysler had already established production and market infrastructures. In contrast, Guangzhou allows "coordinating global inter-firm product development" (Jin, 2007) because it covers growing strategic market areas and provides outstanding logistical advantages for export and import conditions with its proximity to Hong Kong and Shenzhen.

Honda's Chinese joint venture partner was China's number one automaker, Dongfeng Train. Prior to establishing Guangqi Honda, Honda already had joint venture experiences of producing component parts and engine systems. Fortunately, Honda completed joint venture contracts with Guangzhou Train and formed another joint venture for producing complete passenger cars. Furthermore, Guangzhou Train was not absorbed into Dongfeng Train Group. Guangzhou Train was lacking in automotive technological expertise and their experiences on passenger cars were minimal. Thus, Honda could strengthen the relationship with Guangzhou city government and maintain their management leadership as well as ownership interests for implementing speed experiences.

7.4.2 Product and Technology Strategy of Honda China

Other global rivals produced previous old models in China. However, Honda's brand strategy was to produce up-to-date high-end product lines. Honda Accord's global acceptance was well known not only in Japan but also in other countries. Honda's product strategy was to introduce the same new model each year in the China market for all other additional product lines other than Accord.

Guangqi Honda kept their early investment amount low and used the production facilities of Peugeot Motors. By taking advantage of Peugeot's production equipment and facilities, Guangqi Honda could introduce the Accord for Chinese customers. In the 1999 Global Quality Contest, Guangqi Honda received the number one quality award for its Accord (Jin, 2007). Guangqi Honda's sourcing of component parts was through local suppliers while engine system and press parts were internally manufactured at its facilities and the localization speed was extremely fast. According to strict QCDDM (Quality, Cost, Delivery, Development, and Management) standards, Honda chose component parts manufacturers, used their products, and thus achieved cost reduction goals. After China became a member of the WTO, Honda emphasized full localization as its strategic priority for cost advantage.

Engineering Honda China Co. Ltd. (EGCH), which was established in July 20, 2004, is supporting Honda's localization strategy in China. As of 2012, EGCH has R&D Centers in Guangzhou and Shanghai with 240 full-time engineers. Shanghai Center also engages new product development for two-wheels as well. EGCH's localization plans for "two wheels" (e.g.. motorcycle) business unit have achieved a mature stage, while the "four wheels" (e.g., automobile) business unit is rapidly moving toward local sourcing of all components parts. The number of engineers is increasing each year. (Note: As of 2012 the number of engineers is 240.) Besides engineering designs and facility expansion, EGCH focuses on preparing local managers for leadership positions. For example, Japanese and Chinese department managers work together to develop local talents. The crucial role of EGCH in China is to provide manufacturing competences (e.g., tooling and production processes) and information gathering for full-scale localization. EGCH's strategy is to: (1) utilize a superb level of tooling for premium value-added impact, (2) support aggressive productivity enhancement efforts in Chinese manufacturing facilities, (3) contribute to Honda's Chinese production strategy thorough manufacturing technology, (4) improve tooling price competitiveness in all engineering. Tooling design for vehicle body is done in Japan. EGCH is responsible for the processes from design and molding. In the case of PT molding, almost all component parts are acquired through local suppliers. Integration of Japanese high technology and low cost component parts results in high-quality products. Besides, procurement expansion effort has achieved almost all instrument panel molding through local suppliers by 2010. DC (Dye Cast) processes (i.e., from product design to processing data) are handled in Japan, while molding processing, assembly, try and inspections are performed in China. The average lifespan of dye cast molding is 100,000 shots. In reality, Honda's three plants target 200,000 shots through preventive maintenance program. In this way, Honda's high-technology capability permits achieving overall facility and equipment cost reduction. In auto body construction area, Honda supports jig, painting, general facility introduction, and stable production. In the

PT facility area, local suppliers deliver main component parts, including newly developed D, T.R, G.H and high-intensity MoG·G. Thus, additional investment in production facilities is kept at minimum.

Honda rapidly expands the scope of local sourcing of almost all component parts in China, while it strategically retains a high value-added portion of engineering design capabilities in Japan. Honda carefully implements its localization strategy on several fronts. For example, in developing any global automobile models, modeling details have to change according to different types of machinery and equipment. In some plants, their particular pressing machines require different molding methods. Although all plants use Japanese machinery and equipment, manufacturing processes are not necessarily all standardized. EGCH's molding in China is based on economies of scale mass production methods for cost efficiency, but in Japan and North America mass-customization aspects are more or less emphasized. For automobile body parts, not all global plants use precisely of the same type of materials. Honda examines materials separately, requirements in each global market region using extensive simulation options first. The production focus of Honda's three plants in China is molding for large size panels. EGCH (Engineering Honda China Co. Ltd) (EGCH) chooses insourcing for high-valued components such as sider panels and takes outsourcing for low- or medium-value items to Chinese suppliers. Three of Honda's plants in China are empowered to make outsourcing decisions on their own. In some cases, EGCH expects its suppliers to handle on its behalf. The outsourcing value ratio by Honda's three plants and EGCH is 2:1. For example, Guangqi Honda handles 1/3 of total outsourcing in China. In reality, EGCH sends molding design details to Guangqi Honda, which then resends them to its suppliers for the precise tasks. In view of its production volume limitations, EGCH has to count on other suppliers for any increasing demand. The ratio of EGCH's insourcing (30%) and outsourcing (70%) is 3:7. As Honda plans to expand its product lines, it soon expects to increase its molding facilities twofold. Thus, the total volume of EGCH's insourcing and outsourcing will naturally increase. Honda intends to maintain an insourcing ratio no less than 30% of total production volume. For this goal, Honda maintains three daily shifts for manufacturing processng and two daily shifts for assembly.

At present, EGCH's main molding suppliers are 4 to 5 suppliers that are owned by a Japanese investment. Most of the engineers are from Korea. For the Wuhan plant, the outsourcing ratio is somewhat different according to Dongfeng Motor Corporation's preference.

The business relationship between EGCH and Honda's three Chinese plants is purely contract-based molding manufacturing. However, determining the appropriate service transfer costs (e.g., molding maintenance) between them remains an issue to be resolved. The total cost make-up of molding includes materials (40%), labor (50%), of which manufacturing process related labor costs (20% to 30%), Japanese design engineering costs (10% to 20%) and other miscellaneous costs (up to 10%). Because labor costs in Japan are relatively high (or much lower in China), it is quite advantageous to accept a larger share of the production costs in China (as of 2012). Take molding process cost as an example. Suppose particular molding processes cost $100 in Japan. Bringing such processes to China requires transportation/logistics costs ($10.00), custom duty ($5.00), and consumption tax ($5.00). Thus, the total cost of molding from Japan is not $100.00 but about $120.00. Thus, it is preferred to do production in China in light of low materials and production labor costs plus other savings from transporation and import taxes. EGCH, therefore, makes a serious effort to control manufacturing and overhead costs to improve price competitiveness. In the past, Honda could sell its products at premium prices in China. Recently, Chinese suppliers produce routine molding products at lost costs. Thus, Honda can no longer afford to charge high prices for its products in China.

For any new model cars, Honda can no longer merely bring Japanese platforms with body design features to China. Instead, Honda may adopt a "catch-all pattern between China and Japan" (i.e., concurrent design work in Japan and manufacturing facility tooling processes in China).

Manufacturing low-cost cars for the emerging markets requires careful materials selection and rigorous quality management. For example, Honda still may enter parternships with firms in China and Thailand for delivering inexpensive cars by using low-cost steel plates for its automobile body parts. The issue is not merely using inexpensive materials. The challenge is how to minimize the differences in quality performance between products made in Japan or these emerging countries. Thus, full scale implementation of such strategic collaboration is not yet feasible because of product quality requirements. In this respect, it is crucial for Honda to develop engineering talents that are able to use innovative technologies and newly developed materials and components parts.

Honda Japan concentrates R&D work requirements. The issue is in developing sufficient number of R&D talents. Honda's option is to develop innovative new technologies thorugh R&D centers in Japan and implement such technologies to manufacturing plants in China. Thus, local plants in China handle the development need for new manufacturing process technologies. The senior management of Honda's plants in China is responsible for sensing work on the changing Chinese market needs. In the past, Honda brought replication models to China from Japan. Recently, Honda China assumes much of new product development in China. Honda Japan carefully takes local feedback from China for further innovation for global markets.

The different local quality standards includes automobile engine size, standard speed requirements (e.g., in China 90 km per hour) for "two wheel" autobicyle affects product quality expectations. The quality standards of "four wheel" automobile in China might not necessarily be the same as those in Japan and North America. However, tooling quality itself cannot be different. Honda cannot compromise essential performance quality standards in any global market. Instead, from a tooling perspective, Honda does not insist that all the interior design details be the exactly same for an automobile that targets customers in the emerging markets. For example, in view of different customer requirements in emerging markets (e.g., prices and customer preferences), Honda tends to reduce the number of manufacturing processes for the interior features while applying uniform exterior body requirements of all its global market brands.

7.4.3 Marketing Strategy of Honda China

Guangqi Honda, facing intensive price competition with its rivals, kept the policy, "No low prices" (Jin, 2007). Such a consistent price strategy allowed its customers to maintain fierce brand loyalty and invited more potential customers. At this time, mid- or premium-priced models were somewhat outdated, and the prices of imported cars remained fairly high. In such a market context, deploying new annual models and focusing on high-end customers, Honda offered its selective product lines with relatively lower prices than the imported cars. Such a marketing strategy became quite successful.

Guangqi Honda also does not invest on the traditional Chinese distribution network. Rather, Honda opened 200 dealers on its own investment and made concerted efforts to provide reliable after-sales services (Jin, 2007). Honda was the first Japanese global automaker that established its own dealership network in China. For the establishment of its own sales network, Honda examined the detailed statistical data such as the population size of every major city and the demand forecast of passenger cars for city customers. Through such data analytics, Honda determined the market size for its product lines and conducted specific target market size analysis for each product line. Based on such adequate market analysis, Honda determined the size of dealerships, locations, and sales network configurations.

Guangqi Honda also built a package sales network system similar to Japanese dealership chains in terms of finished cars sales, after services, parts availability, and information feedback (Jin, 2007). Guangqi Honda provided extensive support for all of its dealerships in regard to customer support services through direct sales, price level determination for engine systems and component parts for all the products sold throughout China, and special training and development for the dealerships that market the models made in China or high-end models imported from Japan. Guangqi Honda also established "advance payment only" plans and thus avoided the usual credit problems of other rival firms that used to bear major write-offs for bad debts in China. In this way, Guangqi Honda steadily expands its market size and production capability in an orderly fashion.

7.4.4 Implementation of Localization Strategy: Establishing Collaboration System and Talents Development

To develop a Chinese model with the Honda brand, the New Production Development Department of Honada China R&D Center requests 50 additional Japanese engineering expatriates. This is to accelerate new product development in China. Adding Chinese engineers, the total number of engineers is about 200. The specialization system between Japan and China also follows the same Honda pattern: new technology development is primarily in Japan and all other business requirements are distributed to global market centers. Honda naturally moves toward applying global standardization. At present, the Chinese engineers and managers are more or less midful to fulfilling their given assignments. Although they participate in platform design areas, any endeavours for creative and innovative design or business solutions are not yet their work norms. In manufacturing processes, these local talents often seriously consider innovative problem solving.

Honda inspires its employees with high goals and to develop talents to help to aspire to achieve outstanding results. Yet, implementing such Honda style is too often quite challenging in China. This requires minimum essential training and education. Afterward, Chinese engineers receive on-the-job training (OJT). According to Honda engineers in China, Chinese engineers with two years of experience are more likely to be exposed to a larger scope of work compared to the counterparts in Japan. Although in China they might make more mistakes than in Japan, these Chinese engineers appreciate the education and training sytem that encourages learning through mistakes. The role of Japanese engineering expatriates is to develop future talents. Their contribution is assessed through the successful performance of Chinese engineers that they train.

For effective human resource management, the compensation system for managers and employees in China is based on Japanese practices that integrates both technical qualification (e.g., professional expertise) and rank system (e.g., department head, assistant department head, team leader). Annual reviewers are conducted. Honda values a rotation of talents among different global plants. For example, in the Fall of 2012 Honda sent engineers from EGCH in China to a plant in Thailand. Such an exchange usually occurs through proper communication among global plants with the approval of Honda Headquaters in Japan. However, it is not uncommon that leadership in different plants discuss such exchange needs (e.g., Chinese engineers from one plant are assigned to another plant) and such arrangements are confirmed in the global leadership meetings. Some exchange programs (e.g., Honda CRV molding) may not involve the mother factory in Japan. Instead, discussions among managers of different plants in China might be more effective in resolving practical manufacturing issues.

Plants in Thailand were established earlier than those in China. Naturally, Thai's engineering capabilities used to be more advanced and their production volume scale was bigger compared to those in China. Recently, the situation is now somewhat different. EGCH regards Chinese market as Honda's global base. As the Chinese market is expected to grow, Honda does not consider any other manufacturing centers besides China. When EGCH started, Honda anticipated receiving assistance through Thai plants, but it soon cancelled such plans because the Thai plants themselves were struggling with their own needs. In some cases, engineers from plants in China support those in the United States and Mexico particularly in applying molding standards to similar product lines.

At present, with increasing Chinese production requirements, EGCH also explained the number of new employees to be hired each year. As of 2012, 30% of employees in EGCH have no more than one year of work experience. According to the 2012 plan, EGCH plans to hire 50 new employees. The selection process includes examining resumes (usually 4 to 5 of final numbers) and on site interviews (final decisions). Professional expertise is a key criteria for non-routine recruitment. Many of such professional talents are mostly from facility maintenance and other manufacturing firms. In 2012, EGCH narrowed down the candidates (1.5 times of final hires), selects them as work interns for six months and put them on-the job training. At the 7th month, those who passed the internship training are finally selected. From January until June, 2012, these 50 interns were all hired as regular employees.

The annual turnover rate of EGCH (as of 2012) is 5%. This is better than that of other Chinese firms (20%+). The wages rates of Honda, Guangqi Hondain particular, are on the top in automobile firms in China. EGCH's average monthly salaries are failry close to the level of Guangqi Honda. Although similar interms of most of human resource management practices, wages rates in China are different from those in Japan. In 2010, Honda Japan increased overall wages and changed rank differentials for Japanese empoloyees after union labor disputes. However, Honda does not apply the same wage structure in China. With relatively short history of EGCH, managers in department level are the highest in rank in China. Soon EGCH considers to change its current system.

Honda invites employee training instructors from its current employees in Japan. Honda also utilizes the retired senior managers as well. The total number of Japanese expatriates is 41 and many of them are for short-term assignment. The engineers hired in China require extensive training and education. EGCH assumes all the cost of instructors from Japan. These Japanese instructors train Chinese engineers with new technical skills through intensive trainng. In 2012 two retirees from Honda are also hired for one year contract basis. In the past, the retirees were hired on three or six month's contract.

It takes several years to train Chinese engineers. At present, the leading Chinese engineer has five years of experiences. Another Chinese engineer, with only two years of experience, is also receiving senior management leadership training in view of his design expertise.

The main roles of Japanese expatriates are: (1) to transfer their experiences and knowledge without engaging in actual production lines. Although it is important to transfer upstream knowledge (e.g., system and detail design), it takes much longer time to do so. Thus, these expatriates focus on molding. In case of design expertise for new product development, actual experiences are crucial. Thus, design engineers from

Japan are dispatched for such training purposes. Assignments for design eningeers and production engineers last usually three months.

For effective communication, Honda China prefers hiring Chinese engineers who have good command of Japanese. All the leader class engineers speak Japanese well. From early years of EGCH, Chinese engineers who have good command of Japanese naturally assume senior leadership.

Chinese engineers have different perspective after receiving three months training in Japan. Yet, their technical skills do not necessarily improve during three months training in Japan. Yet, they train other Chinese engineers after returning to China. The president of EGCH has the authority to make major facility expansion decision (e.g., panel press equipment purchase). The same president also can send any leaders to other global plants for exchange programs. Five to six out of 21 Japanese expatriates that came to China have had other overseas assignment.

For its dynamic future, EGCH is now implementing a three year Global All Engineering Innovation Project since 2012. Specific plans include: (1) in view of intense competition with Chinese suppliers, various benchmark studies gather information about the consistent winner elements. Honda share vital benchmark lessons with other affiliated business units; (2) try to make component parts produced in China to other global market regions; (3) in the future if Honda finds ways to perfect challengeing design and manufacturing processes in China, Honda may no longer need to rely on tooling manufacturing in the United States.

7.5 TOYOTA'S GLOBAL SUPPLY CHAIN MANAGEMENT (SCM) IN CHINA

Since 2011, Toyota has maintained a dominant market share presence in the United States; however, in China sales of Toyota products have been much less productive. In 2011, the brand ranked eighth with unit sales of 506,000. Toyota established a 50% ownership in joint ventures among three Chinese firms: Zheil Train, Tenjin Nikki Train, and Sisen Nikki Train. Each of these three firms is somewhat unique. For example, Tianjin Toyota focuses on mini-cars (i.e., Vios and Corolla) and mid-sized cars (i.e., Crown), and Sisen Nikki Toyota on large cars (i.e., Land Cruiser). Different from Japan, Toyota produced selective few product lines in China with a large-scale production (Figure 7.5).

Ford Trails in Asia's Two Big Markets

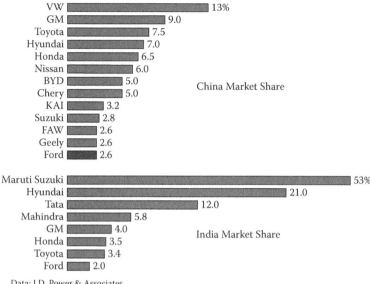

Data: J.D. Power & Associates

FIGURE 7.5

Global automobile market strengths in China (From J.D. Power, 2012; http://seeking alpha.com/article/202264-top-auto-companies-in-china-india.)

Toyota implemented its proprietary Just In Time (JIT) practices (known as the Toyota Production System or TPS) to fit the production system in China (White et al., 2001). TPS holistically views the production process as a means to remove "MUDA" (Japanese term for the removal of waste in a process), which includes wastes found in idle capacity, non-value-added work activities, and the use of material resources. The TPS and through the use of KANBAN methods, the workforce is cross-trained in various functional skills that allow for task flexibility in transitioning easily from one operation to another. Implementing the TPS has been challenging to the Chinese management style and has resulted in slow adoption of the Toyota methods. Likewise, predicting Chinese product demand has also been a challenge; government policy changes, tax rates, market intervention, and such are exogenous factors that influence Toyota's ability to properly forecast demand. For example, in 2009, the Chinese government decided to reduce automobile income taxes by 5% for all the automobiles under 1,600 cc engine sizes. Immediately then, Toyota's Vios and Corolla showed rapid increase in sales volume. Yet, with an unexpected demand surge, huge stockouts and inventory shortages occurred. From January to April, 2009 the sales volume actually decreased compared to that of 2008 (Economic Information,

2009). In the rapidly growing Chinese market, what matters most is not about eliminating all forms of wastes (MUDA) but avoiding missing major sales opportunities through unreliable demand forecasts.

The TPS as mentioned before has been a challenge in transferring this production culture to China; Chinese national culture, value systems, educational level, and consumer mindset are different from those of Japanese people. Compared to China, the demand patterns of the Japanese automobile market is fairly stable and thus demand forecast is highly reliable (Tseng, 2004; Tomino et al., 2009; 2011). However, in view of turbulent market conditions in China, it is challenging for Toyota to implement Toyota's flexible production and marketing system. A crucial element of global SCM is sourcing of component parts. Toyota's local sourcing percentage is 70% (e.g., Corolla and Crown) to 85% (e.g., Camry). The intermediate-term goal is to move up to 90%. Currently, about 15% to 30% of components parts are brought in from Japan. Thus, major natural disasters on March 11, 2011, heavily disrupted the supply flows. The total sales volume of new cars were reduced up to 35% compared to that of 2010. Logistics cost and lead time reductions of component parts require the overall increase in the localization ratio. In China, supply and demand in terms of product lines and volume requirements are uneven. The Chinese automobile market needs stable economies of scale production of diverse product lines, and thus supply and demand patterns would become more predictable. Then, Toyota production methods would be applicable in China just as in Japan.

For steady growth in the Chinese market, it is imperative for Toyota to move forward a broad scope of localization that includes both sourcing component parts and building marketing networks. Their speedy decision making should allow better production and market responses in case of frequent government policy changes. Its production and marketing capacity should fit to rapid market expansion requirements through implementation of the Toyota Production System (TPS) in Chinese contexts.

7.6 STRATEGIES OF OTHER JAPANESE GLOBAL FIRMS

7.6.1 Strategy of Yaskawa Electrics of China

Increasing global demand for cost competitiveness requires that the Japanese distribute their technology-intensive research and development

(R&D) capabilities to other parts of the world for faster innovation speed. The Drives and Motion Division of Yaskawa Electric Corporation (YEC) is an example of such a move. YEC specializes in drives, power modules, motors, and amplifiers (Figure 7.6). According to a new report published by IMS Research, the Chinese servo system market is expected to become a $1 billion market by 2012. Japanese firms dominate in the Chinese servo system market (e.g., servo motor and servo drive). YEC and Mitsubishi Electrical Corporation (MEC) are the top two leaders followed by Matsushida Electrical Corporation, DELTA (Taiwan), Siemens (Germany), and other Chinese firms.

Recently, Taiwanese and Korean companies' entry to this market put greater pricing pressure on local Chinese suppliers.

Initially, YEC did not invest for local R&D functions. The engineers at Japanese headquarters were responsible for developing products that reflect the Chinese market reality. Yet, they experienced failures with their lack of understanding of the motor usage patterns and business environment

Yaskawa Spindle Drives

Yaskawa SGDK, SGDH, CIMR-MXL and CIMR-MXN Series with test station

Yaskawa CACR-SR Servopack

Yaskawa CACR-IR Servopack for CNC and Robots

FIGURE 7.6
Yaskawa's products in China. (From Yaskawa China, Inc., Drives & Motion Division.)

of Chinese firms. Afterward, YEC became successful through localizing R&D processes of servo motor products. The dust and oil, heavy work environment of Chinese local suppliers often results in malfunctioning products. YEC developed customized products that are resistant to dust and oil intrusions in the system. The development of such products considers the requirements of the Chinese manufacturing work environment and involved 4 years of major investment from 2003 to 2006.

Other electrical products are for elevators and air conditioners. ABB, Siemens, and YEC occupy the top three positions in the market. Mitsubishi and Fuji Electric Corporation focused on the mid-range market. ABB and Siemens are strong in the large electric division, while YEC is versatile in all electric product divisions. Its marketing strategy is characterized by using repair agents. Its repair agents respond to any maintenance needs of the products. Thus, all the detailed customer information is not necessarily available to YEC on a real-time basis. For servo motors YEC maintains direct responsive customer service operations, not using its repair agents.

7.6.2 Strategy of Panasonic China

Another good example of local sensing capability is Panasonic China. In 2005 Panasonic established the China Life Research Institute to develop products that respond to the local needs. Its household goods (refrigerators and washers) provide an example of local market responsiveness. The senior management team consists of nine Chinese managers and one Japanese director. Their function is to research consumer use patterns, actual home environment, and most marketable product design options. One successful case is to reduce the size of a refrigerator up to 45 cm in view of the Chinese average kitchen size. It also benchmarked LG India's successful case and developed products that provide enough space for women to put in their cosmetic items. Another successful project was to develop a washer that contains AG removal devices. The product idea was based on the particular data discovery that suggests that many Chinese consumers do not use machine washers for cleaning their underwear clothes and rather do washing with hands. Further inquiry revealed that Chinese consumers regard pants and skirts as dirty and rough and thus do not want to mix those with their underwear items. Thus, the new Panasonic washers enhanced the sensing capability for strong bacteria removal and thus their market share was substantially increased.

7.6.3 Strategy of Clarion China

Clarion is one of many rising stars in the emerging markets—particularly in China. Its main products are car audio and other automotive component parts. In the past the strategic role of Chinese operation was to become a cost center as a production base for global markets. Yet, the new emphasis has been to make it a profit center for the growing Chinese domestic market. In China, Clarion has multiple production facilities that satisfy more than half of its global production requirements. Approximately 70% to 80% of Chinese production is for export purposes of global markets. In this sense, the global factory (i.e., cost center) concept is reasonable. Clarion China's production facilities intend to satisfy the growing needs of emerging economies. Clarion plans to increase its current 180-member R&D team (2010) to 600 (2012) and 1,000 (2015). In the past, the products developed in China were mostly simple ones like car audio, which were derivatives of Japanese models. China's rapid automobile market growth requires Clarion to respond with more innovative products that fit Chinese unique market characteristics. Thus, the previous marketing strategy based on Japanese customers no longer appeals to Chinese customers who demand value products that reflect broad Chinese cultural and market contexts.

In the meantime, Clarion China emphasizes information sharing of sample cost estimation details. Original equipment manufacturers (OEMs) are eager to learn the market trends of products such as car audio and car navigation systems. For this reason, Clarion thoroughly investigates the changing features of the Chinese automobile industry and strives to engage with Chinese customers. Clarion sends its design engineers to Japanese and other global automobile manufacturers. In contrast to other component parts suppliers, Clarion aims to implement a differentiation strategy with special attention to improving the level of product integrity. Thus, Clarion overcomes a lack of customer-based information through technological discovery practices and moves toward a solution-based discovery business model rather than a simple modularization strategy.

Clarion also seeks cost reductions through using common platforms of product architecture. To reduce overall development costs, Clarion China operates R&D centers for global product models in China. Clarion reexamines the quality practices of its component suppliers and makes efforts in design standardization and information sharing. For low-cost products, Clarion has completed platform design, improved cost competitiveness, and thus achieves rapid product customization requirements for each individual national market.

7.7 CONCLUSION

This chapter provides in-depth case analyses of Komatsu, Yaskawa Electronics, Panasonic, Clarion, and Toyota. Each of these prominent Japanese global firms experienced successful market positioning in China. Successful cases of Japanese firms in the Chinese market suggest that their market strategy is based on new supply chain management that implements active localization practices in terms of sensing local market needs, development of Chinese suppliers, and context-driven marketing rather than bringing their domestic products with little variations. These firms effectively use linkage competence, which integrates both technology and customer competence. From the product architecture perspective, these firms also integrate their high-technological competence (i.e., closed integral architecture for technological excellence) with the reality of uneven quality performance of local suppliers (i.e., open integral architecture for reasonable quality performance and market context accommodations).

8

Strategies of Japanese Firms in the Indian Market

Increasingly, Japanese component parts suppliers sustain their global advantage by utilizing manufacturing capacities and market strategies in India. This chapter deals with the strategic practices of Japanese manufacturers—particularly Toyota, Denso, Honda, and Seiko-Epson. These firms not only use India as their production basis for global markets but also provide their own products that satisfy Indian customers.

8.1 INTRODUCTION

This book presents (1) three types of competencies that form network capability—technology competence, customer competence, and linkage competence; and (2) the concept of product architecture as a crucial dimension of product strategy. Chapter 3 covered the cases of Japanese global firms in China. In this chapter, the focus is on Japanese global firms in India, particularly the cases of Toyota, Denso, Honda, and Seiko-Epson.

8.2 STRATEGY OF TOYOTA INDIA

The key for a successful market strategy in emerging markets is to integrate technology competence into sensing and translating local market needs through customer competence. For this purpose, Japanese global firms move away from the previous focus on product development based on their technology competence and replication of their domestic market-driven product development models. Here, we discuss Toyota's strategy in the Indian market.

8.2.1 Toyota Kirloskar Motor (TKM) and Toyota Kirloskar Auto Parts (TKAP)

In 1997 Toyota established Toyota Kirloskar Motor (TKM), a joint venture with an Indian firm, and since then it has marketed several product lines including Innova and Corolla Altis. Among them, the most successful model was the Innova and Etios model. Innova is the Indian version of Toyota's global strategic brand called IMV (innovative multipurpose vehicle). Its production was the fourth in Southeast Asia next to Thailand, Indonesia, and the Philippines. IMV was truly an epoch-making project in that all the main processes (e.g., component parts sourcing, production, and logistics) are simultaneously implemented in 10 countries and then the products are supplied to 140 countries. Toyota Kirloskar Auto Parts (TKAP), as a part of IMV, produces major engine parts (e.g., transmission) in India. All the auto parts that TKAP produces are exported all over the world to those that use IMV product lines.

The TKAP business unit is quite strategic for Toyota. The president of TKAP explained the main reason why Toyota made India as the base of IMV as "it recognized the strengths of India auto-manufacturing potential for global market" (Shimada, 2005). Certainly, Indian auto manufacturing has several advantages. First, it has solid makers for manufacturing facilities. India has an unusual basic manufacturing infrastructure capacity, which is quite rare among developing nations. India is more advantageous than China in this respect. Such technological capability is based on its long history of auto manufacturing. For example, before World War II, Nippon Steel Corp.,* the Japanese largest steel maker, received technological assistance from India's Tata in regard to steel technology know-how. Although Tata's growth after the war was not as rapid as it should have been, its technological foundation was quite stable. A machining industry like TKAP requires heavy manufacturing process technologies. The fact that India has such manufacturing process technology firms suggests

---

* Nippon Steel and Sumitomo Metal in October, 2012.

India's potential for manufacturing competitiveness. With stable growth of manufacturing process technology makers, India is quite able to design and market high-quality products just like other advanced nations from the United States and Europe.

Second, India's large domestic market is steadily growing. The market size advantage allows many firms to implement economies of scale of production, and their global competitiveness is also formidable. For example, over 380 million Indians (72 million households) have an annual household income of over $10,000 (http://pppinindia.com/india-large-growing-domestic-market.php). This is expected to increase to 550 million by 2010. The economic reforms since the early 1990s have unleashed a new entrepreneurial spirit creating a vibrant economy supported by rising per capita income. Fast-growing disposable incomes, increased availability, and use of consumer finance and credit cards complement the keenness of the average Indian to adapt to and assimilate global trends. This has led to the creation of a rapidly growing consumer base and one of the world's largest markets for manufactured goods and services. Growth in key sectors like infrastructure, services, and manufacturing continues at almost 12% p.a. (by the year). The market for basic goods such as groceries and textiles is already large, driven by the demands of an enormous population. Markets for other products are equally large and growing rapidly. Over 100 million telephone subscribers, growing at over 25 million p.a., over 8 million TV sets, and 4 million refrigerators are sold annually with a growth of over 20% p.a. and total production of vehicles is likely to exceed 10 million in 2005 to 2006, up from 8.6 million in 2004 to 2005 (in 1998 to 1999, this was only 4.2 million). In addition, India was the fastest growing domestic market in the world in September 2011 with 18.4% year-on-year growth (http://centreforaviation.com/). Traffic growth in the Indian market exceeded the growth rate seen in China (9.7%) and Brazil (7.5%) in September 2011 and was considerably more robust than the global growth rate of 3.8%. India's domestic aviation market expansion has been the strongest in the world, tripling in the past 5 years, according to the IATA, to become the ninth largest aviation market in the world.

Third, India has caught up with the global trend of FTAs among many nations. In the automobile industry most nations require firms to pursue local sourcing options and thus international comparative advantage (i.e., labor-intensive nations focus on their labor cost advantage while technology/capital–intensive nations seek their technological advantages) is not well practiced. Since India has established FTA with other nations (e.g., India and Korea free trade agreement in 2011), the automobile industry also shows an international comparative advantage just like the electronics industry.

Fourth, India has abundant skilled human resources. Indians are fluent in English and they are quick to learn Japanese. Since India is a nation where many diverse languages are spoken (note that there are more than 15 different major languages in India), Indians have a greater ability to reasonably guess what others say in foreign languages. TKM, with the support of TKAP in the above-mentioned contexts, was able to succeed in the product development of car models such as Inova and Etios that fit the particular demands of Indian consumers.

8.2.2 Development of Etios Sedan

Toyota's product development strategy for the Indian market went far beyond its development patterns for the Japanese domestic market. Etios Sedan (that has been popular among Indian consumers) illustrates this point. Etios is Toyota's first successful emerging market-driven product. The project leaders started from a zero base (i.e., do everything new for the Indian market requirements) including its platform design and manufacturing processes. Etios is quite different from the other Toyota models that are marketed in Japan, the United States, and Europe. For example, Japanese passengers do not want direct exposure to the cold air from a car's air conditioner. Yet, Indians love to get direct access to cold air in the car. Recognizing Indian consumers' preference for auto air-conditioner functionality, Toyota installed the air-conditioning unit in Etios in the ways Indians wanted. Toyota benchmarked the new product development practices of Korean household electronics firms and Hyundai–Kia that successfully defended their market leadership in the Indian market. Toyota also accommodated additional space for Indians who like to put their "Ganesa" (Hindu religious statues) inside their automobiles. Many Indians also walk on barefoot so Toyota provided special soft covers in the guide rail of the front seat. In view of much of the unpaved Indian road system, Toyota installed an additional cover for the lower engine parts area. Thus, shock absorber anti-dust performance is enhanced, which in turn benefits shock absorber longevity in dusty regions (Figure 8.1).

All these features indicate Toyota's commitment for the Indian market and reflect the practical needs of Indian customers in their product design and manufacturing processes. An additional three aspects of Etios' development strategy are noted for further discussion here (Park and Amano, 2011).

Toyota Etios Sedan

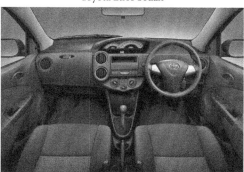

FIGURE 8.1
Toyota Etios' sedan front section—inside space and guide rail and lower part cover.

First, a new product development team visited India numerous times and maintained collaborative relationships with Indian local R&D teams. The Japanese chief engineer who planned and executed the Etios model project visited India several times and observed the riding habits and demand patterns of Indian customers. He also toured many regions of India—total 200,000 km—by car. He insisted the field adaptation test of the Etios prototype in India at least four times (instead of one time in Japan). Since Toyota established Toyota Kirloskar Motor (TKM) in 1997, the key competitive challenge was how to successfully market its models for market leadership in India. Toyota senior management leadership accepted the fact that its previous development platform focusing on the advanced market (e.g., Japan, North America, and Europe) does not fit customer needs in emerging markets like India. For translating the local needs in product design and manufacturing, it became obvious that Japanese engineers alone could not adequately reflect all local customer requirements. Toyota very closely collaborated with local Indian engineers of TKM. The Etios model was born in the course of these Indian engineers working together with Japanese counterparts.

Second, a crucial element of emerging market needs is price competitiveness. This requires localization of component parts and development of an Indian suppliers' network. In the case of the Etios model in India, the goal of drastic cost reduction was achieved through bold product design. Take steel plates as an example. According to the Japanese chief engineer responsible for the Etios development project, all the component parts for the Etios model were sourced from Indian suppliers. India's Tata Steel Company supplied steel plates. Different from Japanese high-quality steel plates, Tata's inconsistent quality performance remained a huge challenge for Etios' product development success. However, Toyota devised a product design that covers this particular quality challenge. Since the highest-quality level of steel plates that Tata could offer was 440 MPa (MegaPascal; 1 MPa = 1 N/mm), not the high-grade level of 500 to 1000 MPa, the design team came up with an option that substantially strengthened product performance with 440 MPa steel plates. Toyota has achieved about 70% of localization in India. By 2011, its goal is to increase up to 90%, including engine and transmission systems as well.

Third, Toyota's innovative product development strategy achieved cost reduction goals and vast performance improvements that satisfy Indian customer requirements through various technological functionality enhancements such as standing oil jet technology for piston cooling, forged crankshaft and connecting rod for durability, EPS (electric power steering) system for fuel efficiency, suspension system for comfortable ride, and shock absorber for anti-dust performance. All these comprehensive product development efforts indicate how Toyota achieved its integral product architecture in Indian market contexts (e.g., India's high temperature, bumps in the uneven road surface and dusty regions, and high gasoline costs).

8.3 STRATEGY OF HONDA INDIA

8.3.1 Nikkei Makers Lead in Indian Motorcycle Market

There has been a substantial increase in motorcycle demand in major cities like New Delhi, Mumbai, and Calcutta with a relatively reliable road system. The growing Indian middle class prefers to use motorcycles for their transportation means. For this vast number of Indian consumers, passenger cars are still relatively expensive, but motorcycles are affordable for their income level. In response, global motorcycle makers have poured their newer models into the Indian market, and India's financial loan system supported such surging consumer appetites (Kadokura, 2006).

According to data published by the Society of India Automobile Manufacturers (SIAM), the sales volume of motorcycles in India has maintained two-digit growth rates each year. The market growth of Japanese motor bicycle manufacturers also shows steady performance in the ASEAN market with their competitive prices and high product quality reputation. The global ranking of India's motorcycle market is next to that of China. By international standards, the diffusion rate in India is still fairly low. As of 2003, per 1,000 people, the Japanese rate is 106.3 and India shows 35.4 (Kadokura, 2006).

India's motorcycle market is huge and its growth potential is enormous. A simulation result based on the Japanese diffusion rate growth up to the climax years suggests that India would show similar patterns of growth—in 2015, 98.2 per 1,000 and by 2020, 131.7 per 1,000. The estimated forecast of its demand in the Indian market is 15,663,000 in 2015 and 18,846,000 in 2020. The annual growth rate in the period of 2005 to 2020 is expected to be 10.5% (2005 to 2010), 7.7% (2010 to 2015), but only 3.9% (2015 to 2020) with the rapid passenger car demand in that period.

In the Indian motorcycle market, 10 (including global rivals from Japan, the United States, and Europe) firms maintain both manufacturing and market networks. The Honda Hero has the largest market share. The Honda Hero was established in 1984 by Honda (Japan) and Hero (India) with each holding 26% of ownership. With the recent termination of such a joint venture, both Honda and Hero hereafter consider separate manufacturing and marketing strategies in India. In 2004 both firms extended technological cooperation for an additional 10 years and thus by the end of 2013 the current form of collaboration relationship would continue.

8.3.2 Honda's India Strategy

Honda is excellent with its technological competence and linkage competence that translate local market needs in its products. Based on such a strategy, Honda maintains an absolute advantage in BRICs markets (i.e., China, Brazil, and India) and other ASEAN markets (e.g., Thailand, Vietnam).

First, Honda exerts strategic efforts in reinterpreting its technological competence in relation to market competence. Such initiatives started in China and now they are extended to Thailand, Vietnam, and India. For example, its products sold in Thailand reflect its unique contexts—especially the prices of motorcycles, which drop exceedingly each year.

In emerging markets, the key for market advantage is in speed and cost competitiveness. Thus, the long-term strategy of emerging markets must consider total low cost strategy. Increasingly, Chinese and Indian indigenous firms introduce their inexpensive models aggressively in the markets. In Brazil, Honda's market share is up to 80% but, Chinese motorcycle rivals steadily challenge Honda's competitive position.

In response to such competitive threats, Honda identifies individual national market needs and translates them into its products that appeal to customers of each nation. In principle, Honda conducts new product design and development by individual country. In practice, Honda defines maximum common denominators based on market research of every country and determines the global model platform first. Low-cost competitiveness for product development and manufacturing is crucial in this vital process. This is the firm's network competency that uses low-cost component parts and materials for all their products. Honda's competitive advantage in emerging markets like China and India is in its ability to utilize sourcing network infrastructure to achieve the best possible choices for multiple customer requirements in terms of quality, cost, and delivery. In other words, Honda integrates its brand reputation, advanced technological capability (environment/safety/efficiency), and economies of scale production capability to sustain its superior market position. For example, Honda developed PCX 150 as a global model by applying such a network development infrastructure—using the sourcing/manufacturing infrastructure of emerging countries while product concept is of advanced nations. It offers the fuel economy of the most frugal scooters, but yet is big enough and powerful enough to carry a passenger and ride on the highway (Figure 8.2).

Honda India rapidly grew with a joint venture with Hero, an Indian firm. Its market share in India exceeds 60%. The primary reason for such market leadership is cost competitiveness based on a high percentage of local sourcing of component parts through India's indigenous firm Hero and other Indian suppliers. The Japanese engineering design team provides product structure and detailed design blueprints, and all the component parts are secured by local Indian suppliers. Product design of

FIGURE 8.2
Honda's PCX 150.

PCX 150 in India accommodates a strong rear structure, which allows three or four people to ride a motorcycle. Thus, PCX 150 is an example of how Honda combines its strong engine performance, local sourcing, and India customer-specific design structure. One serious concern is that from 2011, Honda India is going to separate from Hero, an Indian partner, and needs to find another Indian partner for a collaborative relationship. This requires a continuous high level of local sourcing as well as product development strategy that satisfies changing customer requirements in India.

8.4 STRATEGIES OF OTHER JAPANESE GLOBAL FIRMS IN INDIA

8.4.1 Strategy of Seiko Epson India

Seiko Epson Corporation, a Japanese electronics company (headquartered in Suwa, Nagano, Japan), is one of the world's largest manufacturers of computer printers, and information- and imaging-related equipment.

With similar market contexts, Seiko Epson's experiences in Indonesia are helpful in discussing Seiko Epson's strategy in India. Seiko Epson cooperated with an Indonesian local marketing firm in developing ink-jet printer L100 and L200 targeting the Indonesian market. The L100 and L200 models do not have any large size of ink tank. In Indonesia, the improved models are not using ink cartridges but substitute ink from a printer tank. In fact, products targeted for the Indonesian market mostly remodeled Seiko Epson's existing products to fit the needs of Indonesian customers. In this context, Epson products in India do not use pure ink from Epson but substitute ink from an attached ink tank. However, this type of model variation resulted in a frequent breakdown of printer functions. In this context, Seiko Epson introduced the new models L100 and L200 (Figure 8.3). Indonesian staff played a significant role in these development efforts. For the purpose of developing products for Indonesia, they displayed a sense of pride for their work and conducted vigorous customer surveys that reflected the customer voice in their products. Through such cooperation, Seiko Epson experienced huge success in the course of sharing vital information in the front end of product development with these native staff members who willingly offered their knowledge of Indonesian consumer needs and preferences.

FIGURE 8.3
Seiko Epson's L100 and L 200; Epson HX-20, Epson LX-300 dot matrix printers.

Seiko Epson applied the market experiences in Indonesia to serve customers in India as well. In India Seiko Epson marketed the same inkjet printers that were highly successful in Indonesia. However, in contrast to the Japanese market trend, the mainstream printers in the Indian market are still dot matrix based. In both Indonesian and Indian markets, printers that use substitute, not pure, ink are the most popular because consumers in both countries are not ready to spend much money for ink usage more than the original printer cost. For this reason, Indian customers prefer using dot matrix cartridges that are relatively inexpensive. A reverse marketing strategy is required. Thus, in response to such customer preference, Seiko Epson adopted a different pricing strategy by charging much higher prices for dot matrix printers and maintenance warranty (one-time purchase) than ink cartridge charges (frequent purchases during printer lifetime). As a result, Seiko Epson secured a much larger amount of total net profits from printers and ink cartridges. In this way, Seiko Epson applied a total profit-based (higher inkjet printer prices plus lower cartridge) rather than consumption-based (lower inkjet printer prices and higher inkjet cartridge) business model.

8.4.2 Strategy of Makino India

The total world market size of the machine tools industry is $65.3 billion, and world leader Japan has 16% of the market share with $10.5 billion. The domestic size of Indian Machine Tools is about $620 million (Suzuki and Shintaku, 2014). Makino Prize produces and markets machine tools in the Indian market. Makino India, a Bangalore-based and well-known information technology (IT) firm, established an Indian subsidiary in 1996. From 2002, Makino India started local production. The total number of employees is about 300. Except for several Japanese managers working in the services area, Indians assume all other management roles in the company. Customers of Makino India are mostly local manufacturers. With outstanding functionality of Makino machine tools, various first- and second-tier Indian manufacturing suppliers are its major customers. The recent global financial crisis affected the Indian machine tools market in the form of a reduction in production and sales. Even so, its large market size still attracts and retains large global firms. The current market hierarchy is in three tiers: upper-end market by Japanese and German firms; middle-end market by US, British, and Korean firms; and low-end market by Taiwanese, Indian, and Chinese firms (Figure 8.4).

The success secrets of Makino India are not only selling machine tools but also providing turnkey business solutions for high-performance machines for its customers. It offers total services from machine tools design consulting to employee skill training services for its major customers. As of 2010, it has developed 750 different types of business turnkey solutions. Its diverse business scope includes one single machine tooling to its entire production system line design. Makino India differentiates its products and services from its rival German firms in that it

India's Share of Imports in Machine Tools 2004–2005

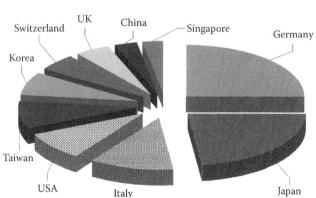

FIGURE 8.4
Indian machine tools market and market share of global and Indian firms.

provides total support solutions for customers to use their machine tools at the optimal levels.

India has an abundant supply of engineers who are highly educated, technically competent, and relatively inexpensive. These engineers are quite capable of handling complex and detailed work requirements as well as the numerous engineering processes. In Bangalore regions, outstanding engineers usually prefer to work in the IT sector. From 2006, Makino India made a strategic investment to secure a high-quality labor force. The Makino Technical Center recruits students from all over India and offers extensive training courses for machine tooling theory, technical knowledge, and liberal arts courses on a total scholarship basis. In this way, Makino India secures high-quality engineers and prepares for sustaining its excellent market share position in India.

8.4.3 Strategy of Denso India

Firms that target emerging markets are not only the finished goods manufacturers (e.g., Toyota, Honda, Seiko Epson, and Makino) but also component parts suppliers. Denso, a leading supplier of advanced automotive technology, systems, and components for all the world's major automakers, operates in 35 countries and regions with approximately 126,000 employees. Global consolidated sales totaled $38.4 billion for fiscal year ended March 31, 2012 (Denso Corporation http://www.globaldenso.com/en) (Table 8.1).

Denso India also recognizes the importance of sensing customer needs in India—particularly price competitiveness. Denso's innovative approach

TABLE 8.1

Denso Corporation Worldwide

Established	December 16, 1949
Head office	1-1, Showa-cho, Kariya, Aichi 448-8661, Japan
Capital	¥187.4 billion (US$2.3 billion)
Net sales	¥3,154.6 billion (US$38.4 billion)
Operating income	¥160.7 billion (US$1,955.6 million)
Net income	¥89.3 billion (US$1,086.5 million)
Employees	126,036
Consolidated subsidiaries	188 (Japan 68, North America 28, Europe 35, Asia-Oceania 51, others 6)
Affiliates under the equity method	31 (Japan 13, North America 4, Europe 2, Asia-Oceania 10, others 2)

Source: Denso Corporation data (April 1, 2011–March 31, 2012).

to designing new products for emerging markets is not using the previous design of existing products. Instead, it starts from a zero base and defines essential minimum functionality and performance requirements and then devises products that would sustain Denso's brand in terms of functionality, performance, and value added. Denso's cost target for emerging markets is in general half of the past products. Since Denso's products are mostly automotive component parts, its customers are primarily original equipment manufacturers (OEMs). To secure customers that market their finished products in India, China, and Brazil, Denso's strategic priority is to sustain superior cost competitiveness and a high-quality workforce that can sense local customer needs.

Denso India became the supplier of wiper systems for Nano, Tata's strategic product vehicle, through developing local Indian engineering talents. For many years Denso's primary customer base has been Japanese makers such as Mariti Suzki, Yamaha, Honda, Szuki, and Toyota. From 2006, Denso participated in Nano product development processes and became the local supplier of its wiper system. It was through the Indian engineers who have been working at Denso for more than 10 years that Denso could develop a strategic partnership with Tata. Under the leadership of an Indian chief engineer, Denso was able to reduce the total cost by 30% to 40% for the ideal product considering the local customer needs (Kim, 2014). At the same time, Denso's customer relationship with Tata by an Indian chief engineer was also quite smooth. Denso India has instituted the training program that selects two Indian engineers who receive 1 year of intensive training in Japan. As of 2011, more than 30 Indian engineers have completed their education and training in Japan. From 2011, Denso also constructed testing labs for India's small and medium suppliers. In this way, Denso has developed an extended network capability that includes both its own R&D facilities for its regular customers of Japanese and Indian OEMs and additional testing labs to serve the needs of small and medium Indian suppliers.

8.5 CONCLUSION

Increasingly, Japanese component parts suppliers sustain their global advantage by utilizing manufacturing capacities and market strategies in India. This chapter deals with the strategic practices of Japanese manufacturers—particularly Toyota, Denso, Honda, and Seiko-Epson. These firms not only use India as their production basis for the global markets but also provide their own successful products that satisfy Indian customers.

Case studies of Japanese global firms in the Indian market suggest that their market strategy is based on new supply chain management, which implements active localization practices in terms of sensing local market needs, developing Indian suppliers, and using context-driven marketing rather than bringing their domestic products with modest variations. These firms effectively use linkage competence that integrates both technology and customer competence. From the product architecture perspective, these firms also integrate their high technological competence (i.e., closed integral architecture for technological excellence) with the reality of uneven quality performance of local suppliers (i.e., open integral architecture for reasonable quality performance and market context accommodations).

9

Strategies of Japanese Firms in the Brazilian Market

Brazil is another thriving emerging economy with a sizable population and a vast natural resource basis. Among the emerging economies, Brazil is experiencing phenomenal growth. This chapter focuses on Japanese firms in Brazil, such as Komatsu (construction equipment firm), Toyota (auto manufacturer), Bridgestone (tire manufacturer), and Epson (personal computer firm).

9.1 INTRODUCTION

This book presents (1) three types of competence that form network capability—technology competence, customer competence, and linkage competence; and (2) the concept of product architecture as a critical dimension of product strategy. Chapter 8 focused on the cases of Japanese global firms in India. This chapter examines the practices of Japanese global firms in Brazil—particularly the cases of Komatsu, Toyota, Bridgestone, and Epson.

9.2 KOMATSU BRAZIL

9.2.1 A Brief Overview

The Komatsu case in Chapter 7 indicated that the large portion of its global market sales is from emerging markets. The Chinese market is the largest (21%), the Latin American market is also sizable (14%), and the prospect of growth is great. Here, we consider the case of Komatsu Brazil (Park and Shintaku, 2014). In Brazil, the company has two plants, one marketing business unit, and ten distribution centers. Komatsu do Brazil Ltda. (KDB) was established in 1970 in response to "the home-made tractor law of 1969" by the Brazilian government. However, with no real sales record and no actual production plant, the Brazilian government rejected KDB's "home-made bulldozer" proposal. Thus, KDB decided to form a strategic alliance with Franco-Nevada Corporation FNV, an indigenous Brazilian heavy machinery maker. Komatsu FNV (KFNV) was formed in 1973. From 1975 on, the large scale of production, marketing, and after-sales services were achieved. Subsequently, it was recognized as a Brazilian home-based manufacturer. Its main product lines are construction and mining equipment. In the Brazilian market, KFNV reports more than 80% of market share for heavy construction equipment. Mining equipment is mostly imported from the United States, Japan, and Germany. KFNV's after-sales services network is extended to 23 states of Brazil. Distribution centers keep adequate inventory of key component parts and services agents handle minor expendable parts. The key point is that KFNV is prepared to assume all aspects of after-sales services needed through KOMTRAX, which reduces the response time in case of any maintenance needs or performance failures. "Domestic firms first" by Brazilian government's protection policy defines the nature of the Brazilian construction machinery/equipment market. Thus, customers' choice options are limited as well. The vast land area dictates very high demand for huge construction equipment with large tires; a small number of profitable coal mines hardly require large-scale shovels or dump trucks. The market leaders are Caterpillar (United States), New Holland (United States), Case (United States), and Volvo (Germany). The market share details of construction equipment makers are Komatsu (20%+), Caterpillar (30%+), and others (15%). Other makers are Hyundai Heavy Industries and Doosan Infra Core (Korea) and SANY (China) that appeal through their production facilities in Brazil.

9.2.2 Construction Equipment Usage Patterns in Brazil and Komatsu's Response

The ratio between urban and rural areas is 9:1 (Figure 9.1). Through the infrastructure expansion, more rapid growth is expected in rural areas. Even with the same types of construction equipment, the usage patterns in cities and farm lands are quite different. In rural areas, the construction equipment needed to

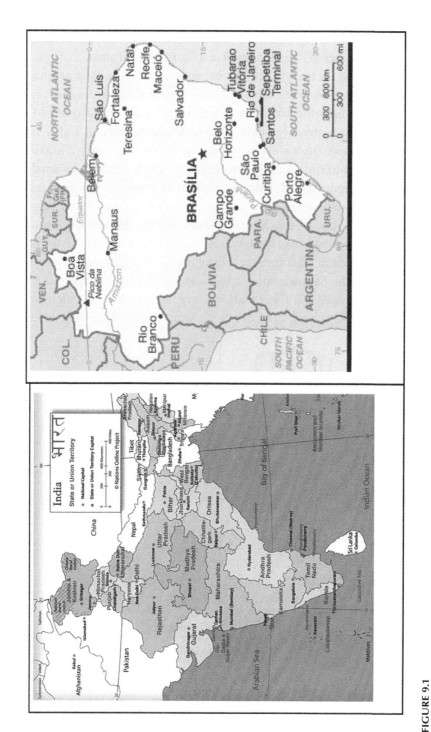

FIGURE 9.1
Major business center cities of India and Brazil.

handle rough areas (e.g., sugarcane fields), the two primary order winners for agricultural machinery/equipment are durability and cost competitiveness. Here we examine cases of Komatsu Brazil in urban and rural areas.

First, the methods of using construction equipment in the cities are presented. The southern, southeastern, and some northeastern areas of Brazil have major cities, but other areas are mostly rural areas. This is quite different from India. Many large cities are scattered throughout India. In contrast, several large cities are concentrated in the southern part of Brazil. São Paulo belongs to the southeastern region in which demand for small construction equipment and hydraulic shovels is growing. For building construction in urban areas, most equipment is not necessarily for large jobs (e.g., 20 tons+) but are much smaller units. For the deep underground work much of the manual work is now automated with machines. For this reason, relatively small machines are mostly used. For laying electric wires underground in the Santos region, small shovels, not back loaders as in the past, are now used. All these machines are made in Brazil by domestic firms. Hydraulic shovels can cover wide work areas (Figure 9.2). Back

FIGURE 9.2
Komatsu hydraulic shovel models.

loaders are not used around the world. Komatsu makes back loaders in Italy and the small size of models shows rapid market growth in China.

Second, we consider the usage patterns of construction equipment in the agricultural sector. In Brazil, different from other countries, more equipment/machinery with moving tires is used because of its vast land area. In the agricultural sector, the areas that the equipment cover are relatively large. Sugarcane farms are widespread in vast regions. Its annual production growth is high. Surging demand for construction equipment is noted with the building of increasing numbers of new sugarcane processing facilities and a corresponding need to prepare larger land areas for growing sugarcane. The ways farmers use their equipment for sugarcane fields are somewhat unique in Brazil. For example, in Brazil they use wheel loaders instead of bulldozers for leveling off the land area. In Japan this is rare because such methods put too much strain on the equipment. Yet, in Brazil it is quite common. Beyond sugarcane, farmers use this construction equipment for cleaning up their farmlands and moving fertilizers. They also use wheel loaders to carry biomass fuel, which is being processed from farmland waste materials. The rate of demand of wheel loaders is 30% of all construction equipment. In keeping up with the steady decline of its prices, its demand keeps increasing.

Even the same construction equipment (e.g., Komatsu's products) is adapted to a variety of usage patterns. Komatsu, for example, provides a user-friendly working recipe for its products that its customers apply in diverse work environments with a great deal of satisfaction. Komatsu differentiates from its rivals by offering service sets as its marketing promotion core and thus established its advantage in the high-end market. Komatsu Brazil strengthens its after-sales service system through its dealerships, which cover 23 states besides Amazonas and its northern neighboring state. The Komatsu marketing unit maintains a necessary level of inventory for key component parts repairs, and its dealerships handle small peripheral items such as filters and engine oils. KOMTRAX requires all the Komatsu products to get maintenance checks after 1,000 hours of operation, and thus, Komatsu is aware of the actual volume needs for replacing particular component parts in advance.

Dealers receive relevant information on the maintenance needs for Komatsu products and necessary component parts are sent at the right time. The response time in Brazil is quite long because of long transportation time. It takes more than 5 days to travel from the southern part of Brazil to the northern part. Thus, Komatsu implements the systematic maintenance check through KOMTRAX about its products. Since specific maintenance need details are communicated through KOMTRAX in advance, all the necessary arrangements are made so that customers receive the needed parts just before the maintenance needs actually occur. With such a system, the overall downtime of Komatsu's equipment is low. The number of regular maintenance items is well defined and naturally, total maintenance costs are quite manageable. At present, Komatsu continues service operation development (SOD) for customer satisfaction and profit enhancement.

9.2.3 Summary

Over the years Komatsu has vigorously caught up with Caterpillar, and currently, it is positioned as number two in the construction equipment industry. Increasingly, Komatsu focuses on the premium market. By using KOMTRAX it offers a high level of rich customer services and thus sustains its market leadership. In 2009 Komatsu developed and introduced hybrid construction equipment (highly energy efficient with oil-fuel engine and electric motor) that is well received as cutting-edge technology and superior quality products in the market.

Both in China and Brazil, competition for hydraulic shovels is becoming intense (Figure 9.3). Recently, Hyundai Heavy Industries and Doosan Infra Core (Korea) and SANY (China) advertised their production in Brazil. These Korean and Chinese makers give service points to customers and use small factories as their dealerships. As discussed in Chapter 7, Komatsu China uses KOMTRAX (i.e., a highly integrated IT system) to sense customer service needs. It also executes a high premium value differentiation strategy through effective communication of its product strengths and an outstanding combination of both hardware and software advantages. However, its competitive challenges come from Korean and Chinese rivals that offer quality products with cost competitiveness.

9.3 STRATEGY OF TOYOTA BRAZIL

9.3.1 Brazilian Automotive Industry

As of 2012, the Brazilian automotive industry is the seventh largest in the world. Most large global companies are present in Brazil including Fiat, Volkswagen, Ford, General Motors, Nissan, Toyota, Mitsubishi,

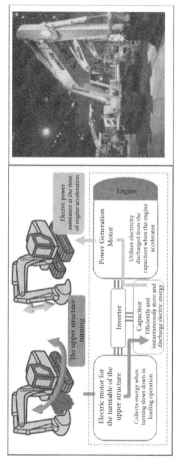

Komatsu Hybrid System

Komatsu Hybrid Excavator

FIGURE 9.3

Komatsu versus competitors (Hyundai and SANY).

Mercedes-Benz, Renault, Honda, and Hyundai. As in India, the primary focus in Brazil is on small-size cars. Brazil's past 10-year production trend shows strong growth for the domestic market with a steady decline in the global market. In view of this trend, Japanese original equipment manufacturers (OEMs) (e.g., Toyota, Honda, and Nissan) all expanded their production volumes in Brazil, and Hyundai-Kia of Korea's production facilities are under construction.

At present, the industry market leaders are mostly European and US global firms such as Fiat, Volkswagen, and GM. The production volumes are 900,000 (Fiat), 700,000 (VW), and 600,000 (GM). Toyota and Honda of Japan have less than 10% of market share. Hyundai-Kia, with no production facilities in Brazil, reports record sales growth. Since Brazilian customers are price-sensitive, the key for new production development and production is cost-competitiveness. Even a slight increase in prices affects the size of customer demand. Popular models, therefore, are small-sized cars with the price range of 30,000 to 40,000 Real (US$15,000 to US$20,000). The sales volumes in Brazil are 200,000 (Fiat UNO) and 300,000 (VW Gol).

9.3.2 Toyota's Entry into the Brazilian Market

In the late 1950s (years after World War II), Toyota built its first global plant in Brazil. Even with this addition, total production volume remained somewhat small. With its enormous distance away from Japan, Toyota Japan strategically focused on European/US and Asian markets (Kumon, 2009). Thus, European and US firms had dominated the Latin American market.

In the 1990s serious changes in the automotive industry occurred. The Brazilian government adopted a free trade policy in regard to automobiles and lowered the tariff rate on automotive products. In 1995 the establishment of Toyota Mercos provided new business opportunities for the automotive industry. Foreign firms are allowed to import their finished products and at the same time build their own plants in Brazil. Toyota's strategy includes expanding production capacity in Brazil to capitalize its growing market potential. Specifically, Toyota built a passenger car plant in Brazil and another commercial truck plant in Argentina. In 2003, Toyota established Toyota Mercos (as a virtual control firm) to oversee the overall production and marketing strategies for Latin American countries.

In 1958 Toyota built a commercial truck plant for producing the Land Cruiser at San Bernard, Brazil (Sao Bernardo plant). For the next 40 years,

Toyota produced the same model truck. With increasing demand for passenger cars, Toyota turned over truck production to an Argentinean plant and focused on passenger car assembly production in Brazil. For this purpose, in 1990 Toyota purchased land space at Indaizba near São Paulo and completed the production project by 1995. This plant assembles the Corolla.

9.3.3 Toyota Brazil: Plants and Quality Management

Toyota's passenger assembly plant in Indaizba has several advantages in terms of distance from suppliers, skilled-labor availability, and industrial water supply. In San Bernard Toyota's parts suppliers are concentrated. With Santos harbor nearby, a logistical infrastructure was also well established. Yet, its strong labor power is based on a long history of industrial tradition.

Passenger assembly plants start with a CKD (completely knocked down) factory. In 1998 it started production. From 2002, it established a press and transformed it into a small- and medium-size plant. Toyota applies the TPS (Toyota Production System) for plant operation and for quality management, and its quality performance exceeds that of other plants in the 3Ts (Taipei, Turkey, and Thailand), which have the best quality reparation among global plans. All the employees hired at this plant have at minimum a high school education. All employees commit to multitask skill training requirements.

Toyota also regards employee training very seriously. Diverse types of training (e.g., intensive fieldwork training of Brazilian employees in Japan, Japanese managers' participation in long-term training in Brazil, new employees' orientation program, leadership development projects) recognize the need to develop human resources capability at multiple levels—addressing strategic, technical, and cultural aspects. All work team members are required to master various types of tasks. On the work floor level, the functional skill level of every worker is defined and measured. Job rotations are fairly routinized for all employees. Such extensive training is useful in promotion decisions (i.e., team member—team leader—group leader—supervisor) and performance evaluations of each employee. In this way, Toyota Brazil achieves high-quality performance in Brazil operations through effective implementation of TPS.

9.3.4 Present and Future of Toyota Brazil

Toyota, just as in India and China, has not yet fully deployed its strategy for emerging markets in the 2000s. Based on its experience with Etios in India,

Toyota Brazil would more vigorously penetrate the Brazilian market and increase their production volumes as well. Toyota Brazil operations had their 50th-year celebration in 2008. Toyota Brazil, thus, has the longest operational history among all global plants. From the San Bernard operations, other expansions included new plants in Argentina (1997) and Indaiatba, Brazil (1998). The prices of Toyota models are Corolla ($30,000; 60,000 Real), Camry ($60,000; 120,000 Real), and Hilux ($40,000; 80,000 Real). By 2000, sales volumes were somewhat modest but recent sales growth is quite noticeable. The production level of Toyota Brazil is not large enough to meet the domestic demand, and the shortage amount is imported. Thus, Toyota Brazil has implemented a plant expansion after 2011. The local sourcing rate of component parts is about 80% and the tariff rate is 35% for the finished cars. Import component parts of CKD are 18%, and as of 2011, it is temporarily 11%. The majority of imports from Japan are mostly engine and transmission parts.

Based on competitive priorities of safety, quality, volume, cost, and timing (lead time) (in order sequence), Toyota engages in its production. The director of plant operations is mostly focused on quality. For quality improvement, Toyota pays a great deal of attention to developing the capabilities of its component parts suppliers. Specifically, the Toyota Manufacturing Quality Leading (TMQL) team goes to the manufacturing and assembly plants of component parts suppliers and provides technical support services in the areas of quality inspection and improvement. In consequence, the market quality evaluation receives consistently high marks. For an example, the quality of Corolla produced in the Brazil plant is as excellent as that of any other global plants. Since the Brazilian market prefers small-size cars, in 2012 Toyota Brazil began manufacturing the Etios model that is successful in India.

9.4 BRAZIL HONDA'S STRATEGY

9.4.1 Brazilian Motorcycle Market

Honda's entry into the Brazilian motorcycle market began with sales by imports from Japan in 1960. Global firms (including Honda) considered actual production in Brazil in response to the 1974 Brazilian government's policy that placed import restrictions on all finished motorcycles (Abo, 2009; Seo et al., 2012). In 1974, Yamaha built its plant in São Paulo, and in 1976 Honda did the same in Manaus. It was 1977 when Honda started large-scale production in Brazil. In the 1970s, the total production capacity in Brazil was no more than 50,000 units. By 1982, the total volume grew to 220,000; but with the prolonged recession, the motorcycle market size shrunk and accordingly motorcycle production experienced a serious reduction. After 1993, the motorcycle market recovered and customer demand steadily grew from 100,000 in 1993 to 900,000 in 2002. At present, Japanese firms are the industry leaders in the motorcycle market, in terms of market share as of 2009, Honda (75.4%), Yamaha (12.2%), and Suzuki (5.3%). The total combined market share of Japanese firms is more than 90%.

9.4.2 Honda's Entry into the Brazilian Market

Taking tax advantages as first importance, Honda put its foot in Manaus. Its plant was completed in 1976 and large-scale production started from 1977. By 2006, annual production volume exceeded one million units (Abo, 2009). By 2007, the total accumulated production reached up to 10 million units. Honda's motorcycle business division is a global leader with 30% of the global market share. By 2010, the accumulated production volume was 14.83 million units. Honda's global production by regions can be compared in terms of the year of achieving the accumulated production volume of 10 million units: Japan (1968), Indonesia (2003), Thailand and India (2004), and Brazil (2007). As of 2007, annual production volume was 5.4 million (India), 3.5 million (Indonesia), and 1.5 million (Thailand). Thus, with annual production that exceeds 1.5 million, Honda Brazil's global rank is third to fourth, similar to that of Thailand.

Initially, Manaus' plants in Brazil started small-scale operations for 125 CC model with 276 employees. Even in Manaus, its plant is 20 km away from the airport and 20 km from its nearest harbor. In this Manaus plant, Honda produces for both Brazil domestic customers and global export models. The total number of product lines is 28. Eighteen of them are for both domestic and global market purposes, and 10 models are exclusively for global export. Major export markets are in 70 countries of North America, Central and Latin America, and Africa.

9.4.3 Honda Brazil's Motorcycle Production and Marketing Strategy

Brazil Honda's plant in Manaus produces diverse models (i.e., small-size to supersized motorcycle). Complex ordering patterns of Brazil customers reflect unique Brazilian contexts such as collar choices, external feature preferences, motorcycle structural support requests that accommodate hilly and mountain regions, and unpaved road conditions. Honda Brazil also prepares a variety of product lines for global export purposes. In China, other local firms introduce cheap, copy versions of Honda models for price-sensitive customers; thus, Honda's share in China is relatively low. However, in Brazil, with mountainous regions and a rugged, unpaved road system, such copy versions from China do not appeal to customers who quickly recognize their quality defects and instead appreciate Honda products' high durability and dependability. Motorcycles, much more than passenger cars, must respond to the Brazilian market contexts and the unique customer needs in their product design and functional performance. Thus, Honda's meticulous attention to Brazilian customer requirements enabled the company to achieve more than 80% of motorcycle market share.

The biggest problem for the Manaus plant is a transportation issue. Brazil Honda produces all sizes of motorcycles—small to super giant size. The total number of component parts is close to 2,000. However, very few Honda suppliers are located in Manaus. Many of Honda's suppliers have their operations near São Paulo. In 2001, out of Honda's 102 suppliers, only 12 suppliers (including seven Japanese suppliers) were located in Manaus, and 60% of them were near São Paulo. In 2006, Japanese suppliers in Manaus increased from 7 to 11 (Abo, 2009).

It takes five to six days to get from São Paulo to Belém, the harbor city in the Amazon region. Then an additional five to six days by ship are needed to transport parts from Belém to Manaus. Thus, a total of 10 days are required to transport component parts from São Paulo to Manaus. Since Brazil is so far away from Asia, it takes at least 30 days from Japan to Brazil. Other Asian countries (China or Thailand) require at least 45 to 60 days of transportation time. Such logistical challenges are quite serious obstacles for other global firms to produce their products in Manaus.

Naturally, the Manaus plant of Honda Brazil has a high rate of internal sourcing (Seo et al., 2012). In 2006, it was 40% (local sourcing rate was 80%—the highest among all Honda's global operations), which is higher than 30% of Honda Indonesia and 20% of Honda Japan (Abo, 2009). Such a high rate of insourcing and localization reflect Manaus's unique sourcing challenges. In neighboring Latin American countries, there is no reliable component parts supplier network. The Brazilian government also requires insourcing requirements by components parts (up to 80% to 90%) according to the government's local sourcing regulation policy directives. Although inconvenient, it is imperative for Honda to build its own insourcing structure or develop local suppliers for achieving government requirements. For this purpose, Honda installed a SED (sales, engineering, development) system and applied it for its global system network.

Domestic sales (other than export to global markets) are handled by the Honda franchise system, which had 530 distribution centers in 2001 and grew to 640 in 2006 (Abo, 2009).

Honda, in contrast to other Japanese firms, could attain a high market share with its early entry to the Brazilian market and its extensive investment. Honda entered the Brazilian market 10 years earlier than Yamaha, and even when the Brazilian economy was in a long recession in the 1990s, it continued to maintain an adequate level of investment. Instead of focusing on limited product lines, Honda's marketing strategy offered a broad set of product lines such as Cave, Scooter, CG XL, and Giant group models. At present, Honda's hot products are mostly from 100- to 120-CC class models from CG groups; yet, Honda still offers a wide variety of models for a growing number of customer segments. In the early 2000s, many Japanese firms withdrew from Manaus. In 2000, Sanyo discontinued its operations of TV, VTR, and the electronic ranges. In 2001, Murata stopped ceramic filter production, and Seiko shut down its operation and returned to Japan. In 2002 Fujitsu also did the same. In such a context, Honda kept its production in Manaus.

The Manaus Economic Priority Zone (MEPZ) offers tax advantages to all member firms and thus financial incentives are substantial. However, to receive such benefits all the final assembly work needs to be completed in Manaus (Seo et al., 2012). For example, the clutch (i.e., one of Honda's key component parts) requires both production and assembly of outer aluminum die casting in Brazil. Thus, Honda's Japanese suppliers operating in Brazil import some parts from Japan, which takes between 4 and 6 months of cycle time. This reflects the distance challenge between Japan and Brazil. With such a long cycle time, different from Japan, Honda Brazil has to implement an annual production plan by which all sourcing requirements from its suppliers are determined. Besides, since the MEPZ is located in the middle of the Amazon jungle, the logistical challenges are enormous. This raises serious concerns for competitiveness in terms of on-time receipt of components parts from suppliers and delivery of finished products to customers in major cities (e.g., São Paulo) which are quite a distance away. In this sense, a real business challenge in Brazil is how to implement supply chain management (SCM) without adequate infrastructure support of an extended supplier network and an efficient transportation system.

9.5 OTHER JAPANESE FIRMS IN BRAZIL

9.5.1 Strategy of Bridgestone Brazil

Bridgestone Corporation is a global tire manufacturer. In 1988 it acquired Firestone. Since then, its key operational priority was to improve production capability of Firestone plants for meeting the demand of Latin America. As mentioned above, with the growth of automobile sales, the demand for tires also increased. New tire plants are being built near São Paulo. In particular, the Firestone plant was built in 1940. Bridgestone, with more than 10 years of continuous training and education for employees, instilled the corporate culture that fits Bridgestone brand values. Bridgestone's initial strategy was to differentiate between Bridgestone brand tires and Firestone tires. As the quality performance of Firestone tires came quite close to that of Bridgestone over 10 plus years, the identical brand power is now established.

The current production capacity of Bridgestone Brazil is 23,000 radial tires for passenger cars; 5,500 radial tires for trucks; and 400 agriculture equipment tires. Bridgestone also exports its products to other Latin American countries and the United States as well. Its market leaders are European and US-based firms such as Pirelli & C SpA (35%) and Goodyear (30%) (*Tire Review,* September 2011). Japanese firms issue quality certificates in Japan, but GM and VW do so in Brazil.

After its acquisition in 1988, Bridgestone Brazil produced and marketed tires in Brazil with the Firestone brand. With continuous quality improvement, Bridgestone started certifying passenger car tires from 1998 and truck tires from 2000. At present, tire plants in Latin America are managed by the subsidiary office of Bridgestone USA in Brazil. Technical support for manufacturing is from Bridgestone Japan and product development is by Bridgestone USA. Tire size and product performance standards conform to the user conditions in Latin America. As in India, the road system in Brazil is not well-paved. Driving distance requirements are big. Thus, tire life should be long with highly durable functionality. Cost competitiveness is also a crucial element. Bridgestone utilizes the old plant facilities to the maximum and keeps manufacturing costs low.

9.5.2 Case of Epson Brazil

In the Brazilian electronics product market, mobile phones, TVs, and PCs have a large potential customer base. Among them, the growth prospect for

PCs is quite good. Brazil Epson produces and markets printers. In keeping up with growth in the PC market, the printer market will expand as well.

In Brazil, high tariffs, sales tax, and other value-added taxes are fairly high according to the domestic market protection policy. Most printers are used for issuing receipts. Epson Brazil develops its business model in such a market context. Epson has developed printers for issuing receipts and other tax documents.

In the printer market of emerging economies including Brazil, the market position of Hewlett Packard is relatively strong. Thus, Epson and Canon are the market followers. In the consumer inkjet printer market, the market shares of major firms are HP 56%, Epson 22%, Canon 18%, and Lexmark 3%. Epson holds an absolute advantage in the business-purpose printer with 84% of the market share. The secret of such market success is based on its strategic approach to develop a printer system for issuing sales receipts according to legal requirements of the government. In Brazil, sales receipts are to be issued for tax purposes. Dot matrix printers are mostly used for this purpose. By law, customers are required to receive the receipts for all transactions. Theaters, cinemas, and drug/convenience stores have to issue receipts for all sales. An E-invoice system has become widely used. Epson's thermal printer with necessary software support allows sales receipt information to be sent to the Brazilian government.

In the meantime, the laser printer market is expected to grow. Samsung would be a key rival. The inkjet printer market has growth potential. As in India and Indonesia, it is crucial to raise the ratio of regular ink cartridge usage. For this goal, Epson's distribution strategy is to make its ink ribbons available in all electronic products outlets, IT distributors, small retail stores, and shopping malls throughout Brazil.

9.6 CONCLUSION

Brazil is another thriving emerging economy with a sizable population and a vast natural resource basis. Among the emerging economies, Brazil is experiencing phenomenal growth. Practices of Japanese firms suggest their commitment to Brazilian market needs in unique ways: Komatsu (e.g., manufacturing and marketing synergies with 2 plants and 10 distribution centers), Toyota (e.g., product design and manufacturing capabilities that satisfy Brazilian domestic demand patterns), Bridgestone (e.g., brand strategies to appeal to higher quality for the Brazilian automobile market), and Epson (e.g., personal computer firm case to integrate product development and customer competence that satisfy Brazilian domestic demand patterns).

Case studies of Japanese global firms in the Brazilian market suggest that their market strategy is based on new supply chain management, which implements active localization practices in terms of sensing local market needs, developing Brazilian suppliers, and implementing contexts-driven marketing rather than bringing their domestic products with modest variations. These firms effectively use linkage competence that integrates both technology and customer competence. From the product architecture perspective, these firms also integrate their high technological competence (i.e., closed integral architecture for technological excellence) with the reality of uneven quality performance of local suppliers (i.e., open integral architecture for reasonable quality performance and market contexts accommodations).

10

Strategies of Korean Firms in the Chinese Market

In this chapter we will introduce supply chain management capabilities of Korean firms. In China, the focus is their effective supplier building strategies. We will introduce supply chain management capabilities of electronic firms (e.g., Samsung and LG). The Korean auto manufacturer (e.g., Hyundai-Kia) is one of the most successful firms. Korean auto suppliers (e.g., Mobis, Hankuk Tire) support Hyundai-Kia and the global competitive strengths of global auto manufacturers (e.g., Nissan, Ford).

10.1 INTRODUCTION

In the turbulent competitive global environment, supply chain management (SCM) is regarded as one of the most effective strategic moves to building a global competitive advantage (Gunasekaran et al., 2008; Tomino et al., 2009; Trkman and McCormack, 2009; Barney, 2002; Park et al., 2013). Customers expect firms to provide them with high-quality products with competitive prices at the right time. Particularly, in an intensely competitive global market environment, firms need to develop their capabilities to design and market innovative products in a timely manner in the ways customers demand.

Increasingly, agile supply chain management is a new condition for competitive advantage in a turbulent environment. The complexity of customers' demands for flexibility, timeliness, green-orientation, and innovativeness requires synergies of multiple layers of external and internal processes such as a stream of changing customer needs, product development processes, manufacturing processes and their suppliers, purchasing and procurements, marketing, and service chain network (Liao, Hong, Rao, 2010; Hong et al., 2009; Hong and Kwon, 2012; Gunasekaran et al., 2014). Such a supply chain management enables firms to improve their long-term business profitability and sustains their competitive advantage. For example, the supply chain evaluation of AMR (Academy of Management Review) research notes that from 2008 to 2011, Apple was rated global number one because of first importance, Apple offers outstanding customer service experiences. Apple was able to do this because it was successful in constructing an optimum supply chain network. Another outstanding example is P&G (Procter & Gamble). It is in a sense a pioneer of espousing supply chain management principles in the first place. P&G generates at minimum 50% of useful ideas of innovative products from its external sources. For value creation and delivery P&G goes far beyond the traditional logistical efficiency and starts from customer needs and integrates its internal resources and external supply chain network ecosystem. Thus, P&G maintains global supply chain leadership and high profitability.

Building such an agile supply chain requires a collaborative network system that supports and complements the focal firm's resource capabilities. For effective SCM construction, a focal firm discovers, develops, and deploys its core competence while making serious efforts to explore and invites other available resources through its large network or innovation ecosystem (Prahalad and Hamel, 1990; Adner, 2006; Lusch, 2011). SCM goes beyond one firm system boundary and collaborates with partners, pursues shared risks and benefits, and evolves into something new and different through continuous and expanding network coordinating mechanisms (Demeter et al., 2006; Kanter, 2012). The motive of forming such a network partnership is for complex customer requirements such as cost reductions, efficient deployment of resources, best services offering options, superior marketing, profitability enhancement, and steady business growth.

Supplier relationships in the Japanese automotive industry suggest three types of partnerships (Halley and Nollet, 2002). The highest kind of partnership is to share extensive knowledge including operations and marketing and form a collaborative system to work together with shared vision (Halley and Nollet, 2002; Chinen, 2006). Such a strategic partnership focuses on their core competence areas and evolves in ways to create and deliver greater customer values and mutual benefits based on their broad set of core competencies (Chiang and Trappey, 2007). Through such a process, focal firms form strategic partnerships with other partner firms that understand their own core competences and provide necessary resources. As supply chains are established with partners, all the participants of the supply chain collaborate for shared vision within the same industry value chain system. Partners that share vision together respond to the changing market demand with flexibility and timeliness. Particularly, in emerging economies like China where market conditions and technological changes are rapid, proper investment and supply chain strategy is crucial for continuous business success (Hong et al., 2006). In this chapter, SCM (supply chain management) of Korean global firms in China is discussed.

10.2 SAMSUNG CHINA'S SCM COLLABORATION STRATEGY

10.2.1 Samsung LCD's SCM System

Samsung LCD's headquarters are located in Tanjung, Korea. In this section we examine Samsung LCD Panel's SCM system and SCM case studies of Samsung China LCD's SCM back-end assembly processes for LCD panels and BLU (Park, 2012d). Samsung LCD's SCM system is called the SLJ-Network (S-LCD JIT Network). In 2004 Samsung built the SLJ-Network for the purpose of ensuring the quality of component parts suppliers and raw materials providers. It was also for sourcing and a logistics environment based on LCD panels. For example, in the course of changing from second to eighth generation the size of substrate grew 34 times the original one. In the meantime, the scale of the plant was expanded from 4.33 hectare (2003) to 47.3 hectare (2007) to achieve SCM integration with its suppliers. The network related to the SCM system includes Enterprise Resource Planning (ERP), Manufacturing Execution System (MES), transportation management system (TMS), and warehouse management system (WMS). Thus, the goal was to utilize all these systems in all production processes.

Building a SCM system between Samsung LCD headquarters and the first-tier suppliers was somewhat smooth because of their prior business relationships. However, the situations between the first-tier and the second-tier suppliers were quite different in view of somewhat irregular order amounts and timing as well as lack of a shared common information technology (IT) system. To resolve this issue, Samsung had a newly constructed SLJ-Network that connected first-tier component parts suppliers and second-tier suppliers, reduced overall inventory levels, and achieved supply chain network efficiency.

Logistics network (both inbound and outbound) is an important element of SCM for Korean firms (Hong and Vonderembse, 2011; Hong and Kim, 2012). The SLJ-Network involves the sequential processes such as order receipts from the marketing department, MP (master production plan), MRP (materials requirement planning), P/O (purchase order), and D/O (delivery order). As of 2007, the cycle time was one week for MRP planning. This is somewhat similar to Toyota's Kanban methods. For the reliability of D/O (e.g., accuracy of arrival time of component parts at destinations), from 2006 SLI-Network uses GLONETS (i.e., Samsung's same internal system) and applies it with all its first-tier suppliers. As of 2007, the number of first-tier suppliers were 100 domestic and 100 global, and since then, total numbers are steadily increasing. For second-tier suppliers, Samsung also built the BLUNET system which is similar to GLONETS for the first-tier suppliers. Only Samsung's LCD headquarters use the BLUNET system. These systems allow both first- and second-tier suppliers to get access to necessary information sites through WEB by putting their MRP plan details. These systems enable the suppliers to forecast future demand from Samsung with greater accuracy and timeliness. According to MRP, Samsung delivers forecasting details to the first-tier suppliers about 13 weeks in advance. In response, the first-tier suppliers reply with RTF (ready to fly). Such communication processes are repeated every week.

Figure 10.1 shows how TMS (transportation management system) and WMS (warehouse management system) are connected to MRP (materials requirement planning). Relevant information is available both to the suppliers and logistics services providers. Through implementing the SLI-Network, practical performance impacts are obvious: (1) There is a large reduction in manufacturing/marketing lead time. The information flows and decision steps from MRP to D/O become much more effective. The previous nine steps (i.e., from customer order receipts to final delivery) were simplified into five steps (thus time requirements were reduced from 290 minutes to 120 minutes) as the ERP system accomplished functional interfaces standardization. (2) The number of component parts for logistics services were also reduced from 142 to 16 items. The number of component parts from second-tier to first-tier suppliers was also reduced from 15 to 5 units. (3) BLU

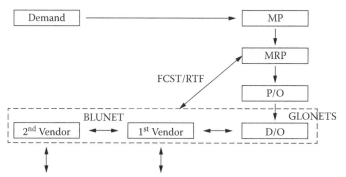

FIGURE 10.1
SLJ-network structure.

(Back Light Units) processes were also simplified from 49 to 27 steps. Korean main plants handle all the front-end LCD panel processes, and the plants in other global market locations assume all back-end processes. Thus, all the back-end BLU processes are integrated in each global market location. GPS (Global Positioning System) also monitors the overall flows of components parts in real time. Through these responsive mechanisms outstanding LCD quality is assured in all logistics processes from one location to the final destinations. (4) There has been a drastic reduction in inventory level. For example, through these improvement efforts, the inventory cycle time changed from 7 days (2007) to 5.2 days in a few years. The average inventory cost was down from $182.1 million to $162.4 million. The corresponding reduction in first- and second-tier inventory turnover time was down to 6.6 and 7.4 (days), respectively. Other additional benefits included warehouse space reduction by 33% and logistics expenses savings by 27%.

10.2.2 Samsung China LCD's Integration of BLU Suppliers

In 2002 Samsung LCD established a manufacturing business division in China. Samsung China received panels with complete cell processes by sea or air and assembled the back-end LCD panel processes in China. Major products are notebook PCs and medium panels for monitors. Recently, Samsung accelerated large LCD TV module productions. For the sake of upstream flows, integration production facilities in China are in the same cluster areas like Samsung's notebook PC. These plants are both very close to the notebook PC market as well.

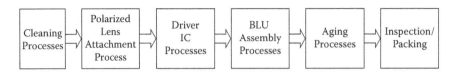

FIGURE 10.2
Module processes flows.

Figure 10.2 shows the panel module processes that include the PAD cleaning process, polarized lens attachment process, Anisotropic Conductive Film (ACF), Tape Automated Bonding (TAB), and Printed Circuit Board (PCB) adherence driver IC process, and BLU (back light unit) assembly process, aging process, final inspection/packing process. In the early 2000s, the polarized lens attachment process was dependent on array/cell processes in Korean plants. Recently, most of these processes have been transferred to Chinese plants and localization of component parts (i.e., use Chinese suppliers for all the necessary component parts).

Samsung China's vertical integration strategy of the LCD supply chain is applied somewhat differently for upstream and downstream. First, for upstream component parts/raw materials integration, Samsung's production cost reduction efforts have achieved almost maximum possible production efficiency attainment and there is little room for additional improvement. Thus, Samsung is now outsourcing BLU assembly and final inspection/packing process to outside suppliers. In the past, Samsung China received BLU from suppliers and completed other manufacturing processes in Samsung China plants. From the latter part of 2007, Samsung adopted LCM (low-cost module) by selecting three BLU suppliers and turned over to them assembly and final inspection/packing processes as well. Hereafter, Samsung's plans are to expand LCM strategy further to integrate with upstream BLU and further reduce production costs and achieve stable BLU component parts supply through BLU supplier integration. Samsung China then focuses high-value-added processes such as PAD cleaning and the driver IC process. Second, integration with downstream suppliers is addressed. Samsung China's notebook PC division is in the same cluster as the LCD panel division. As the LCD market becomes saturated with ease of entry, many small and larger firms compete based on the cost advantage of component parts that are modular in design and easy-to-set-up manufacturing assembly operations. Thus, both notebook PC panels and LCD panels share common business needs for achieving sustainable cost competitiveness.

10.2.3 LCM (Low-Cost Module) Strategic Challenges

However, in the course of integrating the supply chain of Samsung China and BLU suppliers, some unexpected issues arose. The central issue was customs clearance. Table 10.1 shows Samsung China's integration process with supplier A, which is located in close proximity with Samsung LCD. Firm A is a leading firm among Samsung China's BLU suppliers. From 2004 on, it engaged in active manufacturing and by 2006 it built its own production facility and became a reliable supplier for Samsung China. From July 2007, this firm kept up with LCM with Samsung China's LCD supply chain integration strategy. Practically, it helped to get Chinese custom clearance of 500,000 units of component parts that went through front-end processes of panel modules from second-tier suppliers. Then, it completed back-end BLU assembly processes and supplied to Samsung's Notebook PC/Monitor division.

Although Firm A is no more than 15 minutes driving distance away from Samsung China LCD, the actual time it took to get customs clearance was more than 5 hours. Such a custom process delayed the lead time and increased an unexpected level of inventory, which naturally put pressure on overall production costs. Thus, work-in-progress LCD panels left the Samsung China LCD facility in the morning and yet they arrived at Firm A in the afternoon and the overstock level increased in between 5,000 to 15,000 units. With such a custom clearance delay, the work that would finish by 1:00 p.m. needs to be extended until 4 to 5 p.m.

In the past, Firm A was able to meet Samsung's 30% cost reduction requirement primarily through its relatively low wages. (Note: Samsung China LCD wages, as a large global firm, are much higher than those paid to workers of Firm A, as a small-scale supplier firm.) However, delay time due to custom clearance wiped out such labor cost advantage because of increased lead time and overstock inventory level. This Samsung China LCD case suggests that

TABLE 10.1

Samsung China's LCM Model and Integration Period with Suppliers

LCM Production Scale	BLU Integration Suppliers	Distance between Samsung China and BLU Suppliers	Integration Period
One million units	A	15 minutes	July 2007
	B	40 minutes	January 2008
	C	40 minutes	July 2008

governmental regulation and custom clearance processes have serious implications on cost competitiveness. Thus, SCM strategy in emerging economies requires careful consideration of these external factors.

In this section we examined the LCM strategy through which Samsung China LCD (i.e., the maker of LCD panels) implemented innovative supply chain integration in the form of production facilities transfers to China and upstream integration with its suppliers. Even after achieving location proximity, BLU suppliers had to resolve Chinese customs issues. Such governmental policy issues matter not merely in China, but in other emerging economies such as Brazil, India, and Russia as well.

10.2.4 Conclusion

Japanese firms have caught up with the first mover global firms from the United States and Europe. Korean firms adopted a fast follower strategy to keep up with Japanese, American, and European firms. Japanese electronics firms, despite their global leadership until the 1980s, remained stagnant in the 1990s. In the meantime, Samsung and LG Electronics, Korean global firms, rapidly established their competitive position in the global markets. Their global SCM integration strategy is an obvious factor for their impressive growth. Samsung China's case in this section suggests that SCM integration does make a real difference in the competitiveness war in emerging markets.

10.3 GLOBAL SCM STRATEGY OF HYUNDAI BEIJING

Hyundai Motor Company is another global firm from Korea that has shown steady growth in emerging markets (Park et al., 2011; Hong and Kim, 2012; Park et al., 2012e). Its market performance in BRICs (Brazil, Russia, India, and China) is comparable to Japanese rival firms such as Toyota and Honda. Hyundai built a plant in St. Petersburg with annual production volume of 150,000 and started small passenger car production from 2011. For the Latin American market, it also constructed a new production facility in Brazil. It accelerates aggressive market penetration efforts in Africa. In Eastern Europe, Hyundai and Kia now have large-scale production facilities in Slovakia and the Czech Republic.

This section focuses on Hyundai's Chinese market strategy. In October 2002, Hyundai formed Beijing Hyundai, a joint venture firm with Beijing

Train, with a 50/50 investment. In 2003, it produced 52,000 and sold 50,000 vehicles—a new history maker that achieved the sale of 50,000 cars in such a short period. In 2010, Hyundai sold 703,000 vehicles and became the number four automotive firm in China and thus sold more than other Japanese rivals. Hyundai's SCM strategy—particularly, research, sourcing, and marketing—different from that of Japanese firms, might be a primary reason why it could report such rapid growth in China.

Beijing Hyundai pours a great deal of its resources into market research in China. In 2011 Hyundai established the Automotive Business Research Institute. A Hyundai senior manager comments, "We can get statistics of US automotive industry easily. But information on Chinese market is not enough. Government policies frequent change and the market dynamics are quite complex. This is why we need this type of research institute here" (*Dongyang Economy Daily*, 2011). Beijing Hyundai grew through quality market research support through such a highly visible and well-funded institute that assists with clarity of market targets and road maps that translate into marketing business. The new products respond to the changing requirements of customers' lifestyles. Preparing for the Chinese government's policy directives is essential to market high-valued products in China.

Beijing Hyundai (BH) adopts economies-of-scale production for mass customization purposes. It introduces the right mix of new models in response to diverse market segments and expanded the volume size per product line. This suggests that BH conducts a high level of market research and its product development processes translate the changing customer requirements very well. BH's production type is MTS (make-to-stock), which is to forecast the customer demand and produce sufficient stock of cars in advance. It responds to the customer needs in a time-based manner and prevents any potential loss of sales opportunities. An unreliable forecast of customer demand has huge negative implications in terms of huge unsold car inventory. In this sense, Hyundai is somewhat different from Toyota that adopts the just-in-time (JIT) production concept.

However, BH implements MTS rather than MTO. In China's huge market size, large segments of customers do not necessarily require the JIT type of production method. Rather, upon making a purchase decision in the dealership, Chinese customers would like to pick up their car and go home right away. BH sells such a large number of cars for each product line that economies of scale production achieve low cost per product unit. Such small customer segments and large numbers of production for each product model require simple-skilled, not multiskilled workers. For example, the rate of automation for press and assembly of the main body is 100%, the stamping process is 60%, and the final assembly process is 10%. Production lines rarely stop. The utilization rate is on average 99.5% (second plant utilization rate), and 98% (first plant utilization rate 98%) as of 2009 (Sioji et al., 2012). In Hyundai, the idea is that an automated process is more reliable than a manual process. Thus, BH is not particularly strong in training and developing multiskilled workers to discover and resolve problems at the floor level through continuous improvement (i.e., KAIZEN activities). Thus, discovery of quality problems is through inspectors, managers, and specialized staff personnel (Sioji et al., 2012; Park et al., 2012c). Characteristics of HB are not emphasizing Kaizen for the workers. Rather, HB simplifies the manufacturing processes in detail so that each worker's portion is small. The total number of work processes is usually twice that of Japanese auto manufacturers. Any workers who are not quite proficient in basic communications can be assigned to production processes. Thus, training and education requirements are fairly small and the amount of training needed for each worker is relatively small. Thus, the productivity of global plants is fairly high (Sioji et al., 2012). This type of human resource plan is quite fit to the Chinese labor market in which the movement of workers among different firms is frequent. Thus, this type of work structure fits not only in China but also in many other emerging economies.

BH also has a very high rate of localization up to 94%—only 6% of component parts are imported from Korea (Sioji et al., 2012). For its global production system, Hyundai's affiliated suppliers move together with Hyundai in China. Hyundai also utilizes local Chinese suppliers. Hyundai invites the affiliated suppliers as suppliers in the emerging markets and thus the extent of vertical integration is fairly high (Park, Oh, and Fujimoto, 2012). For peripheral items, BH increases the volume of sourcing from Chinese suppliers and maximizes the effect of cost reduction. For strategic items BH maintains a stable supply with high-quality emphasis. In all other items, a cost reduction effort is key for their cost-competitiveness strategy (Sioji et al., 2012). In this way, BH invites affiliated firms to China as strategic partners for speedy growth initiatives and expands the supply base through Chinese local suppliers to achieve both total cost reduction (i.e., raw materials plus logistics) and quality manufacturing processes.

Another BH success factor is to segment customer requirements by region and respond to their needs with the right mix of products. BH, in contrast to Japanese makers, uses both subdealers and satellite sales offices. In this way, BH covers not only coastline big cities and surrounding regions but also small and medium cities and other rural areas as well. With its national network of marketing and distribution, BH could achieve such rapid growth by 2009 (Sioji et al., 2012). In keeping up with the Chinese government's policy that reduced the income tax by 5% for promoting automobile distribution for rural residents, BH also had a series of special promotion activities for these target segments.

In this way, BH's DSCI (demand and supply chain integration) includes careful examination of the impact of Chinese government policy changes, rapid translation into development of products that fit customer requirements, and execution of the large economies of scale production at low cost.

10.4 HANKOOK TIRE STRATEGY

In 1941 Hankook Tire started as the first Korean tire company. It is still the largest among Korean tire firms. In the past, all its employees worked in Korea. As of 2009, its global operation has about 14,000 employees. In 1962, it exported its products to South East Asian countries such as Thailand and Pakistan. Its market share in China is 25%, the largest in China. The pattern of such phenomenal growth of Hankook Tire is somewhat different from Korean Economic Miracle. Different from other Korean global firms (e.g., Samsung and Hyundai) that produce semiconductors for large oil tankers ("chips-to-ships"), Hankook Tire focused only on tires.

Hankook Tire is still relatively small compared to the other global leaders such as Bridgestone, Michelin, and Goodyear. It is the seventh largest tire manufacturer in the world. Yet, its growth is faster than any other tire companies in the world. In 1962, its first export to other countries, its global sales also increased $100 million (1980), $400 million (1993), $500 million (1995), $600 million (2002), $700 million (2003), $1 billion (2005), $2 billion (2006), $3.5 billion (2007), and $3.7 billion (2008). Between 2000 and 2006, its annual growth was 18.2%, and afterward it maintained a similar rate of growth 20.7% (2008) and 18% (2009), which is the highest among the global tire companies. Since 2000, most firms experienced slow growth in the global recession, yet it has maintained a rapid growth pattern.

10.4.1 Market Reality

Hankook Tire (HT) changed its global focus in the 1990s after completing its solid domestic advantage in the 1980s. It started as one of the SMEs (small and medium enterprises) and went through serious global business challenges such as the oil shock in the 1980s and the Asian Financial Crisis in the late 1990s. In 2000, it also feels tremendous cost burdens with increasing raw materials costs and fluctuating oil prices. As of 2011, Korean workers' average annual wages are now up to the level of $50,000 per year. With these external and internal factors, HT is required to implement serious quality management initiatives and global strategy for emerging markets.

10.4.2 Strategic Focus/Organizational Leadership

In view of a dynamic global market reality, in the 2000s HT has pursued a global marketing strategy with a set of bold initiatives such as decisive investment strategy, cost competiveness, and aggressive management style. HT's strategic focus is to bring a steady stream of high-performance new products (e.g., research and development [R&D] investment) and corporate brand enhancement (e.g., diverse marketing, differentiated customer services). During the Asian Financial Crisis in the 1980s and the global recession in the 1990s, HT had vigorous investment in the European Union, North America, and China and expanded its global market basis. In 1994 HT established a Beijing branch and marketed the tires that were imported from Korea. In 1998, HT built production plants in Jiaxing, Zhejiang, and Huaian, Jiangsu. At this time, EU and North American markets were saturated with limited growth potential and Korea was going through financial crisis. HT strategically targeted its growth potential in China.

This type of bold initiative (i.e., seeking growth opportunities out of crisis contexts) is based on strong organizational leadership. *First, an aggressive and bold management style was adopted.* In 1990, HT switched to a professional management system. Cho, a first professional CEO, is an aggressive management proponent. During the Asian Financial Crisis in 1997, most firms stopped daring to invest for new businesses and instead downsized their marketing efforts. Cho did the opposite. At the outbreak of the Asian Financial Crisis, HT was about to start operation of another new plant in Gumsan, Korea, and was in the process of constructing other plants in China. Like other firms, HT was struggling to generate additional capital. Cho visited banks and other capital venture firms and spoke about the need to focus on long-term growth needs beyond the immediate recession pressures. With his tireless efforts, HT was able to sustain its China projects without any delay.

Second, premium quality management and design management strategy were supported by cutting-edge technology. In a sense, Cho's stubborn insistence on premium quality is behind HT's outstanding growth. According to Cho, investment concentration on R&D was key for sustainable growth as a globally competitive firm. Over the years, Korean firms' tire quality is some of the best in global standards. Hankook invests at least 5% of its sales on R&D and maintains research centers in Korea, China, Japan, Germany, and the United States. He emphasized that HT was selected as a supplier for global automotive firms like GM, Ford, and Audi for its outstanding quality reputation. Cho is also keen in the area of design. He believes that design is performance. One might wonder why design is so important to tires. However, tire design quality has much to do with noise level, speed, and car performance.

Third, a differentiated marketing strategy was implemented. In July 2004, Hankook Tire opened the first T'Station, a high premium distribution franchise, in Anyang, Korea, for brand enhancement in keeping up with its marketing strategy. T'Station is a comprehensive auto-service center that promises the same prices, standardized services, and high level of customer satisfaction. T'Station sells auto parts such as tires, wheels, and batteries, and also offers automotive operational services including wheel alignment and vibration adjustment line balancing. The perception of a traditional tire service center was dirty and outdated. With the rising standard of living in Korea, customers began demanding clean and comfortable service stations. T'station's marketing strategy is to offer high-quality services with readily available automotive parts at competitive prices. This strategy is very successful. The clean and attractive T'Station invites many women drivers to premium services.

Furthermore, Seo, the second professional CEO appointed in 2007, implemented effective management and marketing strategy based on his global perspective from 17 previous years of fieldwork experiences in the Middle East, the United States, the United Kingdom, and Germany. His global leadership was instrumental in transforming HT into a global tire manufacturer. During his tenure as CEO, Seo strengthened regional headquarters in Korea, North America, the European Union, and China and formulated marketing strategy according to a market maturity level.

The impressive outcomes of such an aggressive and bold investment strategy, premium quality focus, and innovative marketing campaigns were demonstrated in China. HT, with 25% of the market share in China, supplies a broad set of tires including luxury models such as Audi A6,

Volkswagen, Hyundai, and Kia. In China alone, HT produces 29 million units—2% of global demand. Its efforts to establish a strong Chinese market distribution network are also noteworthy. In April 2007 it opened its first T'Station in Shanghai, China, and by 2009 it had about 20 T'Stations. By 2013 it opened an additional 300 T'Stations in the four major cities—Shanghai, Beijing, Guangzhou, and Tianjin—and expanded its distribution network in China and in other countries and plan to open an additional 6000 networks by 2020 (Jung, 2014).

Seo's top priority since his early years was to transform HT into a "global major tire manufacturer" (Kim, 2009). For this overarching goal, he emphasized service quality innovation and brand image enhancement. Besides regular channels of advertisement in business magazines, newspapers, and technology media outlets, HT has become an official sponsor of two major sports events in China, which are CCC (China Circuit Championship) and CRC (China Rally Championship). These concerted efforts communicate HT's differentiated business image and premium brand.

10.4.3 Product/Value Innovation

HT's business philosophy is summarized in "Kontrol Technology," which produces premium quality tire products for global market competitiveness. Kontrol Technology refers to HT's business philosophy and principles that cover innovative R&D and production and distribution processes. The *K* is from "kinetic" (i.e., dynamic movement of tire) through which perfect "control" of technology (i.e., all the interactive elements among driver, automobile, and road impact) is achieved. Kontrol Technology is to affect all aspects of global standards of outstanding tires in terms of product functionality, safety, sense of touch, environmental friendliness, and value. Creative and practical HT design and technology receive a very good response from global markets and many overseas partners show interest in technology transfer. Six percent of HT's employees are dedicated to R&D, and 5% of its revenues are invested in R&D. Its R&D offices are located in Korea, China, Japan, Germany, and the United States. HT's R&D investment reaps the benefits in the form of top product awards and highly favorable reviews from recent German professional automotive business periodicals. HT's Bentus Tire was selected as the best product by *AutoBild* in 2008 and *Auto Zeitung*. Auto Motor and Sport awarded Bentus Tire the sole top brand award. J.D. Power tire customer surveys reported that in terms of customer satisfaction it was tenth in 2004 but in

2007 it moved up to the fifth most satisfying brand, outperforming global leader brand Bridgestone.

In particular, in view of 2003 and its successful transformation as a market-driven company, HT was featured as one of the outstanding 250 global consumer goods enterprises in 2008 by Deloitte, a global business consulting firm. In keeping ahead of the automotive industry trend, HT has engaged in eco-friendly R&D efforts for years. In 2006 HT was certified with the Swedish eco-friendly "Nordic Ecolabel." After 2.5 years of investment of $11 million, in 2007 HT introduced a new product "Enfren," which is characterized by a vast improvement in fuel efficiency and a drastic reduction in carbon dioxide emissions. HT's Enfren eco Eco-Friendly All-Season Performance tire also received the highest rating certified by the Korea Energy Management Corporation (KEMCO) for Energy Efficiency Grade for Tires (based on its rolling resistance)—the first-ever achievement for any tire in Korea. Enfren eco also set a new standard in Japan for eco-friendly tires by receiving the highest mark, AAA (by rolling resistance), possible under the labeling system measuring the fuel efficiency of tires—a feat no other international brand in the market had previously achieved.

It is designed specifically for fuel-efficient and hybrid vehicles and features a high silica rubber tread compound that lowers rolling resistance by 21%, increases wet and dry handling, and helps to improve fuel economy. The actual fuel saving per year is about $400. Furthermore, for every 1 km, carbon dioxide emission is decreased by 4.1 g. For 10 years of an estimated driving distance of 200,000 km, the total effect of CO_2 reduction is 820 kg, and thus its impact on environmental protection is outstanding. "Enfren" is the abbreviation of "environment friendly" and besides its eco-friendly product name, it shows outstanding benefits in terms of safety performance, personal comfort, and smooth driving. HT's continuous efforts to introduce eco-friendly products resulted in Optimo 4S (i.e., an all four seasons tire), which received the certification of Blue Angel by the Federal German Environmental Agency—the only tire among all global tires—May 2008.

In 2009, *AutoBild*, the world best automobile periodical along with *ADAC*, reported HT's Optimo 4S as the best of the global nine leading brands. HT's Bentus S1 evo was recognized as the world's best performing tire by *Auto Bild Sportscars*, *Sport Auto*, and *Auto Zeitung* (Germany's leading automobile periodical) in 2008. CEO Seo said, "HT's Icebear W440 and Optimo 4S are developed based on Kontrol Technology (i.e., the synergy of HT's technology development-orientation and its unique business philosophies) to perform well even in the worst weather condition" (Kim, 2009).

10.4.4 Strategic Alliance

In the 1970s HT formed a technology transfer contract with Yokohama of Japan, the seventh-largest tire manufacturer. However, by 1998, as the results of its vigorous R&D efforts for years, HT's Research Office recommended the discontinuation of such a relationship with Yokohama. In 2003, HT entered a strategic alliance with Michelin, the global top tire maker. Based on HT's sense of confidence on technology management, it strengthened marketing initiatives from 2000. In spite of the outstanding quality and product performance, HT's brand was not so high in the global market. In 2004, HT's CEO said, "For the next level of strategic leap, HT needs to raise up its brand recognition" (Kim, 2009). For this, HT expanded its exposure through sports marketing through sponsorship of professional baseball and basketball games and consistently increased its global advertising campaign.

As an effort of such initiative, HT engaged in joint marketing with diverse companies such as Kia Motor Company and Sony Computer Entertainment Korea. In 2008, HT participated in a joint marketing campaign with Kia which was to promote the new model, Porte Moving Studio along Bentus S1 Noble, HT's new product. HT plans to continue such joint marketing efforts with other global firms to enhance its brand image that is connected with other outstanding global brands.

10.4.5 Global Market

HT has 14,000 employees worldwide and 70% of its sales are from the global markets outside of Korea. According to the report of *Modern Tire Dealer*, a US tire periodical, in the January 2009 issue, HT was the seventh largest in the world and third biggest Asian tire firm in terms of annual sales. HT markets its products to 185 nations, 4 continental headquarters, and 20 overseas offices through global marketing initiatives based on strong localization. Five R&D centers maintain global technology leadership. Through five production centers in three nations (i.e., one in Korea, two in China, and one in Hungary), HT focuses on serving its global customers with high-quality tire products. By 2010, the annual production goal was 10 million tire units. With $250 million of investment in the Korean Keumsan Plan, the goal of the annual tire production volume was 5 million by the end of 2009. The future production plant location is countries in South East Asia (e.g., Thailand, Vietnam, and Indonesia).

HT China achieved the number one position in market share of passenger car tires within 4 years of its operations. The sales also increased almost four times in 2007 ($916 million) compared to 2002 ($238 million). HT's senior manager said, "Our early success is partly because we approached Chinese market through thorough market research. Another reasons are strategic relationship with OEM (Original Equipment Manufacturers) (e.g., Changchoon First Automotive and Shanghai Volkswagen) and aggressive domestic distribution network." HT China supplies its products to 40 automotive manufacturers such as GM, FAW, Volkswagen, Beijing Hyundai, and Nanjing Fiat. HT achieved global sales in their tire product line in 2009 ($4.8 million sales and 549,300 net profit), which suggested healthy growth even in the midst of a global recession.

HT achieved its historic record of sales in 2009 because of (1) drastic increases of completed-car production volumes in China and (2) reliable production from the Hungary plant established in 2007 and growth of the EU market. Also, there was a demand surge for HT's ultra-high performance tire (UHPT), which has received excellent market acceptance for its reputation for high quality and performance in the global markets. In particular, in 2009 HT's domestic sale (Korea) of UHPTs was 72% above the previous year's sale. With its steady supply to the premium quality automobile manufacturers such as Audi and Volkswagen, HT's global sales also showed an impressive 129% increase compared to the previous year.

From 2010, HT has concentrated on marketing UHPT and other eco-friendly products in emerging markets (e.g., Latin America and CIS). In 2013, HT attained sales of $7 billion (Oh, 2014). With HT's unique Control Technology, it will continue to enhance its global brand power and establish its market leadership through eco-friendly and fuel-efficient products, effective distribution network, and global marketing campaigns (e.g., popular professional sports marketing).

10.5 CONCLUSION

In this chapter we examined the SCM strategy of Korean global firms in three different industries (i.e., electronics, automotive, and tire) in China. All these firms are similar in their successful localization efforts. With a deep understanding of rapidly growing emerging markets, these firms strategically align with Chinese government policy changes and dynamic customer requirements. These firms develop their supply chain capabilities through integrating affiliated Korean suppliers, and local Chinese suppliers, and outsourcing arrangements using effective operational and social control mechanisms (Kang et al., 2012, 2014). With the IT evolution, big data utilization supports developing innovative business models that are instrumental to develop and deploy outstanding products that are cost-competitive, with reliable delivery and excellent quality.

11

Strategies of Korean Firms
in the Indian Market

This chapter explains the localization strategy of Korean firms (e.g., Hyundai, LG, and Samsung). It is crucial for global firms to translate their home-based technology competence into emerging-market-driven technology competence. The real key for success in emerging markets such as India is to offer products that fit the needs of customers in a local area. Korean firms utilized sensing competence first. Through leverage of market competence, they extended their technology competence.

11.1 INTRODUCTION

This chapter explains the localization strategy of Korean firms (e.g., Hyundai, LG, and Samsung). It is crucial for global firms to translate their home-based technology competence into emerging-market-driven technology competence. The real key for success in emerging markets such as India is to offer products that fit the needs of customers in a local area. Korean firms first utilized sensing competence. Through leverage of market competence, they extended their technology competence. In a turbulent competitive environment, the key for sustainable competitive advantage is to consistently offer differentiated products and services to complex global market segments (Ulaga and Eggert, 2006; Skarp and Gadde, 2008). However, pioneering emerging markets require different market approaches than past North American or European market-based strategies.

Korean global firms have been catching up with Japanese rivals. Recognizing the limitation of the small domestic market in Korea, these firms targeted a much larger global market and thus changed their focus in their product development strategies (Park, 2009; Park and Amano, 2011; Park and Shintaku, 2014). In other words, they adopted a different market strategy for emerging economies. The real challenge of the localization strategy of these global firms is how to maintain their organizational integrity while offering products and services that fit the complexity and scale of global market demand.

Korean global firms have experienced success as they moved away from their narrow domestic market and pursued a localization strategy in different segments of global markets. In particular, their success in India is a classic case. In this chapter, we present the cases of localization strategy of Korean firms in the Indian context. We specifically focus on the cases of three global firms from Korea—Hyundai Motor Company, LG Electronics, and Samsung Electronics.

11.2 HISTORICAL BACKGROUND OF KOREAN FIRMS' ENTRANCE TO INDIA

For a long time, India remained somewhat unfamiliar to Korean firms. India's tropical monsoon weather, its location in Southeast Asia, and cultural and religious diversity all made the Korean people less likely to pursue potential business opportunities. India is the second largest country in terms of population next to China, with the seventh largest land size. Most of the people (more than 80%) profess the Hindu faith. It covers the huge areas from the Himalayan Mountains covered with snow in the north to the tropical forest regions in the south. India has 14 common languages including Hindi and English. India became independent in 1947 after 200 years of colonial rule by England. By 1980 it became obvious that India's inward-looking economic growth policies had not necessarily resulted in systematic infrastructure efficiencies and adequate global competitiveness of Indian firms. However, since Rao, the Prime Minister installed in June 1991, pronounced the liberal and open economic reform policies, India showed an annual average growth rate of 6%. By the mid-2000s its growth rate increased to 9% per year. In 2008, India also experienced somewhat of a slowdown in the annual growth rate below 7% due to price increases of raw materials and economic recessions in the United States, Europe, and Japan. From 2009 on, it was expected that the economic growth rate would exceed 7% per year (Park, 2009).

Korea and India established a formal diplomatic relationship in December 1973. Since then, Korean firms regarded India as a strategic major market and took steps to develop partnerships with Indian firms. In September 2008 Korea and India formed a Comprehensive Economic Partnership Agreement (CEPA) after 12 bilateral negotiations and after resolving serious disputes in regard to trade conditions of a broad level of products and services. Through due legislative processes of both countries, CEPA has become effective since 2010 (Cho, 2008; Park, 2011b). Korea's export to India was about 0.8% of its total global export amounts as of 2000 and since then it shows a consistent upward growth trend. Korea's import from India also suggests a steady increase from 0.7% of the total global important volumes (SERI, 2007). The investment status indicates that after the mid-2000s, overall bilateral trade and direct investment are expected to grow further. Korean global firms take the lead for investment in the Indian market. Since the late 1990s, these Korean global firms (e.g., Hyundai, LG, and Samsung) engaged in aggressive investment. Both LG and Samsung maintain market leadership in India in household goods and flat panel display (FPD) TV. Over the years Hyundai has positioned itself as the number two auto manufacturer in India in terms of production and its product lines such as Santro, Verna, i10, i20, and Sonata, which all show top record sales. In terms of investment amounts, more than 90% from Korea is from Korean large global firms (i.e., global firm investment orientation) in India. More than 80% of investment is concentrated in the manufacturing sector. In this chapter, the focus is on the localization strategies of three Korean global firms in India.

11.3 LOCALIZATION STRATEGY OF HYUNDAI MOTOR INDIA (HMI)

Foreign firms become successful in the Indian market as they consider unique cultural contexts and develop their products and work with the native leadership. For example, Nokia dominated the mobile market in India with more than 70% of market share until the mid-2000s. It added several crucial functionality options (e.g., dust-free number button, nonslippery hand grip, internal flash function) and secured market leadership. Nokia developed such a model after learning that hundreds of thousands of truck drivers often have to use mobile phones on dark highway roads for frequent stops without proper lighting. Hyundai Motor, Samsung, and LG also are successful in India because they have developed their marketing strategies in response to unique Indian customer requirements. In the next section, we discuss localization strategies of Korean firms.

11.3.1 Investment Goals in Indian Context

With Prime Minister Rao's economic liberalization policy, the automobile market was also open in India. Several global firms rushed into India. In 1983, the Indian government and Japanese Suzuki established Maruti Suzuki as a joint venture firm. Since then, India's automobile industry was infused with a great deal of energy. Hyundai Motor Company (HMC) could not afford to lose the investment potential in India. In 1996, HMC leadership predicted that in view of the high rate of growth in gross domestic product (GDP), India's potential for automotive market would be enormous. Thus, HMC decided to move into India to capitalize on the huge domestic market and use its production plants there as a solid global export base. In May 1996 HMC received the approval of the Indian government for the right for business operations. In October of the same year construction of the first plant started; by May 1998 it was completed, and by September 1998 the mass production system was in full swing. The initial investment was $700 million and the Indian government allowed HMC to operate alone without any Indian joint partner. It was unprecedented in that most industries in India were state owned and HMC alone exercised 100% ownership and registered as Hyundai Motor India Ltd. (HMI).

HMC had a bold and speedy decision-making process through which it considered lessons from the failed joint investment experiences of Daewoo, another Korean firm, with another Indian partner and thus it pushed for a single owner investment option. At that time, the maximum allowed ownership ratio for foreign firms was 51%, and thus HMC alone could not claim all the ownership interests. However, HMC, with economies of scale production, achieved more than 70% of the localization target (i.e., utilize the suppliers in India) and within 4 years of its operation. HMC also guaranteed active technology transfer to other Indian suppliers and thus the Indian government gave permission to HMI for 100% of ownership interests.

HMI's single ownership option was crucial for its success in the Indian market. The joint investment option in India required serious collaboration challenges with Indian partners. In fact, Daewoo Motor Company had to abandon its initial investment plans with its inadequate understanding of the Indian market and serious issues with Indian partners. HMI's first plant is located in Chennai in the State of Tamil Nadu in view of multiple advantages in terms of logistics, human resources, infrastructure, and state government support. Tamil Nadu State government provided its wholehearted support in the form of fast administrative priority procedures through which HMI could arrange purchasing of a plant location, getting an investment permit, and securing infrastructure supports (e.g., electricity, industrial water supply, road, and communication network) within a relatively short period of time. Thus, HMI could complete the plant within 17 months instead of the initial prediction of 3 years (SERI, 2007). Hyundai Motor India Ltd. (HMI) is recognized as one of the most successful global investment cases in India. Since HMI exported Santro to Nepal in December 1999, its accumulated export volumes as of 2006 were more than 500,000 cars. At present, HMI exports to more than 60 countries including the European Union, South East Asia, the Middle East, and Central and South America with Santro, Verna, i10, and i20. Santro is the bestselling product line of HMI both in India and the global markets (Park, 2009). By 2001 (after 3 years of operations in India), 67,000 Santros were sold. Its sales recorded the number one position in the greater than 1,000 cc product category. Since then, annual sales were 250,000 (2005), 489,000 (2008), and 600,000 (2010)—domestic sales (247,102) and the remaining were all for global markets.

From its early years HMI introduced new models each year for customer loyalty, reflected the requirements of Indian customers in the new product features, and maintained a 24 hours a day, 365 days a year after-service (AS) system. In marketing areas, HMI's success factors include high quality and sufficient numbers of marketing and service dealerships. In fact, the number of dealerships increased from 320 (2010) to 340 (2011). For remote areas where timely services are not readily available, the number of AS shops increased from 625 to 700. HMI also expanded the scope of collaboration with Indian firms in the areas of joint marketing strategy and development of component parts suppliers.

HMC constructed a second plant in 2007 to respond to the increasing customer demand in India and increased the production capacity to 600,000. As a global auto manufacturer, HMC is developing India as a strategic global production base. The first plant focuses on productions of Santro, Verna, Avante, and Sonata, and the second plant focuses on Santro, i10, and i20, which is the most popular model in India.

11.3.2 Localization Strategy: Local Adaptive Product Development and Marketing Strategy

In the same period, Maruti Suzuki—the joint venture firm by Japanese Suzuki and the Indian government—was maintaining 82% of market share in the small car market in India. HMI challenged Maruti Suzuki's position in 1998 by aggressively marketing Santro. Prior to its massive marketing campaign, HMI conducted detailed market research that suggested that in the mid-sized car market the market potential of a small car with engine displacement less than 1000 cc is enormous. Based on this result, HMI decided on Atoz as its initial production model. Additional market research focused on the special preferences of Indian customers. The customer response to Atoz was not very favorable. Since Atoz's rear feature looked somewhat similar to an auto-mini street taxi, its overall image was somewhat cheap. In light of such market research, HMI began a massive design image improvement. For further examination of road conditions, HMI engineers and managers engaged in road tours of the entire nation. They discovered that the cars must handle various tough circumstances such as (1) in the summer the temperature goes up to 40 Centigrade, (2) most of the roads are not well paved and are very dusty, and (3) in the rainy monsoon season with lack of sewage infrastructure the car has to go through water overflowing roads.

HMI decided to challenge Maruti Suzuki, which was marketing the old models (but remained as the dominant leader with 82% of market share in the small-sized car segment). With its superior position Maruti Suzuki's marketing approach was primarily producer centered, not customer driven. Noticing this, HMI's strategic focus was to develop cars that fit customer preferences, Indian weather, and road conditions while basic model features are similar to what was marketed in Korea.

Another of HMI's strategic priorities was to keep the promise with the Indian government that more than 70% of component parts should be from local suppliers. Since customs on component parts were in the range of 27% to 42%, the parts localization target was important for cost competitiveness. Initially, the defect rates of the main engine and transmission were high, but with systematic technological support, the issues were steadily being resolved. As of 2012, HMI has established a comprehensive supply chain through which more than 90% of component parts of Santro including all the major components (e.g., main engine and transmission) are all procured through suppliers in India. HMI's marketing strategy is highly customer driven and thus, the focus of product lines in India has been small-sized cars, in contrast to its focus on mid-sized cars in North America and Europe. In view of the Indian weather with high temperatures and extreme moisture plus challenging road conditions, HMI strengthened the cooling capability and air conditioning functionality. The enhanced brake power also supported the suspension lifespan.

HMI also made serious efforts in enhancing Santro to be drivable in Indian weather conditions. Once Santro's smooth large scale of production was waiting for final shipment to customers, on the delivery day, an unexpected crisis occurred. Many of the cars waiting for delivery did not start (due to engine failure). Upon investigation the reason was simple—with extreme heat the water in the engine oil was all vaporized and the sulfur element in the engine oil paralyzed the connection lines of the pumps. Later, HMI found the solution by using a carbon substance for coating the rectifiers. Another issue was water damage on the car because of heavy rain in the monsoon season in India. Many customers complained that their cars did not start in the rainy season. That's because of the water damage in the engine control unit (ECU). At first HMI tried to put the ECU in the left side of the car instead of its bottom. HMI developed a car to be waterproof and ECU to be water resistant.

HMI engaged in promotion activities for its brand recognition. Based on the large cities, HMI established its own extensive dealership network and engaged in concerted marketing campaigns. HMI motivated dealers to consider building showrooms for its new models that were still in production. By the early quarters of 1998 HMI invited many dealers to the factory and instilled confidence in their new models. By August 1998, 60 dealers completed showrooms for HMI's new models prior to their market introduction. In this way, HMI prepared both sides of its supply and demand chain network by completing 100% of repair services for component parts and dealership readiness. For marketing and promotion, HMI put forth Shahrukh Khan, a legendary Indian actor, who was enormously popular among the Indian people. As Khan became the advertising model for its products, the once unknown Hyundai's name was widely recognizable. At that time, Indian people did not feel close to Hyundai from Korea. However, Khan's advertising effect was huge. Six sequels of HMI's promotion campaign for Santro launch with Khan in the forefront planted in the Indian mind a very favorable image of Hyundai.

In October 1998, Santro's market introduction started steadily toward a huge success. The initial sales performance was not impressive, yet the nationwide marketing campaigns and excellent customer service received the attention of the customers. After 6 months, its sales quickly picked up. With increasing orders, HMI concentrated in the large scale of production. The nationwide strike of the truck drivers' union resulted in serious component parts shortages. HMI could not afford to stop its production. Thus, HMI deployed other available means of transportation including emergency hospital vehicles and school buses and secured the needed component parts for the production process and fulfilled all delivery order commitments. Through such extraordinary efforts, HMI gained customer confidence through its quality products and reliable delivery performance.

When the emission standards were enforced by the order of India's Supreme Court, HMI's performance was reported as excellent. This event helped the Indian public perceive that Santro was based on cutting edge technological capabilities. Through the initial success of Santro, all its subsequent models (i10 and i20) received very favorable reviews from customers. In 2007 i10 received the Car of the Year Award and in 2008 it received awards in five categories of excellence. From February 2009, HMC opened its global customer-centered websites (http://www.hyundai .com). Its goal was to upgrade with newer content and design features and to integrate country-specific websites for expanding global marketing capabilities and enhancing brand image. HMC's comprehensive strategic coordination (e.g., outstanding front-end preparations and well-executed collaboration in production processes, local market adaptive marketing efforts, and single ownership investment) allowed HMI to experience a huge success in India.

11.3.3 Human Resource (HR) Policies: Develop Native Leaders and Education/Training at Headquarters

HMI has focused on maximizing work productivity and organizational efficiencies through due consideration of India's cultural characteristics (e.g., its social system and religious influence) and implementation of a fair reward system, a scientific task approach, and effective communication. HMI also hired and placed Indian natives in high levels of management leadership and allowed them to assume leading roles in the organization.

Thus, it removed unnecessary conflicts between Korean expatriates and Indian native managers, which in turn motivated the passion and devotion of the Indian managers. Accordingly, HMI provided rigorous education and training to its employees. HMI invites manager trainees in all departments to the Ulsan factory and Korean headquarters and offers necessary education and training for knowledge-intensive work requirements and specific functional skills. Such learning and training processes allow every worker to have a sense of identity and responsibility. HMI has paid special attention to nurturing constructive labor-management relationships. India by law allows multiple labor unions, third-party mediation, political activity involvement, and forbids employee termination without due process.

HMI has formed a labor-management coordinative team with representatives from management and labor, respectively (i.e., 7 from labor and 6 from management—a total of 13 members), and has a formal monthly collaborative meeting. HMI also built a small-scale Hindu temple for employees' religious activities, thus showing respect for Indian culture and religion. From 2009, HMC has implemented a global internship program to support its oversea plants. From 2009 to 2012, HMC had more than 100 interns beyond English-speaking countries such as China, India, Czechoslovakia, and Slovakia. These interns major in the languages of these countries. HMC strategically tries to develop these global marketing talents in advance.

━━━━━━━━━━

11.4 SAMSUNG INDIA ELECTRONICS (SIE)

11.4.1 Investment Context and Strategic Priority

In 1995 when Samsung first set its feet in India, it was not even possible to get an adequate supply of industrial water. However, Samsung paid attention to India's huge market potential. In the early years, it was joint investment with little success. After Samsung was allowed to have sole ownership investment, by 2007, after 13 short years, its market share was LCD TV (44.1%) and monitor market (44.9%). In response to such rapid market growth, Samsung constructed the factory in Noida with an annual production capacity of 1.5 million TV units. In 2007, it also completed another 1.5 million unit TV production capacity plant in Chennai. Dehradun of the north also has an outsourcing plant for air conditioners. With such a large scale of investment, the total TV production capacity in India became 3 million units. In this way,

Samsung completed building a huge supply chain network that covers India and Southeast Asian TV markets.

Samsung allocated $30 million for a plant in Chennai, Tamil/Nadu State of southern India with a total 322,000 m² of plant size. In November 2007, it started actual production. By 2011 Samsung planned to invest the total amount of $100 million for the following 5 years and use it as the production base for Southeast Asian markets. India's TV market shows about 20% annual growth. Samsung also focused on its emerging market strategy through building a massive production base in India, which is the second largest in terms of population with the fourth biggest purchasing power in the world.

Samsung now has 15 large TV production bases in countries like Korea, Mexico, China, Slovakia, Hungary, Thailand, Indonesia, Brazil, Vietnam, India, Russia, and Malaysia. Such an extensive supply chain network is to meet the global digital TV demand and sustain its number one global market leader position. In this context, the role of the Indian market is quite important.

According to GK, a market research firm, Samsung India (SI) has maintained the number one position in LCD TVs from 2006 to 2012 in terms of sales volume. Its aggressive premium product strategy, local market reality-based product development practices, and local production supply network base are contributing such impressive success records. Samsung's mobile phone market share in India is number two—next to Nokia. By 2010, its plan was to expand the production volume up to 20 million and use India as the production base for South East Asian markets. Up to 2007, SI still imported component parts. In 2008, four Korean component parts suppliers decided to invest $5 million to form production clusters in India.

11.4.2 Localization Strategy: Pursuit of FPD TV–Based Premium Strategy

Samsung's localization strategy is premium product strategy based on FPD (flat panel display) TV. From the latter half of 2007, Samsung showed the visible outcomes of its localization strategy in the form of premium products. In 2006, Samsung discontinued marketing the curved brown tube TV and instead focused on LCD and plasma TV marketing for premium products strategy. Samsung transformed its 5,000 marketing and distribution networks including brand sales offices and superstores to carry only plasma and LCD TVs. Among brown tube TVs Samsung increased the display space for SlimFit TV, another premium product line.

In view of the general noise level in India, Samsung enhanced TV speaker volume power, and easy-view functionality by remote control. Samsung also developed India-market-specific SlimFit TV and differentiated its product offerings from its rivals. In the meantime, the CTV market in India is 12.5 million units as of 2008 ($21 billion), and by 2011, 23% annual growth of sales was expected. As of 2008, FPD TVs (i.e., LCD plus plasma TV) annual sales were $5.3 billion (25% total TV market). By 2010, the market grew to $19 billion (more than 50% of total TV market) and in 2011, $28 billion (62% of market share). In this way, the Indian TV market is becoming rapidly premium-TV centered.

Only 5% of India's population is upper-middle class, whereas 40% is a very poor class, with extreme differences between the rich and the poor. With inadequate electricity supply, power failure is quite frequent. Every household electricity product has a voltage stabilization device and refrigerators should have enough ice packs. Such product accommodation to India's reality is crucial for SI's quality performance and customer satisfaction. Samsung also shows impressive records in the product lines of washers and dishwashers. Samsung's washers are popular because of memory functions that remember the status prior to power failures and sensitive treatment functionality of clothes (e.g., India's traditional women's costume—the Shari). With an inadequate supply of water, customers prefer to reuse water and appreciate SI's second-round washing process features.

SI offers both cost-competitive and premium value products. With the integration of localization and premium product strategy, SI successfully implanted the brand image, "Samsung products = premium quality." In November 2007, SI selected Indian Olympic athletes from shooting, archery, and boxing as Samsung's Olympic Dream members and supported their expenses to the Beijing Olympic games and thus used sports marketing for Samsung brand awareness.

Samsung's R&D efforts include Samsung India Software Center (SISC), which is one of the primary Samsung's global R&D centers. From SISC, Samsung develops cutting-edge technologies for the LCD collar TV, camcorder, computer, and MP3. In particular, SISC successfully developed TV's high-definition and multimedia interfaces plus multimedia slots for LCD TV for global market leadership. Samsung increased R&D personnel from 300 to 400. As of 2010, more than 1,000 people would be placed in R&D areas.

In addition, Samsung maintains SISO (Samsung India Software Operations) in Bangalore. SISO specializes in diverse areas of technology development such as wireless terminal, network infra, networking Soc (system on chip), digital printing, image solutions, multimedia, memory and communication technology whereas SISC concentrates on digital media products. As of 2010, 450 patent applications were submitted. Fifty percent of SISO researchers are engineers from prestigious Indian engineering schools like IIT.

Samsung also regards India as the global component parts supply base center. A key criterion for supplier selection in India is price. Samsung also develops a training program for its electronic component parts production. Based on its experiences with Indian firms, Samsung applies similar training programs to other Samsung factories in Indonesia, Korea, and China in relation to quality control and production processes.

11.4.3 HR Policy of Management–Employee Relationships: Continuous Improvement by Field Employees

Samsung India Electronics (SIE) encourages the suggestions of its employees for quality and productivity enhancements. Each year more than 60,000 suggestions are submitted. Anyone whose suggestions are of value for quality and cost reduction efforts receives 500 to 20,000 rupees. For a TV assembly line, employees usually receive 3 weeks of training. Each TV team assembly line has 15 members and one female employee assembles four component parts simultaneously. In India, women are not allowed to work beyond 8:00 p.m. SIE considers using male employees in view of such labor hour restrictions for women. In general, SIE's proactive initiatives make Indian workers' productivity relatively higher than other overseas plants.

The authors' actual observation in a Noida color TV plant suggests that its productivity is higher than any other plants including those in Korea. Between 2004 and 2006 it received for 3 consecutive years the Manufacturing Value Innovation Award. Since 2006, SIE welcomed 56 engineers from Vietnam, Mexico, Thailand, Malaysia, and Hungary for the benchmarking purpose of Indian plant's productivity performance. Ten or more SIE engineers were also sent to other overseas plants to offer training for other plants in other countries.

In Samsung's Korean headquarters, more than 120 Indian engineers are working as regular employees. At least 250 engineers are in short-term projects. Through continuous innovation activities, SIE sustains a high level of productivity in India and other areas are quite interested in learning the secrets of such high performance. Behind such impressive records, the outstanding leadership of the CEO of SI who has had extensive experience in Korea, Mexico, and Bangladesh TV plants should certainly be noted.

11.5 LG ELECTRONICS INDIA (LGEI)

11.5.1 Investment Contexts and Strategic Priority

India's 28 large states are almost like individual nations with amazing variety and diversity. The two common languages are Hindi and English. Its constitution formally recognizes 19 languages. In such an incredible environment, LG is successful with its "bare feet running management styles." LGEI is a subsidiary of LG, which has 100% ownership. Established in 1997, LGEI is the number one household electronics firm in India through its highly popular product lines such as the color TV, electronic range, washer, and air conditioner. LGEI's Noida plant is in New Delhi for targeting Northeastern India. Its second plant is in the region of Pune near Mumbai with the Southwestern India market. Both of these plants produce GSM mobile phones, TVs, refrigerators, air conditioners, and washers. The third plant is under construction. For the development of outstanding R&D resources, LGEI established a software research institute in Bangalore.

In 1997 LG Electronics formed LEGI in India with an initial investment of $30 million. Within 9 years the total assets increased to $500 million. The total sales were $1.8 billion (2005) and $2.1 billion (2008). As of 2008, the total number of employees was 3,527 of which consited of 27 Korean managers and 3,500 Indian employees. The total number of dealers was 2,000 (as of 2008), distribution centers 150 (2008), and service stations 1,100 (2005). LG has built distribution and service infrastructure networks just like well-connected blood vessel lines all over India.

LG's market share is number one in major products such as color TVs, refrigerators, washers, air conditioners, electronic ranges, and DVD players. LG also maintains one of the top three market leaders in PCs, monitors, and mobile phones (GSM). The level of trust and appreciation of LG products among Indian customers is quite phenomenal. LG management considers three important factors for LG's market success in India: (1) producing global premium quality products, (2) localization efforts, and (3) a strong dealer network that covers rural areas. In the next section, we will discuss a further localization strategy.

11.5.2 Localization Strategy: Customer-Driven Marketing and Premium Product Strategy

LG India (LGI) is well known for its marketing strategy that builds on India's unique cultural tastes and national sensibilities. By 1997 LGI invested to establish its own brand with its 70 different product lines. For all the new product development efforts, LGI's long-term focus was to establish the brand image that its Korean technological capabilities translates India's deeply held cultural values and customer preferences into excellent products.

Prior to LGEI's entry to India, Sony was the only global household electronics firm in India. After establishing LGEI as a sole ownership business entity, LGEI produced products as an OEM with a vast network of Indian suppliers. Since the productivity of Indian suppliers remained below LG's global standards, LGEI deployed its senior-level managers on the production floors, working and eating together with the Indian workers and tried to discover the root causes of production-related issues. Through such intensive engagement, there was real change in Indian managers and workers in regard to work attitudes and drastic productivity improvement followed.

India uses at least 10 different region-unique languages. LGEI added language channel features for Indian customers to choose any of 10 different languages. It was a huge success. Sony, on the other hand, adopted the product strategy that merely sells the old Japanese models in India. The responses of Indian customers were not as favorable as those toward LG products. In general, India's electricity is in short supply and the voltage power is unstable. Thus, there were frequent accidents involving TV condenser explosions. LGEI, thus, developed a special condenser that can endure unstable voltage flows and attached it to its TV. In such a way, LGEI developed component parts that fit India's unique circumstances.

LGEI also empowered native Indian managers for all marketing efforts. LGEI recruited and developed Indian managers who knew customer preferences, tastes, and requirements. These managers were allowed to handle 99.9% of marketing responsibilities along with corresponding decision-making authorities. LGEI also developed drum-based washers and dishwashers with direct drive functionalities. LGEI imported component parts for dishwashers from Korea and assembled them in India with CKD methods. On the first day of sales, 4,000 dishwashers were sold. At that time, they were priced from 40,000 to 80,000 rupees. Drum-based washers are produced at the Pune plant. LGEI stresses the product's strength in terms of washing time and water usage reductions and extends product warranties up to 7 years beyond the 2-year warranties that its competitors offer. LG's mobile phones have higher speaker volumes considering the substantial noise level (similar to Central and South America) in the road environments in India. LGEI's refrigerators offer 21 color variations and various flower feature designs that Indian people like. In view of the dusty environment in India, refrigerators or air conditioners are not sold in a white color. LGEI also provided additional accommodations such as a door lock function for refrigerators and utility receipt cases for storing valuables such as women's cosmetics items.

By the end of 2010, LGEI also developed refrigerators with one door only, which are in premium quality at low prices. Such spacious refrigerators are popular for vegetarian Indians who prefer to store a large amount of fresh vegetables. LGEI's success has a lot to do with its unique product development efforts that serve the crucial needs of customers. For this purpose, as of 2010 more than 400 people are working in the areas of R&D. In LGEI more than 4,000 Indian employees are working together with no more than a handful of Korean managers. In particular, Indian managers assume leadership positions in the Pune plant.

In the meantime, LGEI also supports healthcare services to serve the needs of people in the region in the Noida industrial complex. Doctors, pharmacists, and nurses provide free medical services for people at large. LGEI also works toward constructing such healthcare facilities at the Pune region where its second plant is located. In this way, LGEI realizes a localization strategy through empowering Indian managers and serves the larger public through socially responsible healthcare services both through service centers and mobile vans.

LG's effective sports marketing is worth mentioning here. LG has been sponsoring Cricket tournaments for more than 10 years and raised its brand awareness among Indian customers. In a sense, Samsung engages in a massive global scale of sports marketing whereas LG prefers country-specific sports marketing. For example, Samsung invests its resources by supporting the Chelsea soccer team to reach out to Europe for brand marketing. LG, in contrast, selects particular countries for highly focused advertising and promotional campaigns. Among them, since 1999 LG has sponsored the Cricket World Cup that has been held in South Africa, India, and Thailand. LG is proud of sponsoring India-specific games like Cricket

World Cup well ahead of its rival Samsung. Samsung, with its enormous financial resources, support the global sports events through sponsoring particular teams and sports events. On the other hand, LG pays more personalized attention to sporting events—one at a time. Specifically, LG engaged in marketing activities that support the national cricket tournaments that are highly popular to Indians. They also translated their cricket fervor into favoring LG products by embedding cricket games within all LG TVs. Another reason for LGEI's success in India was its careful target on the affluent upper-middle class. In its early years LG focused on the top 5% of the upper-middle class with high premium prices. Their purchasing power and consumer behaviors affected the other new customers who later joined as buyers of LG products. Finally, a logistics and services network was constructed that is well connected like a cobweb structure. From its early years of operation LG established 18 regional offices. Later, its enlarged service and logistics infranetwork included 1,800 distribution centers and 85 service centers. In contrast to other foreign firms that pay relatively inadequate attention, LG allocated half of its Korean managers for specialized after-services. LG also utilized a professional female workforce for sales efforts and recruited highly qualified talented women. LG's women sales force system was new in Indian business practices, which certainly contributed to the sales and distribution of its broad ranges of products to Indian affluent and affording customers.

11.5.3 HR Policy and Management–Employee Relationships: Native Leadership and Incentive Systems

Another of LGEI's success factors is empowerment of native human resources. Indian managers take charge of organizations in LG India. Directors of marketing and human resources are native Indians. Korean executives focus primarily on production and finance. Indian native leaders handle the areas of marketing products and services for their customers. Incentive systems are mostly performance based. Indians prefer objective evaluation criteria. For example, IT firms that have many IT experts announce the performance criteria on the office websites in advance and conduct actual evaluations accordingly. LGEI adopted an incentive bonus system (0% to 1,600%) based on the performance outcomes of each employee from 1990 to 2007. In fact, 5% and 15% of employees receive 0% and 1,600% of incentives. From 2008, this system was modified and the incentive ranged from 0% to 200%.

11.6 CONCLUSION

In this chapter, we have examined the localization strategy of Korean global firms in India. It is worthy to mention the differences of strategy practices between Korean and Japanese global firms in India. Korean global firms started their localization strategy from the mid-1990s. Initially, their focus was on the domestic market (i.e., India) and from the mid-1990s they expanded to the global markets beyond India. The three cases of Korean firms discussed in this chapter represent successful examples of localization in India. Hyundai's and Samsung's localization strategies show strong leadership from Korean headquarters while LG seems to emphasize developing Indian local leadership. Thus, not all Korean firms take similar patterns of localization strategy, and in fact, unique corporate cultures more or less impact the nature and scope of localization.

The domestic market contributes largely to the growth of the Indian economy. More than 60% of the annual growth rate is attributed to domestic consumption. The size of India's consumer market shows rapid growth each year. The demographics of the Indian consumer market also indicate real changes in terms of total disposable income and formation of distinct (i.e., upper, middle, and lower) income distribution. In the past the center of the premium market used to be the traditional upper-middle class of an older age group. At present, the center is moving toward an upper-middle class of a younger generation. These influential income groups are characterized by "strong nuclear family value commitment." This generation is also called "Generation Me" (*LG Weekly Economy*, January 31, 2007). India's median age is 25.4 and more than 70% of the population is under 35 years of age. In this sense, India is the youngest nation in the world. As a vast number of the poor and young imitate the consumption patterns and lifestyles of upper- and middle-income classes, new consumer trends are expected to spread at a record speed. Thus, it would be crucial for firms to develop new products that appeal to and satisfy the tastes, cultures, and styles of the emerging generation of ambitious, young, affluent, and trendy consumers.

12

Strategies of Korean Firms
in the Brazilian Market

LG and Samsung have effectively executed their global market penetration strategies through empowered local human resources. This section examines LG's and Samsung's global marketing and global supply chain management with a particular focus on the Brazilian market. In view of the accelerating needs of infrastructure building (e.g., roads, ports, and railroads), the global strategies of global Korean construction firms are also noteworthy in the form of consortium formation and network building.

12.1 INTRODUCTION

LG and Samsung have effectively executed their global market penetration strategies through empowered local human resources. This section examines LG and Samsung's global marketing and global supply chain management with a particular focus on the Brazilian market. In view of the accelerating needs for infrastructure investment (e.g., roads, ports, and railroads), the global strategies of global Korean construction firms are also noteworthy in the form of consortium formation and network building. The competitive position of Korean firms in the BRICs market—particularly in China and India—is noteworthy. Similar patterns of growth of Korean global firms in Brazil are also observed in Brazil. Thus, the focus of this chapter is the localization strategy of Korean global firms in the Brazilian market.

12.2 STATUS OF KOREAN FIRMS IN BRAZIL

Korea and Brazil established a formal diplomatic relationship in 1959. For years there had been little progress in an economic partnership. Yet, since 1990, these two nations have made significant economic, political, and cultural interactions. In recognition of increasing trade volumes between Korea and Brazil, in 1996, Kim Youngsam, then the Korean president, made an official visit to Brazil. For more vigorous and diverse engagements the heads of two states agreed to form a twenty-first century committee that remained active until 1999. However, for a long time the Brazilian government's overall Asian policy was mostly focused on China and Japan. In 2001, Fernando Henrique Cardoso became the first Brazilian president that visited Korea for an official visit and there was a real turning point for strategic relationships between two nations.

The scope of products that Korean firms offer in Brazilian market include TV, computers, mobile phones, LCD, pharmaceuticals, and textiles goods. Just as in China and India, major Korean global firms made a big stride in Brazil as well. From 1995, Korean firms showed their visible market presence in Brazil. After 2004, Korean firms expanded to other neighboring nations near Brazil (e.g., Argentina, Peru, and Chile). The names of major Korean global firms that are active in Brazil are electronics firms (e.g., Samsung and LG), steel manufacturers (e.g., POSCO), and automotive manufacturers (e.g., Hyundai). The main reason for these firms' entry to Brazil is for local production to avoid high tariffs. In particular, their presence in the areas of Manaus was mostly for tax incentives. For example, in Manaus, these firms receive special treatments for corporate tax, manufacturing product tax, customs, product distribution service tax, PIS/COFINS, and city tax.

12.3 LOCALIZATION STRATEGY OF KOREAN FIRMS IN BRAZIL

In 1995 a Korean electronics firm put their feet in the Manaus region. Like Japanese rivals, Korean global firms also chose Manaus for tax incentives. For example, LG started its operations in Manaus in 1995 and started manufacturing TVs, VTRs, and electronic ranges. Samsung also started in almost the same period. At this time, both LG and Samsung were searching for new markets beyond North America and the European Union. At this time, they thus entered India as well. With the Asian Financial Crisis that hit Korea, many Korean firms were subject to International Monetary Fund (IMF) management control. Thus, Korean firms had no extra capital to stretch their operations in these emerging markets. So Samsung, for example, withdrew all its business units except PCs, from Brazil. Around 2000, Korea finally overcame the financial crisis ("IMF Crisis"). These Korean firms started their massive investment in Brazil. Samsung, thus, established a TV brown tube plant in Brazil. In the same period, Samsung constructed similar plants in Malaysia and China. Samsung's brown tube plant supported TV manufacturers in Manaus.

In the meantime, LG started DVD production in 1999. By 2001 it established the second plant in Manaus. In the 2000s Korean firms targeted São Paulo, the largest Brazilian market base, and constructed a plant for information communication equipment products. Within a 2-hour driving distance from São Paulo, Samsung set up the Campinas plant for mobile phones and information communication product items. LG also built another plant in Taubate, 130 km away from São Paulo for diverse lines of monitors and mobile phones.

In this period, Japanese electronics firms showed poor market performance in Brazil and their available capital was quite limited (Ooki et al., 2010). As Japanese firms became somewhat passive in their market strategy, Korean firms aggressively expanded their production capability near São Paulo and secured their market advantage in a relatively short time. These Korean firms quickly responded to the changing market reality through their facts and bold investment decisions. As the market demanded LCD TVs from 2006, LG and Samsung developed huge production capacity. By 2010 Samsung and LG's LCD TV market share in Brazil was more than 60%. Even for the entire TV market, Samsung and LG maintain the number one and two market leader positions with their combined total 30% of market share. In the brown tube TV era, Japanese firms such as Sharp and Toshiba had a high market share. As the market switched to LCD TV, the market leadership was transferred to Korean firms.

Furthermore, in the 2000s there was a mobile phone boom in Latin America. Korean firms responded well to these emerging product markets and established product recognition among Brazilian customers. For mobile phones, Samsung and LG are fiercely competing with Nokia for market leadership. Samsung has held the top position since 2010. The majority of production volumes of mobile phones are handled in the plants around São Paulo (i.e., Campinas and Taubate). At present, the production base of PC monitors and other electronics items is also nearby São Paulo. Since they have two factories in Manaus and São Paulo areas, these Korean firms can adjust the production volume of these products according to changing tax incentives.

Samsung and LG are unique in that the history of their operations, the scope of global supply chain management, their localization dimensions, and the impacts of their strategic and operational management are noteworthy, for example, in 1995 when Korean electronics firms arrived at the region of Manaus, Brazil. Like Japanese firms, Korean firms chose this region for a preferential tax advantage. For example, LG built its manufacturing plants (e.g., TV, VTR, electronic ranges). Samsung started its operations in the same time period. At that time, these two Korean firms decided to target emerging markets (India and Brazil) other than North American and European markets.

As soon as they started their operations in Brazil, the Asian Financial Crisis hit Korea very hard. Samsung withdrew from Brazil all other business lines except PCs. However, LG Electronics decided to stay. After 2000, Samsung aggressively made investments and established a TV brown tube manufacturing plant. This plant supplied brown tubes to TV manufacturers in Brazil and contributed to the economic growth of the Manaus region. LG's first plant started DVD production in 1999 and in 2001 a second plant was established in Manaus. For the purpose of targeting the São Paulo area which is the largest Brazilian market, Samsung also constructed mobile phone manufacturing plants in Campinas that are 2 hours driving distance away from São Paulo. LG also built its plants in Taubate, which is 130 km away from São Paulo and produces various sizes of monitors and mobile phones. In this period, Japanese electronics firms did poorly and their financial resources were tight (Ooki et al., 2010). When Japanese firms were somewhat passive, Korean firms in contrast made heavy investment in Manaus and São Paulo areas and thus established market advantage. Korean firms in particular made timely investment decisions in response to rapid market changes and thus attained outstanding market growth rates. At this point, the combined market share of LCD TV by Samsung and LG is 60%. They also maintain the top two positions in the mobile phone market as well.

12.3.1 Samsung Brazil

By 2010, Samsung attained the number one position in Brazil for LED TV (42%), 3D LED TV (63%), mobile phones (33%), monitors (40%), HDD (51%), and printers (34%). By 2010 the total sales of Samsung Electronics in Brazil were $4 billion, which is more than 50% growth compared to 2009 and thus more than 60% of Latin American sales are from Brazil alone. It is expected that after 2011 Samsung will maintain 50% plus growth in the Brazilian market.

It is worthy to note Samsung's supply chain management strategy for TV and mobile phones. Samsung's branding strategy is to clarify the message, "Samsung products = cutting-edge products" and thus the target market segment is high income groups. Its promotional efforts are geared toward airport and road signs, major event promotions, and high-class department stores.

In view of two market segments (i.e., high premium product and low priced markets) in Brazil, Samsung's new product development strategy of LCD TV monitors is consistently toward high quality and premium products. Among its full product lines of 15-, 17-, 18-, 19-, 21-, 24-inch TVs, the highest demand is for 15-inch TVs. For its distribution strategy, Samsung uses channels for high premium products with total services offerings, and its products are visibly available in major airports, shopping centers, high-class hotels, and professional soccer playing events.

Electronic products with their relatively short product life cycles require rapid systematic responses and yet Japanese management is not quite strong in this area. In consultations of experts Samsung takes deep consideration of cultural sentiments and changing tastes of people in Brazil. Rapid decision making and clear role definitions are also key strengths. Samsung supports timely decision-making processes through effective information flows via Galaxy smartphones for every employee since 2009.

Success factors of Samsung mobile phones are worthy to examine. First, marketing and production integration efforts are important successful factors. SCM integration from 2008 is to connect Samsung's marketing and production functions. Average components inventories are no more than 3 to 4 days and such inventory level reduction affected its pricing strategy. With ESCM, Samsung's production and marketing plans are completely integrated. Besides, large-scale field distribution centers are all connected with EDI, and daily real-time sales volumes are available as well. With such SCM integration basic mobile models are specialized into

50 and the total number of models including all the derivatives is no more than 300. Samsung's customization strategies serve four communication business leaders. Such small total model numbers have impacted overall cost reduction as well. Since the product life cycle of the mobile phone is relatively short and the logistical time requirements (in view of Brazil's vast land size) are quite long, small numbers of models control change of scope and thus attain cost efficiency.

Second, sensible and timely local needs-based product development practices are noteworthy. For example, Brazil Samsung developed mobile phones that are capable of handling 20-digit Brazilian employee identification numbers through its mobile phone camera and immediate deposit options.

Third, it built effective global supply chain management supported by strong social-culture sensitive marketing and promotional programs. For local market orientation, Samsung made serious efforts to recruit and keep high-quality human resources. Advertising and promotional activities are well-coordinated along with its effective operations and integrative supply chain system.

Product design of mobile phone hardware is done in Korean head offices, and component parts are freely selected from local areas. Thus, Samsung Brazil achieves low-cost production through using component parts from local suppliers while premium branding strategy allows its products to be well accepted throughout Latin American countries with 570 million potential customers. Samsung Brazil also marketed highly differentiated products with unique functionalities. In April 2008 Samsung first introduced a TV-phone (SGH-V820L) and several touch-phone models (GT-S5230). Thus, it has become a technological trend set leader with distinctive premium brands. Samsung also enacted dual SIM mobile phones that allow users to have dual phone numbers for private and social life usages and thus attained 40% high market growth rate.

In August 2010, 33 miners experienced a major industrial accident in San Jose, Chile. Samsung delivered a beam project phone (GT-i7410) through which these miners were able to watch their family programs and soccer games. Such a social service effort has reaped huge unexpected goodwill and brand image. Samsung also supported cultural events in the name of Samsung Live with Brazilian top actors including Tania Kalil for 1 month in 2009 along with Brazil's largest communication firm Vivo and Claro. In this way, Samsung's premium brand image has been established in Brazil and Latin America.

12.3.2 LG Brazil

LG Electronics (LGE) established two plants: LGEAZ (LG Electronics da Amazonia Ltda at Manaus—the center of the Amazon region) and LGESP (LG Electronics de São Paulo Ltda at Taubate near São Paulo) since 1995. Over the years LG Electronics integrated all business processes including product development, production, marketing, and after-services. Three recent years' growth rate is about 35% per year. Some of the products from these two plants occupy the top market position in Brazil. The market share of LCD and plasma TVs is more than 30% and plasma display even reaches 50%. LCD monitors, general monitors, and air conditioners are doing very well not only in Brazil but also in other South American countries—particularly Argentina and Chile. Then what are key success factors of LG's rapid market growth?

First, LGE turned a crisis into an opportunity for growth in Brazil. In its early years, customers had little awareness of the LG brand and product positioning was a real challenge. LGE considered the amazing market growth potential in Brazil. It went through serious financial and business restructuring and committed to substantial long-term and strategic investment and established itself as a solid global firm in Brazil.

Second, LG focused on its business image based on brand advertising. LG recognized the long-term efforts required to establish a distinct brand image in the minds of consumers through consistent investment management and differentiated marketing and communication strategies.

Third, LG offered unique after-services and focused on strategic logistical centers. Brazil LG established highly visible large distribution centers at the strategic locations (e.g., Porto Alegre, Say Paulo, Rio de Janeiro, Salvador) and provided extensive support and growth incentives.

Fourth, oral effect advertisement and strategic partnership were done. Each distribution center secured LG Digital Space in which the most recent cutting-edge, innovative products were made available through various promotional campaigns (e.g., distribution events and LG tour in annual carnivals) and came close to the Brazilian people's lives.

Fifth, it carried off sports marketing through soccer games. In view of Brazilian's soccer enthusiasm, LG became a major sponsor of the São Paulo Football Club—the national championship team ranking number one or two. LG also organized Copa LG for the promotional campaigns during the 2006 World Cup Games.

Sixth, the LG Music Festival has been performed in major cities for cultural enhancements among the growing youth market.

Seventh, it did premium marketing for the 47 million strong high-income groups—25% of the total population—through the first-class department stores and specialty outlets.

Eighth, it managed foreign exchange–related business risks, production standards–directed regulatory risks, complex tax system risks, and human resources risks. In view of high inflation rates and corresponding enormous fluctuating foreign exchange rates in Brazil, LG expanded exports to the neighboring nations and maintained a healthy rate of working capital. Complex tax systems are quite disadvantageous to global firms from other countries. LG responds to these tax challenges through outstanding legal services through native law and consulting firms. Brazil's labor laws are comprehensive, and labor unions are assertive. LG is quite accommodating to the demands of Brazilian labor unions. LG also utilizes region-based incentives for competitive growth.

In conclusion, LG's brand strategy (i.e., strategic positioning) in the Brazil market is based on product leadership and develops differentiated communication and marketing efforts that appeal to Brazilian sentiments and tastes.

12.3.3 Comparisons of Samsung and LG

Samsung and LG are two well-known Korean global firms. This section highlights their common strengths and obvious differences (Park, 2011a). These two firms are common in terms of (1) rapid production systems in Korea, (2) product offerings that reflect local needs and changing requirements, and (3) diverse marketing strategy (sports marketing in particular). Both Samsung and LG adopted benchmarking of US, European, and Japanese global firms for their product strategy (product design in particular) and Japanese style of production methods. Thus, Samsung and LG selected various advantages and developed their unique global production system and supply chain strategies.

At the same time, several differences between Samsung and LG are mentioned here.

First, human resources management is a representatively different practice. Samsung utilizes regional professionals who are sent from Samsung Korea and second-generation Koreans in Brazil. On the other hand, LG uses Brazilian natives for the key leadership. Thus, LG has much more vigorous leadership development.

Second, production line systems are also different. Samsung uses cell lines in all its global operations. Cell lines require a team leader (6 to 8 years of experiences) who is able to train team members for multiple skill-based competencies. With rapid growth in Brazil, the challenges are a small number of cell leaders in spite of large pools of workers. Thus, Samsung has to use a more specialized workforce that divides and separates work content. In contrast, LG's TV line is conveyor-line based. The senior manager of LGA in Manaus said, "TV demand in Brazil is almost explosive. Apart from conveyor methods, it is almost impossible to meet production volume requirements in view of such rapid market growth" (Park, 2011b). In the Brazilian market, LG's market share of LCD TVs is somewhat reduced but it is mainly due to the slow production response to the phenomenal growth of customer demand level. One LCD TV requires an average of 6 seconds (TAKT time) and thus conveyor-line methods seem to be most appropriate. Such a "speed production" system allows LG to secure a high rate of market share—LCD TV (30%, number one), PDP TV (59%, number one), and audio (31%, number one).

Third, product strategy is distinctively different. Samsung, once withdrawn from Brazil during the Asian Financial Crisis, pursues a premium strategy through massive resource investment. For TV products, Samsung primary marketing efforts are for the LED TV and 3D TV and thus do better than LG in premium products. For mobile phones, Samsung achieved a number one market leader position in touch phones and smartphones. On the other hand, LG kept up its operations, not withdrawing as Samsung did. Instead, LG has attained successful localization and thus maintains a loyal customer base in Brazil.

12.4 CONCLUDING REMARKS

This chapter is devoted to studying the market strategy of Korean global firms (Samsung and LG) in Brazil. These firms have experienced rapid growth through their massive investment and owner-based rapid decision making and IT system integration. Their strategy is quite different from Japanese firms that focus on North American and European markets. These firms targeted the emerging economies in the 1990s and established a strong business presence in India and Brazil and deployed their financial, marketing, and production resources for rapid expansion and growth.

Japanese firms were more cautious about uncertain political contexts in India and policy changes of the Brazilian government and thus remained passive for more than 20 years in realizing these market potentials (Ooki et al., 2010). The Brazilian government's numerous policy changes since the 1970s have dictated that these global firms revise and refine their business models. To Japanese firms these emerging markets were almost forgotten. By the 2000s the market growth rates in India and Brazil were too obvious and yet Japanese firms could not afford to make large investments with a lack of resource support from their headquarters in Japan. Korean firms have made aggressive investment in India and Brazil immediately after they overcame the Asian Financial Crisis in the 2000s. Investment timing and amount depended on political conditions and economic policy changes. Yet, timely and bold investment in these emerging economies is crucial for their global strategy success. In this sense, Korean global firms have made serious policy adjustments and organizational system building efforts in response to these rapid environmental changes. Their bold decision-making styles for tapping the growth potential of these emerging markets are instrumental for their successful market performance. It is worthy to observe and study further how these Korean firms supply chain management as an essential aspect of their global market strategy. Their global supply chain management certainly provides rich theoretical and managerial implications and thus deserves further research attention in that it is quite different from the global supply chain strategy of large firms from the United States and the European Union.

13

Concluding Remarks and
Future Research Issues

In this book we have presented three essential elements of network capabilities in terms of technology competence, customer competence, and linkage competence. We then provide product architecture as an important foundation of successful product strategy in the emerging economies. All the successful global firms from Japan and Korea do not merely extend their respective domestic product models to the emerging markets. Instead, they recognize the unique customer needs (i.e., sensing competence) and offer products and services that satisfy the needs of these new customers. For this purpose, both these global and indigenous firms develop network capabilities for their sustainable competitive advantage. In view of increasing importance of base-of-pyramid (BOP) markets, firms' strategies in global BOP markets and future prospects are briefly summarized in this concluding section.

13.1 COMPARISON OF JAPANESE AND KOREAN GLOBAL FIRMS VERSUS INDIGENOUS FIRMS FROM BRICs

Based on the product architecture perspective, in this book we have clarified the organizational processes of Korean firms and the positive role of the Korean government in achieving rapid catch-up with the Japanese firms (Amsden, 1989; Hong and Hwang, 2011). With their modular architecture excellence, several Korean firms have also achieved their global competitive advantage over Japanese firms. Based on extensive field visits and executive interviews, we have presented the strategic and operational practices of Korean global firms in the emerging economies (i.e., India, Brazil, Eastern European countries, and China).

This book also focused on the global strategy of Korean and Japanese global firms and outstanding growth of several indigenous firms from BRIC nations (i.e., Brazil, Russia, India, and China). Several Korean global firms in electronics and automotive industries are noted as primary export engines of Korea. Roubini and Mihm (2010) regard Korea as an economic powerhouse that is innovative, dynamic, and highly skilled labor forces. They also give a high mark on the outstanding growth rates of Korean global firms. By adding Korea as a very dynamic competitor nation along with other BRICs (i.e., Brazil, Russia, India, and China), the notion of BRICKS is introduced (Adams et al., 2013). Behind such recognition, the phenomenal growth of Korean firms and the active and sustained support of the Korean government must be mentioned. The Korean government's free trade agreement (FTA) policies are being implemented more rapidly than those of any other nation.

The localization strategy of successful Korean firms in China, Brazil, and India suggests several common factors. Starting from the mid-1990s, they accelerated the localization implementation efforts in the emerging economies. Their initial focus was to meet the market demand of the respective countries of India, China, and Brazil. From the latter part of the 1990s, the scope of localization expanded to support the increasing growth requirement of global market sales. Large-scale investment, decisive and timely decision making by the owner-management and innovative utilization of information technology (IT) infrastructure are their key success factors. While Japanese counterparts mostly focused on North American and European markets by the mid-1990s, Korean firms have kept their strategic priority in India, Brazil, and China and rapidly deployed their resources to target these growing markets.

Japanese firms were less sure of the promising emerging markets opportunities in view of India's volatile political circumstances and frequent changes in Brazilian governmental policies. Japanese firms revised their business models in response to the Brazilian government's seemingly inconsistent economic policies since the 1970s. In the 2000s, as India and Brazil were about to take off with their rapid economic growth, Japanese firms were less aggressive with resource constraints from Japanese prolonged domestic recessions. In contrast, Korean firms, immediately after the Asian Financial Crisis, adopted aggressive investment policy directions in India and Brazil.

However, at the headquarters' level, no global firms had sufficient capital to meet the needs of all the global markets including the emerging economies. Thus, effective investment decisions for market growth in emerging economies require careful consideration of timing, changing political contexts, and economic policies.

Figure 13.1 shows how Japanese and Korean global firms apply their product strategy from a product architecture perspective. In general, Japanese firms implement an open-integral strategy based on their strong integral architecture development capability and cost-competitive performance of local component parts suppliers. Korean global firms mostly adopt an open-modular architecture with their speedy and bold decision making. Their products, based on open-modular architecture, have very short product life cycles (PLCs). Figure 13.2 shows how Korean firms pursue their brand strategy in the form of open-modular products design differentiation. They are extremely market responsive by applying short PLC (i.e., introduction-growth-maturity-decline). Besides, they implement an effective supply chain strategy that combines design differentiation, functional differentiation by market segments, timely market offerings of new products, and integration of production and marketing.

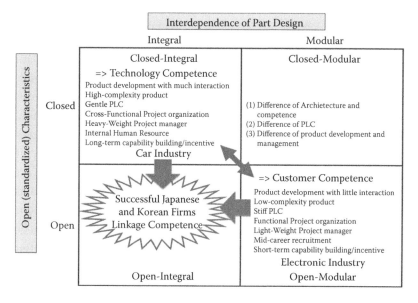

FIGURE 13.1
A model of successful Japanese global firms in emerging markets.

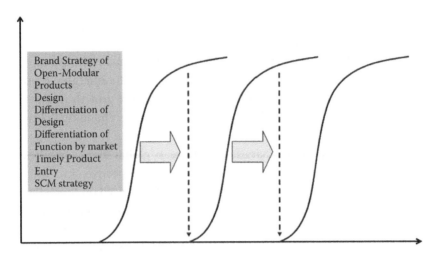

Brand Strategy of
Open-Modular
Products
Design
Differentiation of
Design
Differentiation of
Function by market
Timely Product
Entry
SCM strategy

FIGURE 13.2
Global strategy of Korean firms.

13.2 EMERGING MARKET STRATEGY: DIRECTION AND PROSPECT

This book presents the research framework in terms of three important elements of network capabilities (i.e., technology competence, customer competence, and linkage competence) and the concept of product architecture for the successful product development strategy. Case studies of Japanese and Korean global firms focus on their responsive market strategies in BRICs' (Brazil, Russia, India, and China) emerging economies. Successful Japanese and Korean firms in these emerging economies are common in that they do not merely offer the products already sold in their domestic markets (i.e., Japan and Korea). Instead, they sense the unique emerging market needs, utilize their own technology competence, and source the component parts through their network capabilities beyond their domestic boundaries. Particularly, these firms effectively deploy their strategic network capabilities in the form of linkage competence, which integrates both technology competence and customer competence. The different patterns of global market strategy reflect their strong mission and unique organizational culture characteristics (Roh et al., 2008; Hirota et al., 2010).

Furthermore, this book examines the successful localization strategy of Korean and Japanese global firms. Korean firms—Hyundai and Samsung in particular—emphasize global integration based on strong CEO leadership from Korean headquarters and effective localization strategy. However, LG (at least in India) implements its localization strategy through empowering local leadership. Thus, localization strategy patterns of Korean global firms are somewhat different depending on their organizational culture and structure. Japanese global firms had entered in the emerging markets years before Korean firms even conceived their localization strategy in India and Brazil. Yet, they did not implement a true sense of localization. Instead, they merely apply assembly methods for their old premium products tested in the Japanese domestic market. As a consequence, they had to watch how their Korean rivals outperform in India and Brazil with the successful implementation of localization strategy (i.e., sense local needs and develop product that fit to the local customers) (Bartlett and Ghoshal, 1989, 2000).

After the mid-2000s, Japanese firms benchmarked the Korean localization strategy in these emerging markets and changed their market strategy. This book, thus, discussed several examples of Japanese global firms including Toyota's localization strategy (e.g., the successful Etios model in India), Panasonic's cube air-conditioner development, and Komatsu's practices in China and Brazil. In comparison to the Japanese and Korean global firms, indigenous firms from BRICs also show phenomenal growth. In the coming years, the competitive landscape in these emerging economies would be dynamic with increasing rivalry among global firms from Korea, Japan, the United States, and European nations and indigenous firms. These leading firms will continue to compete and collaborate for their long-term global market strategy.

13.3 NATIONAL AND FIRM LEVEL COLLABORATIONS AMONG BRICS AND BEYOND

On July 14, 2014, Xi Jinping of China met with Vladimir Putin of Russia in Fortaleza, Brazil. In this meeting they affirmed continuous China-Russia cooperation intent in diverse areas as energy resources, science and technology, aviation and aerospace, transportation infrastructure and Russia-China Western Gas Pipeline Agreement. At the 2014 BRICS Summit, Leaders of the BRICS (Brazil, Russia, India, China and South Africa) emerging market nations launched a $100 billion development bank in their practical step toward shaping their own international financial system. Such international level collaboration often accelerates firm level strategic alliances on multiple fronts. Visible presence of Chinese firms at the 2014 World Cup includes a long list of Chinese-made advanced technology products. Yingli Solar has become the first and only renewable-energy company to become an official sponsor in both South Africa and Brazil World Cups. Nuctech Co Ltd. in Beijing has provided security scanners in nine of the 12 World Cup stadiums, as well as at one-third of Brazil's airports. Other companies such as Huawei Technologies and Comba Telecom Systems (China) Ltd use Brazil as a springboard to further explore other markets and achieve a global brand awareness. Mega-scale regional economic integration efforts along with enormous infrastructure development plans are in progress among these emerging economies. BRICS are also pursuing strategic initatives as leading players and fiercely guard vital strategic interests in various forms such as Russia's Eurasian initiatives, India and China's parternshisp with ASEAN nations, Brazil with the Initiative for the Integration of the Regional Infrastructure of South America (IIRSA) and South Africa on African Regional Integration and Development. It is all the more worthy to observe how global firms, regardless of their origin, would face challenges and opportunities arising from dynamic BRICS market, promising regional bloc alliances, and turbulent global markets.

13.4 FIRM LEVEL STRATEGIES IN GLOBAL BOP MARKETS

The development of emerging markets for low-income populations (i.e., bottom or base of the pyramid, BOP) has become important for multinational companies (MNCs) and other organizations. Recognizing the huge demand of enormously large populations for very low price consumer products, the challenge for MNCs is to reconfigure the whole of the corporate process accordingly. There has been increasing research attention to the need for engaging constructively with the poor through innovative, contextualized, and sustainable strategies (London and Hart, 2004; Prahalad, 2005; Simanis and Hart, 2008; Viswanathan et al., 2009; Ramachandran et al., 2012). Recent research on the BOP has called on firms to initiate market-driven interventions to pursue economic, environmental, and social outcomes. In response, business firms and researchers have engaged at length with the creation of new products and services for BOP consumers. Discussions on this issue have centered on the needs, the constraints, and the unique resources of BOP: a term that refers to the approximately four billion people of the world with a per capita income of less than $2 per day, the majority of whom live outside the confines of the formal economy (Prahalad and Hammond, 2002; Prahalad and Hart, 2002; London et al., 2010; Ramachandran et al., 2012).

BOP markets imply new price/performance ratios, new forms of production and distribution, redistribution of competences, shared value, and radical innovation (Acosta et al., 2011; Berger and Nakata, 2013; Gold et al., 2013). Many firms consider BOP markets quite challenging to tackle, whereas others struggle to realize the markets' economic potential (Kacou, 2011; Cholez et al., 2012; Kistruck et al., 2013). In view of the enormous need for BOP consumers, it is crucial for organizations to reconfigure the value chain process to reduce prices, penetrate the most distant zones, and possibly facilitate demand fulfillment with more creative financing systems. "BOP theory," developed by leaders of this movement within multinationals explicitly heralds the "moral" influence of this innovation strategy for shared value for larger stakeholders (Fourcade and Healy, 2007; Porter and Kranger, 2011; Cholez et al., 2012; Calton et al., 2013).

From the corporate point of view, BOP markets represent a major challenge: reaching out over four billion potential consumers in the emerging economies at large while implementing sustainability practices (Sridharan and Viswanathan, 2008; Hong et al., 2012c; Youn et al., 2013). Recent literature has highlighted the demand for products and services in BOP markets and their profitable potential and emphasized the long-standing, informal marketplace traditions, entrepreneurial energy, consumer creativity, and community orientation (Hammond and Prahalad, 2004; Rangan et al., 2007; Viswanathan, 2007; Viswanathan and Rosa, 2007; Viswanathan and Sridharan, 2012). The economic chasm and the considerable social divide between mature/affluent and BOP markets suggest that the factors determining effective product development will be significantly different across these contexts. Product and service needs in established markets are shaped by consumer life experiences amid stable economic capabilities, infrastructural development, rule of law, and marketing principles. In contrast, product and service needs in BOP markets are characterized too often with chronic resource constraints in multiple fronts and thus relatively weak consumer life experiences (Chakravarti, 2006; Viswanathan, 2007; Viswanathan and Sridharan, 2012). From the standpoint of large global firms wanting to develop market innovations in BOP contexts, the above contrasting consumer life circumstances can cause significant problems for their product developers in contending with product motivation completely alien to them (Mahajan and Banga, 2005; Viswanathan and Sridharan, 2012).

Successful BOP market strategy requires empowering the poor people into potential producers and consumers. In this field of literature, the strategic management literature has introduced several models to consider strategic innovation at the BOP (Anderson and Billou, 2007; Anderson and Markides, 2007). The literature has then produced a framework to appraise BOP and devise the routes and opportunity channels for MNCs as they move into these uncertain markets. It has also suggested other hybrid forms of linkages between these markets and development policies involving private firms and other local, national, and global institutional entities.

A key question regarding these BOP markets is the discovery of existing consumption practices, partnership/entrepreneurial-based dynamics, and the politics of local and national institutions (Cholez et al., 2012). For this goal, we summarize discussions on BOP markets in nine different streams as below.

First, strategic choices of firms in international goods and service markets in BRICs contain huge segments of BOP markets within. Spers and Wright (2013) introduce the critical strategic dimensions to operate in international BOP markets in terms of prices, promotion, distribution, products, innovation, entrance into markets, and processes. Their longitudinal and comparative research with the multiple Brazilian firms suggests that the main reason for entrance in international BOP markets is increased long-term sales and earnings. They also show that critical strategic dimensions are brand management, adequate product mix, process innovation, relationships with stakeholders, and corporation culture strengthening.

Cholez et al. (2012) also follow BOP theory and companies' actual innovation. They define the BOP markets, consumers, and local heterogeneous configurations of actors. Based on fieldwork with an MNC (specializing in electrical equipment) operating at BOP markets, they examine how managers explore the paradoxical frontiers of profit by consumption and aid the poor populations with limited means. Thus, realistic business BOP policies require a diversity of alternative business model configurations.

Ramachandran et al. (2012) seek to redirect attention toward the dynamic of the long-term engagement between the firm and the BOP producer. Using rich qualitative data from an Indian firm, they examined how the engagement between Fabindia and communities of handloom artisans in India has persisted over a period of five decades. As a result, they found that, even as it encountered changes in the external environment and pursued newer organizational goals, Fabindia repeatedly renewed its engagement with handloom artisans and facilitated progression in poverty-alleviation outcomes. They also suggest a process model that highlights the role of innovative management practices in sustaining engagements between firms and BOP producers over time. Additionally, they propose the concept of the "bridging enterprise"—a business enterprise that originates at the intersection of specific BOP communities and the corresponding nonlocal markets—as an interpreter and innovator reconciling the interests of stakeholders across the pyramid.

With respect to the geographical scope, the economic variables are fundamental to the choice of markets, especially the GDP, growth rates of income per capita, PPP (purchasing power parity) income, and exchange rates. In this respect, the greater the openness, the more the multinational companies can benefit from global and local middlemen (Khanna et al., 2005; Khanna and Palepu, 2006; Spers and Wright, 2013).

Kuada and Sorensen (2000), Kirsch et al. (2000), and Kirkbride and Ward (2001) also highlight the issues that involve the population (e.g., population composition and rates of population growth), politics, and governance (e.g., levels of corruption; weight of popular-goods markets in investment funds and forecasts of political transition), relations among ethnic, regional, and linguistic groups (e.g., the power centers in each country—bureaucracy, media, society). Calori et al. (2000) supplemented this view on the economy, politics, and society by analyzing the product market, labor market, and capital market, as follows: (1) product market, involving the gathering of information about consumers, consumption patterns, market survey, and advertising; (2) labor market, considering that it is usually necessary to recruit talent for companies, both at higher hierarchical levels and at lower levels, including middle managers, engineers, and plant supervisors; (3) capital market, considering that it is necessary to have accurate information about the market and companies, it is also necessary to assess the corporate governance, local laws, and joint-venture agreements; and (4) the importance of the cultural distance between emerging countries like Brazil and the markets where the companies are expected to do business.

Second, in terms of developing markets, classifications of Mahajan and Banga (2005) are noteworthy: rich and super rich, middle class, poor, and rural people. This classification of segments is essential to a better understanding of the operation of BRICs firms as well as Brazil in international popular-goods markets, detailing the focus of their operations and the potential for doing business in low-income segments (Spers and Wright, 2013).

Third, pricing decisions in emerging markets result from integrated actions of the individual business units, their headquarters, and the regulatory influences of the countries where they operate (Hill, 2005; Prahalad, 2005). The pricing strategy may consider predatory pricing (e.g., use of the price variable as a competitive weapon to put weak competitors out of business), multipoint pricing (e.g., strategies in a market that have an impact on prices of competitors in another market), and the external policies (e.g., antidumping policies). It is also important to analyze the degree of participation of local partners in the pricing strategy, with the purpose of tailoring such strategy to the specific needs and conditions of the popular goods markets (London and Hart, 2004; Prahalad, 2005).

Fourth, promotion dimension (e.g., branding, advertising, and other marketing approaches) in local markets includes standardizing or tailoring to the local market, educating customers in popular-goods markets, and interfacing with innovative customers (Keegan, 1989; London and Hart, 2004; Prahalad, 2005; Spers and Wright, 2013). It is also important for local partnerships to obtain information about customers and promote the product (London and Hart, 2004; Prahalad, 2005).

Fifth, the channel distribution decision is not necessarily simple (Spers and Wright, 2013). It is crucial to analyze all infrastructure and customer challenges relevant to the operation in popular goods markets including the nature of the products, tastes, and buying habits of consumers, market competition and transportation options, and concentration and fragmentation of retail systems (Keegan, 1989; Hill, 2005; London and Hart, 2004; Prahalad, 2005). Companies seek low-cost and effective distribution systems suitable to peculiar market requirements. Forming partnerships with local distribution channels is desirable to promote products among consumers of the popular-goods market, replacing or supplementing traditional methods of product promotion. In general, it is effective to standardize products or services and satisfy the specific requirements of BOP consumers. It may often be necessary to create new solutions through new products or new services fitting to the large low-income segments (London and Hart, 2004; Ricart et al., 2004; Sánchez et al., 2005; Prahalad, 2005).

Sixth, the key for the development and use of innovation and technology is how appropriate they are in the markets where they operate (Rangan et al., 2007; Spers and Wright, 2013). For BOP markets, the use of hybrid solutions may be useful with the application of advanced technologies, but considering a limited infrastructure, standardized interface systems might be suitable for heterogeneous consumers of popular-goods markets (Prahalad, 2005). For this, it is also necessary to decentralize the business structure, expand the technological platforms, and incorporate the specific features for low-income markets.

Seventh, regarding product development opportunities in the BOP markets, several new factors have emerged (Donaldson, 2006; Talke et al., 2009; Copestake and Camfield, 2010; Spers and Wright, 2013). The literature suggests that there is now a stated need for high-quality products and cutting-edge technology in BOP segments, raising participation possibilities even for large global businesses (Prahalad, 2009; Copestake and Camfield, 2010). BOP consumers often exhibit a great deal of flexibility in their product use (e.g., sheltering from rain with plastic bags; using a single detergent across multiple cleaning contexts—clothes, utensils, baths; and leveraging the "missed calls" feature on cell phones to communicate efficiently) and thus expect firms to market products with multifunctional product design. BOP context-driven design processes should be consistent with local conditions and local usage patterns (Donaldson, 2006; Kandachar and Halme, 2007). Thus, BOP markets present unique product development challenges that demand fundamentally different approaches (Viswanathan and Sridharan, 2012).

The entry choices for BOP markets include acquisitions, establishment of a new business, or a variation of these alternatives (Johanson and Vahlne, 1977; Cavusgil and Ghauri, 1990; Hart and Milstein, 1999; Kuada and Sorensen, 2000; Hitt et al., 2001; Cui and Lui, 2005). Other possible entries to BOP markets are exports, licensing, strategic alliances, mergers and acquisitions, establishment of a subsidiary, franchise, manufacturing contracts, turnkey contracts, or management contracts. MNCs also consider the peculiarities of popular-goods markets and collaboration with non-traditional partners for aggressive market entry (London and Hart, 2004; Meyer, 2004; Cui and Lui, 2005). The market entry timing also depends on the target market positioning in the form of pioneers, leaders, or followers.

Eighth, in terms of the supply chain processes, the activities can be concentrated in the country of origin, distributed, or duplicated in each country (Spers and Wright, 2013). Prahalad (2005) argued for the practical aspects of BOP markets in terms of the benefits of economies of scale, the actual number of resources used in production, manufacturing environmentally sustainable products, and realistic options of serving a large popular-goods market without causing the destruction of natural resources. Serious country-level benchmark studies need to examine how a vast size of customers with limited disposal incomes are served with various products offerings and service arrangements (Hong et al., 2012a).

Ninth, development of small and medium enterprises (SMEs) as viable supply chain partners and "hidden champions." SMEs are essential to develop deep and broad supply chain capabilities and at the same time the growth of SMEs arc quite related to effective supply chain partnerships (Hong and Jeong, 2006; Wynarczyk and Watson, 2005; Hong et al., 2013a). Innovative SMEs move beyond narrowly defined regional and domestic markets and penetrate global markets with their unique products and delivery methods (Oh et al., 2009; Hong et al., 2013) The pioneering work of Herman Simon (1992, 2009) recognizes the overall impact of excellent SMEs (i.e., hidden champions) on the macro-economic strengths and overall quality of living. In view of the huge challenges for BOP markets, global supply chain capabiliites need further enhancement and thus the role of SMEs deserves increasing research attention.

In spite of these pioneering research efforts, the BOP markets have not yet been adequately explored in the mainstream of general strategy, innovation, product development, and operations management research. There is a growing need to investigate BOP markets with solid theoretical models, develop testable research questions and propositions, and engage rigorous field-based studies and large-scale empirical research projects.

13.5 COMPETITIVE ADVANTAGE OF FIRMS IN EMERGING ECONOMIES

However, in regard to exploring the frontiers of science with adequate budgetary support, the United States still maintains a relative advantage in its innovation capabilities (Kumar and Puranam, 2012). The majority of the Nobel prizes awarded for science go to academics at US and European universities doing basic research. In the short run, such basic research develops new knowledge that may not seem to have any immediate real-world applications. Yet, in the long run it is such strength of basic research funded by university or government grants that builds the long-term competitive advantage of the country. Over time, new knowledge created through such efforts may result in breakthrough products and services. In the foreseeable future, emerging economies, including Brazil, Russia, India, and China, will continue to compete with developed countries in this domain. In conclusion, the competitive advantage of firms in emerging economies requires effective translation of customer needs into successful products and services through their unique network capabilities. Customers of these emerging economies, including BOP markets, will continue to seek innovative, noble, and fantastic products that value their shared purpose expressed in terms of cultural, social, economic, and technological norms. The real challenge of firms thus is to strive to satisfy their undying hope for a sustainable and meaningful life.

References

Abdelkafi, N., Pero, M., and Blecker, T. (2011), "NPD-SCM alignment in mass customization," Fogliatto, F. S., DaSilveira, G. J. C. (eds.), *Mass Customization: Engineering and Managing Global Operations*. Springer Series in Advanced Manufacturing, London: Springer, pp. 69–85.

Abo, T. (2009), "Japanese factory in Brazil," Yamazaki, K., Chun, U., and Abo, T. (eds.), *Management of Japanese Companies in Latin America*, Tokyo: Chuokeizai, pp. 120–136.

Acosta, P., Kim, N., Melzer, I., Mendoza, R., and Thelen, N. (2011), "Business and human development in the base of the pyramid: Exploring challenges and opportunities with market heat maps," *Journal of World Business*, Vol. 46, No. 1, pp. 50–60.

Adams, J., Pendlebury, D., and Stembridge, B. (2013), *Building BRICKS: Exploring the Global Research and Innovation Impact of Brazil, Russia, India, China and South Korea*, Thomson Reuters.

Adner, R. (2006), "Match your innovation strategy to your innovation ecosystem," *Harvard Business Review*, Vol. 84, No. 4, pp. 98–107.

African Business (2013), "Embraer—Made for Africa? (June), p. 50.

Aircraft Value News (2010), "Residual values of Embraers' corporate jets remain solid" (November 8), p. 3.

Akamatsu, K. (1962), "A historical pattern of economic growth in developing countries," *The Developing Economies*, Vol. 1, Issue Supplement No. 1, pp. 3–25.

Alon, A., and Dwyer, P. D. (2012), "Globalization and multinational auditing: The case of Gazprom and PwC in Russia," *Behavioral Research in Accounting*, Vol. 24, No. 1, pp. 135–160.

Amsden, A. H. (1989), *Asia's Next Giant: South Korea and Late Industrialization*, New York: Oxford University Press.

Anderson, J., and Billou, N. (2007), "Serving the world's poor: Innovation at the base of the economic pyramid," *Journal of Business Strategy*, Vol. 28, No. 2, pp. 14–21.

Anderson, J., and Markides, C. (2007), "Strategic innovation at the base of the pyramid," *MIT Sloan Management Review*, Vol. 49, No. 1, pp. 83–89.

Asanuma, B. (1997), *Organizations of the Japanese Firms—the Mechanism of Innovative Adaptation*, Tokyo: Toyo Keizai Shinposha.

Automotive Manufacturing Solutions (2013), "Restructure & revolution for AvtoVAZ" (July/August) (www.automottvemanufacturingsolutions.com), pp. 30–33.

Baldwin, C. Y., and Clark, K. B. (2000), *Design Rules: The Power of Modularity*, Cambridge, MA: MIT Press.

Barney, J. B. (2002), *Gaining and Sustaining Competitive Advantage*, Upper Saddle River, NJ: Pearson Education.

Bartlett, C. A., and Ghoshal, S. (1989), *Managing across Borders*, Cambridge, MA: Harvard Business School Press.

Bartlett, C. A., and Ghoshal, S. (2000), "Going global: Lessons from late movers," *Harvard Business Review* (March–April), pp. 132–142.

Benner, M. J., and Tushman, M. L. (2003), "Exploitation, exploration, and process management: The productivity dilemma revisited," *Academy of Management Review*, Vol. 28, No. 2, pp. 238–256.

Berger, E., and Nakata, C. (2013), "Implementing technologies for financial service innovations in base of the pyramid markets," *Journal of Product Innovation Management*, Vol. 30, No. 6, pp. 1199–1211.

Brown, S. (2013), "An interview with Wickham Skinner, emeritus professor at Harvard Business School," *International Journal of Operations & Production Management*, Vol. 33, No. 1, pp. 104–110.

Brusoni, S., and Prencipe, A. (2001), "Managing knowledge in loosely coupled networks: Exploring the links between product and knowledge dynamics," *Journal of Management Studies*, Vol. 38, No. 7, pp. 1019–1035.

Burgelman, R. A. (1991), "Intraorganizational ecology of strategy making and organizational adaptation: Theory and field research," *Organization Science*, Vol. 2, No. 3, pp. 239–262.

Calori, R., Atamer, T., and Nunes, P. (2000), *The Dynamics of International Competition*, London: Sage Publications.

Calton, J. M., Werhane, P. H., Hartman, L. P., and Bevan, D. (2013), "Building partnerships to create social and economic value at the base of the global development pyramid," *Journal of Business Ethics*. Vol. 117, No. 4, pp. 721–733.

Cavusgil, S. T., and Ghauri, P. N. (1990), *Doing Business in Developing Countries: Negotiations and Entry Strategies*, London: Routledge, 1990.

Chakravarti, D. (2006), "Voices unheard: The psychology of consumption in poverty and development," *Journal of Consumer Psychology*, Vol. 16, No. 4, pp. 363–376.

Chase, R. B. (1998), *Production and Operations Management: Manufacturing and Services*, Boston: Irwin/McGraw-Hill.

Chen, Y. J. (2011), "Structured methodology for supplier selection and evaluation in a supply chain," *Information Sciences*, Vol. 181, No. 9, pp. 1651–1670.

Chiang, T. A., and Trappey, A. J. C. (2007), "Development of value chain collaborative model for product lifecycle management and its LCD industry adoption," *International Journal of Production Economics*, Vol. 105, pp. 1–15.

China Press (2010), "The retail expansion plan of 25 stores of Apple in China," (February 26).

Chinen Hajime. (2006), MFCS theory of New Times, Hakutousyobou. (In Japanese.)

Cho, S. Y. (2008), "Outlook and current state of India—ASEAN FTA," *Export Bank Overseas Economies* (August), South Korea Export Bank: Seoul. (In Korean.)

Cholez, C., Trompette, P., Vinck, D., and Reverdy, T. (2012), "Bridging access to electricity through BOP markets: Between economic equations and political configurations," *Review of Policy Research*, Vol. 29, No. 6, pp. 713–732.

Christensen, C. M., Verlinden, M., and Westerman, G. (2002), "Disruption, disintegration and the dissipation of differentiability," *Industrial and Corporate Change*, Vol. 11, No. 5, pp. 955–993.

Chung, C. (2012), "What is common marketing strategy of Apple and Tata?," *Chosun Biz* (March 12).

Clark, K. B. 1985. "The interaction of design hierarchies and market concepts in technological evolution," *Research Policy*, Vol. 14, pp. 235–251.

Clark, K. B., and Fujimoto, T. (1991), *Product Development Performance: Strategy, Organization, Management in the World Auto Industry*, Boston: Harvard Business School Press.

Copestake, J., and Camfield, L. (2010), "Measuring multidimensional aspiration gaps: A means to understanding cultural aspects of poverty," *Development Policy Review*, Vol. 28, No. 5, pp. 617–633.

Cui, G., and Lui, H. K. (2005), "Order of entry and performance of multinational corporations in an emerging market: A contingent resource perspective," *Journal of International Marketing*, Vol. 13, No. 4, pp. 28–56.

Daikin Annual Report (2012), *Annual Report 2012*. Daikin Industries (March 31), pp. 1–62.

Danneels, E. (2002), "The dynamics of product innovation and firm competences," *Strategic Management Journal*, Vol. 23, pp. 1095–1121.

Demeter, K., Gelei, A., and Jenei, I. (2006), "The effect of strategy on supply chain configuration and management practices on the basis of two supply chains in the Hungarian automotive industry," *International Journal of Production Economics*, Vol. 104, pp. 555–570.

Doll, W., Hong, P., and Nahm, A. (2010), "Antecedents and outcomes of manufacturability in integrated product development," *International Journal of Operations and Production Management*, Vol. 30, No. 8, pp. 821–852.

Donaldson, K. (2006), "Product design in less industrialized economies: Constraints and opportunities in Kenya," *Research in Engineering Design*, Vol. 17, No. 3, pp. 135–155.

Dongyang Economy Daily (2011), "Hyundai sets about taking Chinese market in earnest" (April 15).

Dougherty D. (1995), "Managing your core incompetencies for corporate venturing," *Entrepreneurship Theory and Practice*, Vol. 19, No. 3, pp. 13–135.

Dougherty, D., and Heller, T. (1994), "The illegitimacy of successful product innovations in established firms," *Organization Science*, Vol. 5, pp. 200–218.

Dunning, J. H. (1979), "Explaining changing patterns of international production: In defense of the electric theory," *Oxford Bulletin of Economics and Statistics* (November).

Dunning, J. H. (1989), "Multinational enterprises and the growth of services: Some conceptual and theoretical issues," *The Service Industries Journal*, Vol. 9, No. 1, pp. 5–39.

Evans, D. S., Hagiu, A., and Schmalensee, R. (2006), *Invisible Engine: How Software Platforms Drive Innovation and Transform Industries*, Cambridge, MA: MIT Press.

Fine, C. H. (1998), *Clockspeed: Winning Industry Control in the Age of Temporary Advantage*, Reading, MA: Perseus Books.

Fixson, S. K. (2005), "Product architecture assessment: A tool to link product, process, and supply chain design decisions," *Journal of Operations Management*, Vol. 23, Nos. 3/4, pp. 345–369.

Fourcade, M., and Healy, K. (2007), "Moral views of market society," *Annual Review of Sociology*, Vol. 33, pp. 285–311.

Freeland, C. (2000), *Sale of the Century*, New York: Crown.

Fujimoto, T. (1997), *The Evolution of a Manufacturing System*, Tokyo: Yuhikaku.

Fujimoto, T. (2001), *Business Architecture: Strategic Design of Products, Organizations, and Processes*, Tokyo; Yuhikaku, Tokyo, edited with Takeishi A., and Aoshima, Y. (In Japanese.)

Fujimoto, T. (2003), *Noryokukochikukyoso* (Capability-building competition), *Chukousinsyo* (In Japanese), English translation: *Competing to Be Really Good* (translated by Miller, Brian), Tokyo: International House of Japan, Tokyo.

Fujimoto, T. (2006), "Architecture-based comparative advantage in Japan and Asia," *MMRC Discussion Study*, No. 94, pp. 1–8. (In Japanese.)

Fujimoto, T., Lee, S., and Ôuyáng, T. (2005), "Product development of Chinese firms: From the viewpoint of dynamic, comparative and process analysis," Fujimoto, T., and Shintaku, J. (eds.), *Architecture-Based Analysis of Chinese Manufacturing Industries*, Tokyo: Toyokeizai, pp. 247–292.

Fujimoto, T., and Oshika, T. (2006), "Empirical analysis of the hypothesis of architecture-based competitive advantage and international trade theory," *MMRC Discussion Study*, No. 71, pp. 1–21.

Gawer, A. (2009), *Platforms, Markets and Innovation*, Cheltenham, UK: Edward Elgar.

Gawer, A. (2010), *Platforms, Markets and Innovation*, London: Edward Elgar.

Ghoshal, S., and Bartlett, C. A. (1990), "The multinational corporation as an interorganizational network," *Academy of Management Review*, Vol. 15, No. 4, pp. 603–625.

Gladwell, M. (2000), *The Tipping Point: How Little Things Can Make a Big Difference*, Boston: Little, Brown.

Gold, S., Hahn, R., and Seuring, S. (2013), "Sustainable supply chain management in 'Base of the Pyramid' food projects: A path to triple bottom line approaches for multinationals?," *International Business Review*, Vol. 22, No. 5, pp. 784-799.

Govindarajan, V., and Trimble, C. (2012), *Reverse Innovation: Create Far from Home, Win Everywhere*, Boston: Harvard Business School Press.

Gunasekaran, A., Lai, K., & Edwin Cheng, T. C. (2008), "Responsive supply chain: A competitive strategy in a networked economy," *Omega*, Vol. 36, No. 4, pp. 549–564.

Halley, A., and Nollet, J. (2002), "The supply chain: The weak link for some preferred suppliers?," *Journal of Supply Chain Management*, Vol. 38, No. 3 (Summer), pp. 39–47.

Hamel, G., and Prahalad, C. K. (1990), "The core competence of the corporation," *Harvard Business Review*, Vol. 68, No. 3, pp. 79–91.

Hamel, G., and Prahalad, C. K. (1994), *Competing for the Future*. Boston: Harvard Business School Press.

Hammond, A., and Prahalad, C. K. (2004), "Selling to the poor," *Foreign Policy*, Vol. 142, pp. 30–37.

Hang, C. C., Chen, J., and Subramian, A. M. (2010), "Developing disruptive products for emerging economies: Lessons from Asian cases," *Research-Technology Management*, Vol. 53, No. 4, pp. 21–26.

Hart, S. L., and Milstein, M. B. (1999), "Global sustainability and the creative destruction of industries," *Sloan Management Review*, Vol. 41, No. 1, pp. 23–33.

Hasegawa, S. (1998), *Theory of Multi-National Corporations Internalization and Strategic Alliance*, Tokyo: Donmungwan. (In Japanese.)

Hasegawa, S. (2002), *Theory of International Business*, Yoshihara, H. (ed.), Introduction to International Business Studies. Tokyo: Yuhikaku, pp. 62–80. (In Japanese.)

Helfat, C. E., and Raubitschek, R. S. (2000), "Product sequencing: Co-evolution of knowledge, capabilities and products," *Strategic Management Journal*, Special Issue, Vol. 21, Nos. 10/11, pp. 961–979.

Henderson, R. (1993), "Underinvestment and incompetence as responses to radical innovation: Evidence from the photolithographic alignment equipment industry," *The Rand Journal of Economics*, Vol. 24, No. 2, pp. 248–270.

Henderson, R., and Clark, K. B. (1990), "Architectural innovation: The reconfiguration of existing product technologies and the failure of established firms," *Administrative Science Quarterly*, Vol. 35, pp. 9–30.

Henderson, R., and Cockburn, I. (1994), "Measuring competence? Exploring firm effects in pharmaceutical research," *Strategic Management Journal*, Vol. 15, pp. 63–84.

Hill, C. W. L. (2005), *International Business: Competing in the Global Marketplace*, Boston: McGraw-Hill.

Hirota, S., Kubo, K., Miyajima, H., Hong, P., and Park, Y. (2010), "Corporate mission, corporate policies and business outcomes: Evidence from Japan," *Management Decision*, Vol. 48, No. 7, pp. 1134–1153.

Hitt, M. A., Ireland, R. D., and Hoskinsson, R. E. (2001), *Strategic Management: Competitiveness and Globalization,* Cincinnati, OH: South-Western College Publishing.

Hong, P., Dobrzykowski, D., and Vonderembse, M. (2010a), "Integration of supply chain IT and lean practices for mass customization: Benchmarking of product and service focused manufacturers," *Benchmarking: An International Journal,* Vol. 17, No. 4, pp. 561–592.

Hong, P., Doll, W., and Nahm, A. (2004b), "Project target clarity in an uncertain project environment," *International Journal of Operations and Production Management,* Vol. 24, No. 12, pp. 1269–1291.

Hong, P., Doll, W., Nahm, A., and Li, X. (2004a), "Knowledge sharing in integrated product development," *European Journal of Innovation Management,* Vol. 7, No. 2, pp. 10–112.

Hong, P., Doll, W., Revilla, E., and Nahm, A. (2011), "Knowledge sharing and strategic fit in integrated product development: An empirical study," *International Journal of Production Economics,* Vol. 132, No. 2, pp. 186–196.

Hong, P., Hong, S. W., Roh, J., and Park, K. (2012a), "Evolving benchmarking practices: A review for research perspectives," *Benchmarking: An International Journal,* Vol. 19, Nos. 4/5, pp. 444–462.

Hong, P., Huang, C., and Li, B. (2012b), "Crisis management for SMEs: An illustration," *International Journal of Business Excellence,* Vol. 5, No. 5, pp. 535–553.

Hong, P., and Hwang, W. (2011), "Operational capabilities and performance toward global supply chain: An overview of Korean manufacturing and service firms," *International Journal of Logistics Systems and Management,* Vol. 8, No. 2, pp. 183–197.

Hong, P., and Jeong, J. (2006), "Supply chain management practices of small and medium enterprises: From business growth perspective," *Journal of Enterprise Information Management,* Vol. 19, No. 3, pp. 292–302.

Hong, P., and Kim, S. (2012), "Business network excellence for competitive advantage: Case of Korean firms," *International Journal of Business Excellence,* Vol. 5, No. 4, pp. 6–20.

Hong, P., and Kwon, H. (2012), "Strategic procurement: A review," *International Journal of Procurement Management,* Vol. 5, No. 4 , pp. 452–469.

Hong, P., Kwon, H., and Roh, J. (2009), "Implementation of strategic green orientation: An empirical study of manufacturing firms," *European Journal of Innovation Management,* Vol. 12, No. 4, pp. 512–532.

Hong, P., Park, Y., and Choi, S. (2013), "Effective innovation strategy of Korean SMEs for emerging markets: A supply chain management perspective," *International Journal of Logistics and SCM Systems,* Vol. 6, No. 1, pp. 11–20.

Hong, P., Rawski, G., and Roh, J. (2012c), "Order winning product strategy, sustainability practices and outcomes: Case for manufacturing firms," *Benchmarking: An International Journal,* Vol. 19, Nos. 4/5, pp. 634–648.

Hong, P., and Roh, J. (2009), "Internationalization, product development and performance outcomes: A comparative study of ten countries," *Research in International Business and Finance,* Vol. 23, No. 2, pp. 169–180.

Hong, P., Roh, J., and Hwang, W. (2006), "Global supply chain strategy: From a Chinese market perspective," *Journal of Enterprise Information Management,* Vol. 19, No. 3, pp. 320–333.

Hong, P., Tran, O., and Park, K. (2010b), "Electronic commerce applications for supply chain integration and competitive capabilities: An empirical study," *Benchmarking: An International Journal,* Vol. 17, No. 4, pp. 539–560.

Hong, P., and Vonderembse, M. (2011), "Emerging global logistics: A case of Korea Express," *International Journal of Logistics Systems and Management,* Vol. 9, No. 2, pp. 141–149.

Hong, P., Vonderembse, M., Doll, W., and Nahm, A. (2005), "Role changes of design engineers in integrated product development," *Journal of Operations Management*, Vol. 24, No. 1, pp. 63–79.

Hymer, S. (1960), *The International Operations of National Firms: A Study of Direct Foreign Investment* (Doctoral dissertation), Cambridge, MA: MIT Press. (Published in 1976.)

Itohisa, M. (2012), "Product complexity and the evolution of Keiretsu system: Network structure for knowledge exploration and exploitation," *MMRC Discussion Study*, No. 412, pp. 1–16.

Jin, C. (2007), *Capability of Chinese Manufacturing Industries*, Tokyo: Shinzansha Press. (In Japanese.)

Jin, J., and von Zedtwitz, M. (2008), "Technological capability development in China's mobile phone industry," *Technovation*, 28(6), 327–334.

Jacobides, M. G., Knudsen, T., and Augier, M. (2006), "Benefiting from innovation: Value creation, value appropriation and the role of industry architectures," *Research Policy*, Vol. 35, pp. 1200–1221.

Johanson, J., and Vahlne, J. E. (1977), "The internationalization process of the firm: A model of knowledge development and increasing foreign market commitments," *Journal of International Business Studies*, Vol. 8, No. 1, pp. 23–32.

Jung, H. (2014), "The reason why Hankook Tire dreams growth like Korean AUDI, *Hankyung* (May 27).

Kacou, E. (2011), *Entrepreneurial Solutions for Prosperity in BoP markets*, Upper Saddle River, NJ: Pearson Prentice Hall.

Kadokura, T. (2006), *The great illustration: Ability of India economy*, Tokyo: Nikkei Press. (In Japanese.)

Kandachar, P., and Halme, M. (2007), "An exploratory journey towards the research and practice of the 'base of the pyramid,'" *Greener Management International*, Vol. 51, pp. 3–17.

Kang, M., Wu, X., and Hong, P. (2009), "Strategic outsourcing for sustainable competitive advantages: Case studies of multi-national corporations (MNCs) in China," *Strategic Outsourcing: An International Journal*, Vol. 2, No. 3, pp. 240–256.

Kang, M., Wu, X., Hong, P., and Park. Y. (2012), "Aligning organizational control practices toward competitive outsourcing performance," *Journal of Business Research*, Vol. 65, No. 8, pp. 1195–1201.

Kang, M., Wu, X., Hong, P., Park, K., and Park, Y. (2014), "The role of organizational control in outsourcing practices: An empirical study," *Journal of Purchasing and Supply Management*, Vol. 20, No. 3, pp. 177–185.

Kanter, R. M. (2012), "Enriching the ecosystem: A four-point plan linking innovation, enterprises, and jobs," *Harvard Business Review*, Vol. 90, No. 3, pp. 140–147.

Keegan, W. (1989), *Global Marketing Management*, Englewood Cliffs, NJ: Prentice-Hall.

Khanna, T., and Palepu, K. G. (2006), "Emerging giants: Building world-class companies in developing countries," *Harvard Business Review* (October), pp. 60–69.

Khanna, T., Palepu, K. G., and Sinha, J. (2005), "Strategies that fit emerging markets," *Harvard Business Review* (June), pp. 63–76.

Kim, E. (2012), Tata sell out $20,000 (USD) in electric cars, *Chosun Biz* (June 28).

Kim, H. (2014), "Product development which local engineers lead," Amano, T., Shintaku, J., Nakagawa, K., and Ooki, K. (eds.), *Emerging Market Strategy*, Tokyo: Yuhikaku. (In press.)

Kim, J. (2009), Hankook Tire CEO, SuhSeung-hwa, *Daily Economics* (June 22).

Kimura, K. (2007), "Product development of China's mobile handset manufactures" (In Japanese), in N. Maruyama (ed.), *China's Industrial Development and Technological Progress in the 11th Five-Year Guidelines*, Tokyo: Institute for International Trade and Investment.

Kimura, K. (2010), "Mobile phone industry in China: The rapid growth and exploration of China's leading mobile phone manufacturers," in Marukawa, T., and Yasumoto, M. (ed.), *Evolution Process of the Mobile Phone Industry: Why Was Japan Isolated?*," Tokyo: Yuhikaku.

Kirkbride, P., and Ward, K. (2001), *Globalization: The Internal Dynamic*, Chichester: Wiley.

Kirsch, R. J., Laird, K. R., and Evans, T. G. (2000), "The entry of international CPA firms into emerging markets: Motivational factors and growth strategies," *The International Journal of Accounting*, Vol. 35, No. 1, pp. 99–119.

Kisruck, G. M., Sutter, C. J., Lount, J. R., and Smith, B. R. (2013), "Mitigating principal-agent problems in base-of-the-pyramid markets: An identify spillover perspective," *Academy Of Management Journal*, Vol. 56, No. 3, pp. 659–682.

Kuada, J., and Sorensen, O. J. (2000), *Internationalization of Companies from Developing Countries*, New York: Haworth Press.

Kumon, H. (2009), "Automotive industry," Yamazaki, K., Chun, U., and Abo, T. (eds.), *Management of Japanese Companies in Latin America*, Tokyo: Chuokeizai, pp. 154–219.

Kupchinsky, R. (2006), "Russia: Gazprom—a troubled giant," *Radio Free Europe* (January 5).

Lee, J. (2008), *Modern VRICs Economy*, Hyungji. (In Korean.)

Lee, J. H., and Kimz, C. O. (2008), "Multi-agent systems applications in manufacturing systems and supply chain management: A review paper," *International Journal of Production Research*, Vol. 46, No. 1, pp. 233–265.

Leonard-Barton, D. (1992), "Core capabilities and core rigidities: A paradox in managing new product development," *Strategic Management Journal*, Vol. 13, No. 1, pp. 111–125.

Levinthal, D. A., and March, J. G. (1993), "The myopia of learning," *Strategic Management Journal*, Vol. 14, pp. 95–112.

LG Weekly Economy (2007), "The future of the Indian economy: New generation change" (January 31), pp. 1–8. (In Korean.)

Li, X., and Wang, Q. (2007), "Coordination mechanisms of supply chain systems," *European Journal of Operational Research*, Vol. 179, pp. 1–16.

Liao, Y., Hong, P., and Rao, S. (2010), "Supply management, supply flexibility and performance outcomes: An empirical investigation of manufacturing firms," *Journal of Supply Chain Management*, Vol. 46, No. 3, pp. 6–22.

Lin, Y., Zhou, L., and Shi, Y. (2009), "3C framework for modular supply networks in the Chinese automotive industry," *International Journal of Logistics Management*, Vol. 20, No. 3, pp. 322–341.

London, T., Anupindi, R., and Sheth, S. (2010), "Creating mutual value: Lessons learned from ventures serving base of the pyramid producers," *Journal of Business Research*, Vol. 63, No. 6, pp. 582–594.

London, T., and Hart, S. (2004), "Reinventing strategies for emerging markets: Beyond the transnational model," *Journal of International Business Studies*, Vol. 35, No. 5, pp. 350–370.

Lunden, L. P., Fjaertoft, D., Overland, I., and Prachakova, A. (2013), "Gazprom vs. other Russian gas producers: The evolution of the Russian gas sector," *Energy Policy*, Vol. 61, pp. 663–670.

Lusch, R. F. (2011), "Reframing supply chain management: A service-dominant logic perspective," *Journal of Supply Chain Management*, Vol. 47, No. 1, pp. 14–18.

Mahajan, V., and Banga, K. (2005), *The 86% Solution: How to Succeed in the Biggest Market Opportunity of the Next 50 Years*, Upper Saddle River, NJ: Wharton School Publishing.

March, J. G. (1991), "Exploration and exploitation in organizational learning," *Organization Science*, Vol. 2, pp. 71–87.

MarkLines (2009), Production adjustment of Toyota, No. 747 (January 27).

Marukawa, T., Yasumoto, M., Imai, K., and Shiu, J. (2006), "A comparison of mobile handset industries between Japan and China" (In Japanese), *Akamon Management Review*, Vol. 5, No. 8, pp. 542–572.

METI (2011), "White paper on international economy and trade 2011," *Policy Planning and Research Office*, Trade Policy Bureau, METI (Ministry of Economy, Trade and Industry), August 2.

Meyer, K. E. (2004), "Perspectives on multinationals enterprises in emerging economies," *Journal of International Business Studies*, Vol. 35, No. 4, pp. 259–277.

Miller, W. L., and Morris, L. (1999), *Fourth Generation R&D: Managing Knowledge, Technology, and Innovation*, New York: Wiley.

Morone, J. (1993), *Winning in High-Tech Markets*, Boston: Harvard Business School Press.

Narayanan, V. G., and Raman, A. (2004), "Aligning incentives in supply chains," *Harvard Business Review*, Vol. 82, No. 11, pp. 94–102.

Nepal, B., Monplaisirb, L., and Famuyiwa, O. (2012), "Matching product architecture with supply chain design," *European Journal of Operational Research*, Vol. 216, No. 2, pp. 312–325.

Nikkei Newpaper (2012), "Entire process of sales efficiency 1 of the Apple Store making in the United States" (April 26).

Nobel, R., and Birkinshaw, J. (1998), "Innovation in multinational corporations: Control and communication patterns in international R&D operations," *Strategic Management Journal*, Vol. 19, No. 5, pp. 479–496.

Nonaka, I., and Takeuchi, H. (1995), *The Knowledge Creating Company: How Japanese Companies Create the Dynamics of Innovation*, New York: Oxford University Press.

Oh, A. (2014), "Hankook Tire, exceeded 1 trillion won, operating profit in 2013," *AutoTimes* (January 28).

Oh, G. (2012), "Psy and intellectual property strategy," *Hankook Newpaper* (October 21).

Oh, K., Cruickshank, D., and Anderson, A. R. (2009), "The adoption of e-trade innovations by Korean small and medium sized firms," *Technolovation*, Vol. 29, No. 2, pp. 110–121.

Ooki, K., Shintaku, J., Park, Y. W., and Amano, T. (2010), "Monozukuri of Brazil Amazon: History of Manaus, industrial city and challenges of Japanese firms," *Akamon Management Review*, Vol. 9, No. 11, pp. 825–848. (In Japanese.)

Orton, J. D., and Weick, K. E. (1990), "Loosely coupled systems: A reconceptualization," *Academy of Management Review*, Vol. 2, No. 15, pp. 203–223.

Park, Y. W. (2009), *Core Competence and IT Strategy*, Tokyo: Waseda University Press. (In Japanese.)

Park, Y. W. (2010), "Product/process architecture in liquid crystal display industry and production location strategy: Case studies of Korean LCD firms," *WIAS Research Bulletin*, No. 2, pp. 45–60. (In Japanese.)

Park, Y. W. (2011a), "Korean electronic industry in growth: Global growth process and localization strategy of Brazil, *JOI*, Special Issue, pp. 23–28. (In Japanese.)

Park, Y. W. (2011b), "Emerging markets strategy of Korean companies: Management strategy of Korean companies and FTA policy of South Korea," *Japan Machinery Center for Trade and Investment Report*, pp. 84–132. (In Japanese.)

Park, Y. W., and Amano, T. (2011), "Localization strategy of the Korean companies in India: The comparison with the Japanese companies," *Hitotsubashi Business Review*, Vol. 59, No. 3, pp. 6–21. (In Japanese.)

Park, Y. W., Fujimoto, T., and Hong, P. (2012b), Product architecture, organizational capabilities and IT integration for competitive advantage," *International Journal of Information Management*, Vol. 32, No. 5, pp. 479–488.

Park, Y. W., Fujimoto, T., Hong, P., and Abe, T. (2010), "Integrated manufacturing and IT strategy for futuristic PLM: A conceptual framework from Japanese firms," International Conference on Product Lifecycle Management, in Papers presented at PLM'10 (CD-ROM), July, Bremen, Germany.

Park, Y. W., and Hong, P. (2012), *Building Network Capabilities in Turbulent Competitive Environments: Practices of Global Firms from Korea and Japan*, Boca Raton, FL: CRC Press.

Park, Y. W., and Hong, P. (2014), "The role of IT for global firms in emerging markets," *International Journal of Business Information Systems*, Special Issue. (In press.)

Park, Y. W., Hong, P., and Hwang, W. (2011), "Building supply chain capabilities: A case study of Korean Hyundai-Kia Motor Company," *International Journal of Logistics and Systems Management*, Vol. 9, No. 2, pp. 238–250.

Park, Y. W., Hong, P., and Moon, G. (2012c), "Implementation of product strategy with differentiated standards," *International Journal of Technology Management*, Vol. 57, Nos. 1/2/3, pp. 166–184.

Park, Y. W., Hong, P., and Park, Y. (2012a), "Product architecture and integrated manufacturing system: A comparative study of Japanese and Korean firms," *International Journal of Business Excellence*, Vol. 5, No. 5, pp. 485–501.

Park, Y. W., Hong, P., and Roh, J. (2013), "Supply chain lessons from the 2011 natural disasters in Japan," *Business Horizons*, Vol. 56, No. 1, pp. 75–85.

Park, Y. W., Ogawa, K., Tatsumoto, H., and Hong, P. (2009), "The impact of product architecture on supply chain integration: A case study of Nokia and Texas Instruments," *International Journal of Services and Operations Management*, Vol. 5, No. 6, pp. 787–798.

Park, Y. W., Oh, J., and Fujimoto, T. (2012e), "Global expansion and supply chain integration: Case study of Korean firms," *International Journal of Procurement Management*, Vol. 5, No. 4, pp. 470–485.

Park, Y. W., and Shintaku, J. (2014), "Expansion into emerging high-end market through the use of IT systems," Amano, T., Shintaku, J., Nakagawa, K., and Ooki, K. (eds.), *Emerging Market Strategy*, Yuhikaku: Tokyo. (In press.)

Park, Y. W., Shintaku, J., and Hong, P. (2012d), "Effective supply chain configurations in the business context of China," *MMRC Discussion Study*, No. 385, pp. 1–19.

Park, Y. W., Shintaku, J., Tomita, J., Hong, P., and Moon, G. W. (2008), "Modularity of flat panel display TV and operation management practices: A case study of LG electronics," The 3rd World Conference on Production and Operations Management, August 5–7, pp. 200–215.

Penrose, E. T. (1959), *The Theory of the Growth of the Firm*, Oxford: Basil Blackwell and Mott.

Peters, T., and Waterman, R. (1982), *In Search of Excellence*, New York: HarperCollins.

Porter, M., and Kranger, M. R. (2011), "Creating shared value," *Harvard Business Review*, Vol. 89, Nos. 1/2, pp. 62–77.

Prahalad, C., and Hammond, A. (2002), "Serving the world's poor, profitably," *Harvard Business Review*, Vol. 80, No. 9, pp. 48–59.

Prahalad, C., and Hart, S. (2002), "The fortune at the bottom of the pyramid," *Strategy + Business*, Vol. 26, pp. 54–67.

Prahalad, C. K. (2005), *The Fortune at the Bottom of the Pyramid: Eradicating Poverty through Profits*, Upper Saddle River, NJ: Wharton School Publishing.

Prahalad, C. K., and Hamel, G. (1990), "The core competence of the corporation," *Harvard Business Review*, pp. 79–91.

Prencipe, A., Davies, A., and Hobday, M. (eds.) (2003), *The Business of Systems Integration*, Oxford: Oxford University Press.

Quinn, L., and Dalton, M. (2009), "Leading for sustainability: Implementing the tasks of leadership," *Corporate Governance*, Vol. 9, No. 1, pp. 21–38.

Ramachandran, J., Pant, A., and Pani, S. K. (2012), "Building the BoP producer ecosystem: The evolving engagement of Fabindia with Indian handloom artisans," *Journal Production Innovation Management*, Vol. 29, No. 1, pp. 33–51.

Rangan, V. K., Quelch, J. A., Herrero, G., and Barton, B. (2007), *Business Solutions for the Global Poor: Creating Social and Economic Value*, San Francisco, CA: Jossey-Bass.

Rauniar, R., Doll, W., Rawski, G., and Hong, P. (2008a), "The role of heavyweight product manager in new product development," *International Journal of Operations and Production Management*, Vol. 28, No. 2, pp. 130–154.

Rauniar, R., Rawski, G., Doll, W., and Hong, P. (2008b), "Shared knowledge and product design glitches in integrated product development," *International Journal of Production Economics*, Vol. 114, No. 2, pp. 723–736.

Ricart, J. E., Enright, M. J., Ghemawat, P., Hart, S. L., and Khanna, T. (2004), "New frontiers in international strategy," *Journal of International Business Studies*, Vol. 35, No. 3, pp. 175–200.

Ro, Y., Liker, J. K., and Fixon, S. (2007), "Modularity as a strategy for supply chain coordination: The case of U.S," *IEEE Transactions Engineering Management*, Vol. 54, No. 1, pp. 172–189.

Rogers, E. (1983), *Diffusion of Innovations*, New York: Free Press.

Roh, J., Hong, P., and Min, H. (2014), "Implementation of responsive supply chain strategy: Case of manufacturing firms," *International Journal of Production Economics*, Vol. 147, No. 2, Part B, pp. 198–210.

Roh, J., Hong, P., and Park, Y. (2008), "Organizational culture and supply chain strategy: A framework for effective information flows," *Journal of Enterprise Information Management*, Vol. 21, No. 4, pp. 361–376.

Roh, J., Min, H., and Hong, P. (2011), "A co-ordination theory approach to restructuring the supply chain: An empirical study from the focal company perspective," *International Journal of Production Research*, Vol. 49, No. 15, pp. 4517–4541.

Rosenzweig, E. D., Roth, A. V., and Dean, J. W., Jr. (2003), "The influence of an integration strategy on competitive capabilities and business performance: An exploratory study of consumer products manufacturers," *Journal of Operations Management*, Vol. 21, pp. 437–456.

Rosenzweig, P. M., and Singh, J. V. (1991), "Organizational environments and the multinational enterprise," *Academy of Management Review*, Vol. 16, No. 2, pp. 340–361.

Roubini, N., and Mihm, S. (2010), *Crisis Economics: A Crash Course in the Future of Finance*. New York: Penguin Press.

Rumelt, R. (1984), "Towards a strategic theory of the firm," Lamb, R. B. (ed.), *Competitive Strategic Management*. Englewood Cliffs, NJ: Prentice Hall, pp. 556–570.

Rupali, K. (2013), "Role of innovation in emerging markets," *Advances in Management*, Vol. 6, No. 9, pp. 11–13.

Sánchez, P., Ricart, J., and Rodriguez, M. (2005), "Influential factors in becoming socially embedded in low-income markets," *Greener Management International*, Vol. 51, pp. 19–38.

Sahin, F., and Robinson, E. P. (2002), "Flow coordination and information sharing in supply chains: Review, implications, and directions for future research," *Decision Sciences*, Vol. 33, No. 4, pp. 505–535.

Sako, M., and Helper, S. (1998), "Determinants of trust in supplier relations: Evidence from the automotive industry in Japan and in the United States?," *Journal of Economic Behaviour and Organization*, Vol. 34, No. 3, pp. 387–417.

Salvador, F., Forza, C., and Rungtusanatham, M. (2002), "Modularity, product variety, production volume, and component sourcing: Theorizing beyond generic prescriptions," *Journal of Operation Management*, Vol. 20, No. 5, pp. 549–575.

Scannel, T. V., Vickery, S. K., and Dröge, C. L. (2000), "Upstream market flexible customizing system and competitive performance in the automotive supply industry," *Journal of Business Logistics*, Vol. 21, No. 1, pp. 23–48.

Schonberger, R. J. (2007), "Japanese production management: An evolution—with mixed results," *Journal of Operations Management*, Vol. 25, pp. 403–419.

Schulze, P. (2009), *Balancing Exploitation and Exploration: Organizational Antecedents and Performance Effects of Innovation Strategies*, Wiesbaden: Gabler.

SERI (2007), "Anatomy of the Indian economy," *Samsung Economic Research Institute*, SERI: Seoul. (In Korean.)

Shimada, T. (2005), *Mega Market India*, Tokyo: Daimond Press. (In Japanese.)

Shimizu, T., Park, Y. W., and Hong, P. (2012), "Project manager for risk management: Case for Japan," *Benchmarking: An International Journal*, Vol. 19, Nos. 4/5, pp. 532–547.

Shimizu, T., Park, Y., and Hong, P. (2013), "Supply chain risk management and organizational decision making: A case study of Japanese major automotive firm," *International Journal of Services Operations Management*, Vol. 15, No. 3, pp. 293–312.

Shintaku, J. (2006), "Positioning Japanese firms in East Asian manufacturing network formation," *MMRC Discussion Study*, No. 92.

Shintaku, J., and Park, Y. W. (2012), "Japan's position in East Asia's IT industrial networks," *SERI Quarterly*, Vol. 5, No. 1, pp. 38–51.

Shintaku, J., Tatsumoto, H., Yoshimoto, T., Tomita, J., and Park, Y. W. (2008), "Architecture based analysis on international technology transfer and international division of labor," *Hitotsubashi Business Review*, Vol. 56, No. 2, pp. 42–61. (In Japanese.)

Shiu, J., and Imai, K. (2010), Advocators of vertical non-integration in the mobile phone industry: Design house and LSI manufacturer, Marukawa, T., and Yasumoto, M. (ed.), *Evolution Process of the Mobile Phone Industry: Why Was Japan Isolated*, Tokyo: Yuhikaku.

Shiu, J., Imai, K., and Tatsumoto, T. (2008), "Market of the product platform and technology platform: The case of China mobile phone industry," *MMRC Discussion Study*, No. 226, pp. 1–21.

Sidhu, J. S., Commandeur, H. R., and Volberda, H. W. (2007), "The multifaceted nature of exploration and exploitation: Value of supply, demand, and spatial search for innovation," *Organization Science*, Vol. 18, No. 1, pp. 20–38.

Simanis, E., and Hart, S. (2008), *The Base of the Pyramid Protocol: Toward Next Generation BoP Strategy* (2nd ed.), Ithaca, NY: Cornell University Press.

Simon, H. (1992), "Lessons from Germany's midsize giants," *Harvard Business Review*, Vol. 70, No. 2, pp. 115–123.

Simon, H. (2009), *Hidden Champions of the 21st Century: The Success Strategies of Unknown World Market Leaders.* New York: Springer.

Sioji, H., Nakata, T., Toyama, E., Seo, Y., Lee, T., Shon, H., Akabane, J., Noro, Y., and Inoue, R. (2012), *Growth Strategy of Huyndai Motor Company*, Nikkan Jidosha Shimbun. (In Japanese.)

Sirkin, H. L., Hemerling, J. W., and Bhattacharya, A. K. (2008), *Globality: Competing with Everyone from Everywhere for Everything.* London: Headline.

Skarp, F., and Gadde, L. E. (2008), "Problem solving in the upgrading of product offerings: A case study in the steel industry," *Industrial Marketing Management*, Vol. 37, No. 6, pp. 725–737.

Snow, C., Miles, R., and Coleman, H. (1992), "Managing 21st century network organization," *Organization Dynamics*, Vol. 20, No. 3, pp. 5–20.

Sridharan, S., and Viswanathan, M. (2008), "Marketing in subsistence marketplaces: Consumption and entrepreneurship in a South Indian context," *Journal of Consumer Marketing*, Vol. 25, No. 7, pp. 455–462.

Stalk, G., Evans, P., and Shulman, L. E. (1992), "Competing on capabilities: The new rules of corporate strategy," *Harvard Business Review* (March–April), pp. 57–69.

Sturgeon, T. (2002), "Modular production networks: A new American model of industrial organization," *Industrial and Corporate Changes*, Vol. 11, No. 3, pp. 451–496.

Suzuki, N., and Shintaku, J. (2014), "The role of local engineers in service solution strategy," Amano, T., Shintaku, J., Nakagawa, K., and Ooki, K. (eds.), *Emerging Market Strategy*, Tokyo: Yuhikaku. (In press.)

Talke, K., Salomo, S., Wieringa, J. E., and Luts, A. (2009), "What about design newness? Investigating the relevance of a neglected dimension of product innovativeness," *Journal of Product Innovation Management*, Vol. 26, No. 6, pp. 601–615.

Tan, K. C. (2001), "A framework of market flexible customizing system literature," *European Journal of Purchasing and Supply Management*, Vol. 7, pp. 39–48.

Teece, D. (1986), "Profiting from technological innovation: Implications for integration, collaboration, licensing and public policy," *Research Policy*, Vol. 15, pp. 285–305.

Teece, D. J. (2007), "Dynamic capabilities and strategic management," *Strategic Management Journal*, Vol. 18, No. 7, pp. 509–533.

Teece, D. J., and Pisano, G. (1994), "The dynamic capabilities of enterprises: An introduction," *Industrial and Corporate Change*, Vol. 3, No. 3, pp. 537–556.

Teece, D. J., Pisano, G., and Shuen, A. (1997), "Dynamic capabilities and strategic management," *Strategic Management Journal*, Vol. 18, No. 7, pp. 509–533.

Teece, D. J., Pisano, G., and Shuen, A. (1990), "Enterprise capabilities, resources and the concept of strategy: Consortium on competitiveness and cooperation," Working Paper CCC 90-8, *Institute of Management, Innovation and Organization*, University of California, Berkeley.

Thomke, S., and Fujimoto, T. (2000), "The effect of front-loading problem solving on product development performance," *Journal of Product Innovation Management*, Vol. 17, No. 2, pp. 128–142.

Tire Review (2011), "Top 25 global tire manufacturers—2010 (September), pp. 14.

Tomino, T., Hong, P., and Park, Y. W. (2011), "An effective integration of manufacturing and marketing system for long production cycle: A case study of Toyota Motor Company," *International Journal of Logistics and Systems Management*, Vol. 9, No. 2, pp. 204–217.

Tomino, T., Park, Y. W., and Hong, P. (2012), "Strategic procurement through built to order system: An analysis of Japanese auto-manufacturers," *International Journal of Procurement Management*, Vol. 5, No. 4, pp. 413–429.

Tomino, T., Park, Y. W., Hong, P., and Roh, J. (2009), "Market flexible customizing system (MFCS) of Japanese vehicle manufacturers: An analysis of Toyota, Nissan and Mitsubishi," *International Journal of Production Economics*, Vol. 118, No. 2, pp. 375–386.

Tomita, J., Park, Y. W., and Hong, P. (2011), "Supply chain management of glass industry: From a viewpoint of product architecture," *International Journal of Services Operations Management*, Vol. 8, No. 3, pp. 390–403.

Trkman, P., and McCormack, K. (2009), "Supply chain risk in turbulent environments—A conceptual model for managing supply chain network risk," *International Journal of Production Economics*, Vol. 119, No. 2, pp. 247–258.

Tseng, M.-C. (2004), "Strategic choice of flexible manufacturing technologies," *International Journal of Production Economics*, Vol. 91, No. 3, pp. 223–227.

Tushman, M. L., and O'Reilly, C. A., III. (1996), "Ambidextrous organizations: Managing evolutionary and revolutionary change," *California Management Review*, Vol. 38, No. 4, pp. 8–30.

Ulaga, W., and Eggert, A. (2006), "Value-based differentiation in business relationships: Gaining and sustaining key supplier status," *Journal of Marketing*, Vol. 70, No. 1, pp. 119–136.

Ulku, S., and Schmidt, G. M. (2011), "Matching product architecture and supply chain configuration," *Production and Operations Management*, Vol. 20, No. 1, pp. 16–31.

Ulrich, K. (1995), "The role of product architecture in the manufacturing firm," *Research Policy*, Vol. 24, pp. 419–440.

Utterback, J., and Suarez, F. (1993), "Innovation, competition, and market structure," *Research Policy*, Vol. 22, No. 1, pp. 1–21.

Vernon, R. (1966), "International investment and international trade in the product cycle," *Quarterly Journal of Economics*, Vol. 80, No. 2, pp. 190–207.

Vickery, S. K., Jayaram, J., Droge, C., and Calantone, R. (2003), "The effects of an integrative supply chain strategy on customer service and financial performance: An analysis of direct versus indirect relationships," *Journal of Operations Management*, Vol. 21, pp. 523–539.

Viswanathan, M. (2007), "Understanding product and market interactions in subsistence marketplaces: A study in South India," Cheng, J., and Hitt, M. (eds.), *Product and Market Development for Subsistence Marketplaces: Consumption and Entrepreneurship beyond Literacy and Resource Barriers*, Oxford: Elsevier, pp. 21–57.

Viswanathan, M., and Rosa, J. (2007), "Product and market development for subsistence marketplaces: Consumption and entrepreneurship beyond literacy and resource barriers," Cheng, J., and Hitt, M. (eds.), *Product and Market Development for Subsistence Marketplaces: Consumption and Entrepreneurship beyond Literacy and Resource Barriers*, New York: Elsevier, pp. 1–17.

Viswanathan, M., Seth, A., Gau, R., and Chaturvedi, A. (2009), "Ingraining product-relevant social good into business processes in subsistence marketplaces: The sustainable market orientation," *Journal of Macromarketing*, Vol. 29, No. 4, pp. 406–425.

Viswanathan, M., and Sridharan, S. (2012), "Product development for the BoP: Insights on concept and prototype Development from university-based student projects in India," *Journal Production Innovation Management*, Vol. 29, No. 1, pp. 52–69.

Voss, C., Tsikriktsis, N., and Frohlich, M. (2002), "Case research in operations management," *International Journal of Operations and Production Management*, Vol. 22, No. 2, pp. 195–219.

Wenerfelt, B. (1984), "A resource-based theory of the firm," *Strategic Management Journal*, Vol. 5, No. 2, pp. 171–180.

White, R. E., and Prybutok, V. (2001), "The relationship between JIT practices and type of production system," *Omega*, Vol. 29, No. 2, pp. 113–124.

Williamson, E. A., Harrison, D. K., and Jordan, M. (2004), "Information systems development within supply chain management," *International Journal of Information Management*, Vol. 24, No. 5, pp. 375–385.

Wynarczyk, P., and Watson, R. (2005), "Firm growth and supply chain partnerships: An empirical analysis of U.K. SME subcontractors," *Small Business Economics*, Vol. 24, No. 1, pp. 39–51.

Yang, M., Hong, P., and Modi, S. (2011), "Impact of lean manufacturing and environmental management on business performance: An international study of manufacturing firms," *International Journal of Production Economics*, Vol. 129, No. 2, pp. 251–261.

Yasumoto, M. (2010), "Final product manufacturers and interfirm labor division under the global market differentiation: Lessons from mobile handset industries," *MMRC Discussion Paper*, No. 300, pp. 1–35.

Yoo, D., Rao, S., and Hong, P. (2006), "A comparative study on cultural differences and quality practices—Korea, USA, China, India, Mexico, and Taiwan," *International Journal of Quality and Reliability Management*, Vol. 23, No. 6, pp. 607–624.

Youn, S., Hong, P., and Nahm, A. (2008), "Supply chain partnerships and supply chain integration: The mediating role of information quality and sharing," *International Journal of Logistics Systems and Management*, Vol. 4, No. 4, pp. 437–456.

Youn, S., Yang, M., and Hong, P. (2012), "Integrative leadership for effective supply chain implementation: An empirical study," *International Journal of Production Economics*, Vol. 139, No. 1, pp. 237–246.

Youn, S., Yang, M., Hong, P., and Park, K. (2013), "Strategic supply chain partnership, environmental supply chain management practices and performance outcomes," *Journal of Cleaner Production*, Vol. 56, pp. 121–130.

Youn, S., Yang, M., Kim, J., and Hong, P. (2014). "Supply chain information capabilities and performance outcomes: An empirical study of Korean steel suppliers," *International Journal of Information Management*, Vol. 34, No. 2, pp. 369–380.

Zhou, H., and Benton, W. C. (2007), "Supply chain practice and information sharing," *Journal of Operations Management*, Vol. 25, No. 6, pp. 1348–1365.

Index

Printed and bound by CPI Group (UK) Ltd, Croydon, CR0 4YY
08/05/2025
01864426-0002